INTERNATIONAL STUDIES

Britain and East Asia
1933–1937

T0382234

INTERNATIONAL STUDIES

PUBLISHED FOR THE CENTRE FOR
INTERNATIONAL STUDIES, LONDON SCHOOL OF
ECONOMICS AND POLITICAL SCIENCE

The Centre for International Studies at the London
School of Economics was established in 1967 with the
aid of a grant from the Ford Foundation. Its aim is
to promote research and advanced training on a
multi-disciplinary basis in the general field of International Studies, particular emphasis being given initially
to contemporary China, the Soviet Union and Eastern
Europe and the relationship between these areas and
the outside world. To this end the Centre offers research
fellowships and studentships and, in collaboration with
other bodies (such as the Social Science Research
Council), sponsors research projects and seminars.

The Centre is undertaking a series of publications
in International Studies, of which this volume is
the sixth.

Whilst the Editorial board accepts responsibility for
recommending the inclusion of a volume in the series,
the author is alone responsible for the views and
opinions expressed.

Also in this series
BLIT: The origins of Polish Socialism
STEINER: The Slovak Dilemma
VAN CREVELD: Hitler's Strategy 1940–1941: The Balkan
Clue
OGUNSANWO: China's Policy in Africa
UNGER: The Totalitarian Party

BRITAIN AND EAST ASIA 1933–1937

ANN TROTTER
Lecturer in History, University of Otago
New Zealand

CAMBRIDGE UNIVERSITY PRESS

CAMBRIDGE UNIVERSITY PRESS
Cambridge, New York, Melbourne, Madrid, Cape Town, Singapore, São Paulo, Delhi

Cambridge University Press
The Edinburgh Building, Cambridge CB2 8RU, UK

Published in the United States of America by Cambridge University Press, New York

www.cambridge.org
Information on this title: www.cambridge.org/9780521204750

First published 1975
This digitally printed version 2008

A catalogue record for this publication is available from the British Library

Library of Congress Catalogue Card Number: 74–76581

ISBN 978-0-521-20475-0 hardback
ISBN 978-0-521-08285-3 paperback

CONTENTS

MAPS

TO IAN H. NISH

PREFACE

It is not surprising that, when the archives of the British Foreign Office for the thirties were opened in 1968, the attention of those interested in British policy in the far east should have first been focussed on the periods of high crisis – the Manchurian Incident (1931–3) and the Sino-Japanese war after 1937. These were the obvious bases from which to explore the assertions that the crisis in the far east in 1931 marked the true starting point of the second world war and that from 1937 there was an inevitable downhill course all the way to the Pacific war. Recent studies of the Manchurian crisis and of Britain and the Sino-Japanese war have changed our appreciation of the pre-war far eastern situation[1] but the years between 1933 and 1937 have remained a hazy and apparently featureless interval. This book seeks to throw some light on them. In fact, these superficially quiet years were marked by vigorous discussion of British policy in the far east and by attempts to direct this policy towards the maintenance of stability in this area. In particular, the British were concerned to find a way of keeping Japan in the ring of world powers and prepared to accept international restraints.

British interest in the far east was conceived to be based on British investment in China and the potential of the China market, and on the defence of the British empire in the far east and the Pacific. To the development of both the commercial and imperial aspects of this interest, the growing power of Japan was the challenger. On one level, British policy was China-centred, based on upholding the Nanking regime as the best hope for commercial expansion in China, on another, the conditions of the day made the state of Anglo-Japanese relations the key to the pursuit of a policy directed towards commercial expansion in China and the maintenance of naval limitation in the Pacific as the essential aspect of a viable imperial defence policy in the area.

Preface

The British were faced by a conundrum. They believed there was room for Britain and Japan in China; they discussed various methods of improving Anglo-Japanese relations; but their search was for a formula which would leave British interests intact. British goodwill was their only bargaining counter. The publicity given to Japanese commercial competition, real and imagined, in other parts of the world was such as to prevent, in the mental climate associated with a world economic crisis, the granting of concessions by Britain to Japan in China or any other market. They were considered neither economically nor politically feasible. Similarly in naval matters, while the British believed adjustments might be possible for the sake of retaining something of the naval limitation agreements of Washington and London, American sensitivity to Japan's naval ambitions was felt to make concessions by Britain politically impossible. In British political circles and in Whitehall, there was evidence of considerable goodwill towards Japan but in reality no concrete way of improving Anglo-Japanese relations could be discovered and in practice British attempts to rehabilitate China only appeared to Japan as a challenge.

Part of the fascination of this period lies in the chronicling which it offers of Treasury influence on far eastern policy. The dual diplomacy which was characteristic of policy-making in which Neville Chamberlain, chancellor of the exchequer, and Sir Warren Fisher, permanent secretary to the Treasury, played an important role in putting pressure on the Foreign Office, helped to obscure the lines of British policy. It underlined the contradictions of a policy aimed at the cultivation of Chinese friendship and of Japanese goodwill and caused uncertainty in Tokyo. Nevertheless, until the outbreak of the Sino-Japanese war, the British tried with some success to keep the Japanese in play despite the unquestioned rivalry of Britain and Japan.

I am grateful to the Centre for International Studies at the London School of Economics and Political Science for the financial assistance which made possible the completion of the research for and the writing of this study. I thank in particular Professors Geoffrey Goodwin and James Joll as chairmen of the Centre for their support and interest. I also thank the committee of the British Federation of University Women for financial assistance granted through the City of London scholarship.

To Dr Ian Nish, Reader in International History at the London School of Economics, who gave generously of his scholarship, advice and guidance, I acknowledge my great debt and express my thanks. Mr E. W. Edwards of the University of Cardiff, Dr Richard Sims of the School of Oriental and African Studies and Professor Usui Katsumi of Kyushu University read the manuscript and I thank them for their helpful criticism and advice. I am grateful also for the interest of Professor W. G. Beasley of the School of Oriental and African Studies and of Captain Malcolm Kennedy. I thank Toshiko Tani, fellow of the Centre for International Studies, for her assistance with translation.

The archives of the Foreign Office and the Treasury form the basis of this study and I thank the staff of the Public Record Office in London for their invaluable assistance. I am grateful to Lord Simon for permission to use the Simon papers and to the China Association and the Manchester Chamber of Commerce for permission to use their papers. I thank the University of Birmingham library for the use of the Chamberlain papers, the University Library, Cambridge for the use of the Baldwin papers, the National Maritime museum for the use of the Chatfield papers, the National library in Canberra for the use of the Latham and Hughes papers and the War Memorial library in Canberra for the use of the Pearce papers.

Finally, I thank the editorial staff of Cambridge University Press for their consideration and my friends in London for their moral support.

A. T.

London
November 1973

East Asia 1933

1 BRITAIN'S FAR EAST PROBLEM

Between the dramatic events of the Manchurian crisis and the outbreak of the Sino-Japanese war, British policy-makers struggled to define Britain's aims in east Asia and her policy towards China and Japan. It was necessary in 1933 to reassess British policy in the light of Japan's success in Manchuria and her departure from the League of Nations; to take account of Japanese commercial competition in China and elsewhere; and to consider British east Asian policy in the wider context of imperial defence problems. Would British help in the reconstruction of China, or Anglo-Japanese cooperation in China, an Anglo-Japanese political understanding, or some recognition of Japan's naval ambitions be the best way to ensure the maintenance of a power-balance in east Asia which would preserve British interests there? The possibilities were discussed repeatedly in Whitehall where the Foreign Office, the Treasury and the defence ministries each had a particular contribution to make to the debate. In these years of uneasy peace in east Asia the relationship between China and Japan ranged between open hostility and apparently imminent *rapprochement*. This state of uncertainty in Sino-Japanese relations relieved Britain, still the western power which played the largest part in east Asian affairs, of any necessity of declaring a commitment to either China or Japan. The circumstances encouraged debate on British policy and, as the *status quo* in Europe was increasingly threatened by German expansion, Whitehall's urge to discover a solution to Britain's problems in the far east intensified. It is necessary first to consider the basis of these problems.

THE BACKGROUND

In a despatch written in December 1918, Sir John Jordan, the

I

British minister in Peking, stated that in his opinion the far east problem might be described as the problem of Japan's position in China.[1] In 1933 this problem remained. When Jordan wrote, Japanese expansion on the Asian continent during the first world war and the temporary distress of the European powers had destroyed that precarious balance in the far east which the imperial powers had hitherto managed to maintain. The war accelerated the decline of British commercial and naval strength just as it accelerated Japan's commercial and political encroachment on the Chinese mainland. As Japan's ambitions grew, so did the clash between her interests and those of Britain in China; and neither the Anglo-Japanese alliance nor the Washington treaties which replaced it solved the British problem of reconciling a desire to check Japan's continuing activities with a need to secure Japanese cooperation in naval matters.[2] To this problem was added in the 1920s the cross-current of growing Chinese nationalism and, though this in one sense added to British problems, it was, nevertheless, to British advantage in so far as it stiffened resistance to the Japanese in China. Successive British governments after 1918 were preoccupied with maintaining international stability and the *status quo* in order to provide the best conditions for the overseas trade on which the British economy depended. This conservative attitude has been described as

appropriate to a wealthy contented Power, with a larger stake in the external world than it was in fact able to defend, and apprehensive as to the effect on its accumulated interests of violence or revolutionary change almost anywhere.[3]

Japan's actions in Manchuria after September 1931 threatened stability in the far east and as such threatened British interests and the international order which Britain wished to maintain. In 1933, therefore, Britain's far eastern problem remained essentially the same as it had been in 1918, the problem of Japan's position in China.

In the mid 1920s the far east had remained relatively quiet. Economic considerations took precedence over political and military considerations and this was conducive to an atmosphere of good feeling among the major powers interested in China. For reasons of her own, Japan avoided clashes with Britain in China and was consequently assessed by Britain's leaders as 'a weak rather than a strong power'.[4] It was even possible to contemplate that Japan might be used to maintain stability in China so that international commerce might flourish the better there.[5] In these circumstances, Britain's influence existed because her strategic situation was not revealed to be perilous. This myth of her imperial power sustained Britain's position in the far east.

Events in Manchuria between 1931 and 1933 demonstrated all too clearly the actual growth of Japanese power, in China in particular, just as they demonstrated that Britain had neither the means nor the heart to oppose Japan there. Japan's overwhelming success destroyed the illusion of co-prosperity among the powers in China and revealed her as the dynamic factor in the far east. In the face of Japanese aggression, Chinese nationalism seemed to lack backbone and both China and the League of Nations were rendered helpless. Most serious for the British, however, was the fact that the unresolved problem of Japan's position in China had exposed the fact that Britain's presence in the far east was sustained by a huge confidence trick.

When, therefore, Japan announced her intention of leaving the League in March 1933, Britain was faced with the necessity of reassessing her own far eastern position and policy and of revising her images of China and Japan. The relationship between China and Japan and the power balance in the far east had to be reconsidered. It was difficult for the British to judge at that stage whether Japan had abandoned the peaceful economic expansion, which had characterised her policy in the 1920s, for military expansionism or whether she was merely attempting to impose some order in that part of China in which Japan was most heavily committed financially. If the first proposition was true, Britain's position in the far east was indeed precarious. If the truth lay in the second, British interests in China could be preserved and the illusion of British power might still be sustained. Moreover, if by 'teaching the Chinese a lesson' Japan had encouraged them to 'put their house in order' at last, she might well have served the interests of all the powers trading there.

Uncertainty about Japan's aims in China added to the problem of reaching a decision about the line Britain should take. The question for the British was whether in the new situation Japan was to be regarded as an invincible rival with aims fundamentally opposed to British interests; or whether she might once more be treated as a possible partner interested, like Britain, chiefly in economic goals. If Japan was to be accepted, the obvious place to meet her half-way was in China. The problem was how to give practical effect to this. It had been possible to contemplate bargaining with Japan in China when Japanese weakness, like British strength, had been over-estimated. It was much more difficult to visualise harmonising Japan's policy in China and the Pacific with British imperial policy and Chinese interests when British weakness could more readily be assessed. It was obvious that, whether or not Japan's policy and methods had changed, Japan's ambitions were unlikely to be contained by British moral influence alone.

The difficulties of Britain's situation in the far east after 1933 were compounded by the very success of her confidence trick in the past. She was herself the victim of a false image, the British public on the one hand and the community of nations on the other, having an entirely inflated idea of the role that Britain had the capacity to play in the far eastern area. It was difficult in the interests of security, if not dangerous, to explode this myth in 1933 and, more than any other government department, the Foreign Office was the victim of the situation. Having played a poor hand not unskilfully for so long,[6] the Foreign Office found itself expected to continue playing great power diplomacy in the far east without any trumps. Japan always held the best cards and any quick tricks taken from her were only too likely to weaken Britain's hand further in the long run. In spite of the difficulties, however, there was no intention of throwing in the hand and abandoning British interests. Politicians and civil servants educated before 1914 to take pride in, and responsibility for, Britain's world-wide interests, assumed that Britain's position in the far east and at the centre of her empire must be maintained, and they were conscious that the British public and the Dominions believed this to be possible.[7]

In formulating principles for the new situation in the far east, British policy-makers obviously could not ignore the sentiments at home which had helped shape decisions in the past. Supporters of the principle of collective security and militant pacifists were incensed by events in Manchuria and wanted action taken to bring Japan to reason. In the case of the brief arms embargo which the British government had imposed in February 1933 and had lasted only two weeks because of lack of support from others, the government had been influenced by these sentiments,[8] but the various other kinds of retaliatory action which were advocated, for example an economic blockade of Japan, were not seriously contemplated.[9] The chief concern of the British cabinet throughout the Manchurian crisis had been that Britain should act as a loyal member of the League. Whether this was from convictions about collective security, from a preference for the inconspicuousness of the League or from considerations of internal policy was unimportant once Japan gave notice of her intention to leave. By March 1933, Britain had to face the fact that the League and the principle of collective security, the main resort of successive British governments since 1918, could no longer be held up as the shield modestly concealing Britain's nakedness in the far east. With Japan's defection, the far east had, in a sense, to become a separate factor in calculations about foreign policy, for considerations of collective security no longer applied.

On the other hand, the far east had never been more in the centre of foreign policy calculations in London. Japan's action there had finally caused the dropping, in 1932, of the rule which had since 1919 caused British strategic planning to be based on the assumption that there would be no major war in the next ten years.[10] The international disarmament conference which had been meeting at Geneva since February 1932 had made no headway by the end of the year and the issue of rearmament had to be faced. The British government was torn between its consciousness of the continuing support for disarmament in the country, demonstrated by the success of Labour candidates at bye-elections in 1933,[11] and its knowledge of Britain's vulnerability in the face of a dangerous situation in the far east and a deteriorating situation in Europe. This paralysing dilemma would have had disastrous implications for Britain's defence strategy in the far east whether or not it had been clear to the British in 1933 that

Japan was embarked on a policy of military expansionism. If over-all strategic readiness was neither a physical nor a psychological possibility for the British in 1933, the question was whether security in the far east could be achieved in some less expensive way. An Anglo-Japanese *rapprochement* apparently offered such a solution; but implicit in such a *rapprochement* was an acceptance by Whitehall of a change in the power relationship between Britain and Japan in the far east and of Japan's activities in China. Given the government's concept of Britain's world role and its interpretation of the British public's opinion of Japan's actions in Manchuria, this solution did not represent an easy way out of the defence dilemma in 1933.

The government's capacity to reach decisions on defence matters was further impaired by its knowledge of the country's economic problems. These problems, which became compelling after September 1931, also affected the thinking of the body of officials upon whose advice the government had to rely. The effect of the crisis had been to heighten the importance and expand the role of the Treasury in both domestic and international affairs. The defence departments and the Foreign Office both suffered as a result of this. In 1932 the Treasury had warned,

The position and future of this country depend on recovery and maintenance of sound finances and a healthy trading position. Without these we cannot provide resources for Imperial or national defence... What has to be considered therefore is one set of risks balanced against another...today financial and economic risks are by far the most serious and urgent.[12]

Inevitably the Treasury became deeply involved in arguments over defence strategy after 1933. The chancellor of the exchequer recoiled in horror from the level of expenditure considered necessary by service ministries after such a long period of rundown; and the Treasury took the lead in a search for an alternative and less costly defence strategy in the far east. In arguments over defence it was possible for the service ministries to defeat the Treasury on the technicalities of tonnage and range and gun size. In arguments about principles of foreign policy which tended to be based on imponderables, it was less easy for the Foreign Office to make a case against a differing Treasury view. The effect of this was to weaken the Foreign Office voice.

The Treasury had the further advantage of having as its spokesman in cabinet Neville Chamberlain, the most active and able member of the front bench. Chamberlain played an increasingly active role in policy decisions relating to the far east after 1933. By the time he became prime minister in 1937 he regarded himself as something of an expert in this field.[13] Chamberlain admitted that 'unhappily' it was part of his nature to try to find solutions to those problems he perceived.[14] This temperament alone would have led him to assert himself in a cabinet in which he regarded the prime minister as 'played out' and his deputy as 'useless';[15] but the persisting conflict between the felt need for rearmament and the necessity for financial recovery must always have given the chancellor a key role after 1933. The priority given to defence requirements in the far east by Britain's defence chiefs meant that Chamberlain inevitably involved himself in the search for a 'solution' to Britain's far eastern problems.

The three foreign secretaries in the period between 1933 and 1937 clearly found it difficult to stand up to the chancellor in matters affecting the far east. Sir John Simon, who was foreign secretary from 1931 to 1935, was the most experienced in far eastern matters as it was he who had guided British policy during the Manchurian crisis. His activities at that time had been criticised at home by those supporters of the League of Nations who felt he had given a half-hearted lead in the application of the principle of collective security; and abroad, particularly in the United States, by those who regarded his response to the Stimson doctrine of non-recognition as inadequate.[16] Simon was, and remains, a controversial figure. In a way he was a victim of the time. To the public, unaware of the extent of the country's strategic and economic weakness, it seemed that Britain's lack of influence during the Manchurian crisis and thereafter must be due to the failings of the foreign secretary. Simon's temperament did not help him. He was apparently wholly unconscious of the effect he produced on others and gave the impression of being 'very pleased with himself'.[17] This did not inspire confidence. Simon's legal training gave him a preference for presenting the pros and cons rather than arguing the case for a particular course of action. This gave some of his exasperated colleagues the impression that he had no policy and needed to be 'kicked from behind' by the cabinet and the Foreign Office before he could be persuaded into action.[18] Simon was prepared to disagree with the chancellor over the policy Britain should follow in the far east but, in the last resort, it was Chamberlain who had his way.[19]

Sir Samuel Hoare who held the foreign secretaryship from June to December 1935 was more preoccupied in this period with the problems caused by Italy's ambitions in Abyssinia than with the far east.[20] He made an early attempt to inform himself of the true value and volume of British trade in China but, having discovered this to be rather less than he had expected, was anxious not to interfere with decisions on aid to China made by the Treasury at that time even when these decisions were criticised by the Foreign Office.[21]

Anthony Eden, who succeeded Hoare as foreign secretary, had considerable experience of foreign affairs and the ways of the Foreign Office. He had been under-secretary of state at the Foreign Office from 1931 to 1933 and minister for League of Nations affairs from June 1935. Perhaps this increased his awareness of the power of the chancellor and the Treasury. Cabinet and Foreign Office records indicate that, at least in matters of far eastern policy, Eden wished to avoid disputes between the Treasury and the Foreign Office.[22]

Differences over policy on the far east reopened wounds which the Foreign Office carried from an earlier and unrelated encounter with the Treasury. To the insult of having lost a battle after the first world war to make the Department of Overseas Trade a part of the Foreign Office had been added the injury of having the Treasury, in 1931, veto an attempt to set up a Foreign Office economic section.[23] The Foreign Office was aware of, and sensitive about, its weakness on the economic side. It happened that economic and political affairs were particularly difficult to separate in the far east and the demarcation lines between technical financial matters which might have been supposed to be the Treasury preserve, and the political matters which were the Foreign Office concern, were necessarily blurred. The antagonism which was felt in the Foreign Office as it seemed that control was being taken out of the far eastern department's hands was not disguised and the result of Treasury influence and inter-departmental rivalry was a dual diplomacy which in no way solved Britain's problems in east Asia.

Some of the difficulties of the Foreign Office in this particular struggle with the Treasury may be attributed to the place of the far east department in the Foreign Office hierarchy. Whatever the importance of the far east in the eyes of the strategists, Washington, Paris and Berlin were posts of greater political importance in 1933. The head of the far east department was a less powerful figure than his counterparts of the American department, the western department or the central department.[24] The far east department had the additional difficulty of trying to create policy for an area whose people and culture were quite exceptionally 'foreign' to members of the Foreign Office, the Treasury and the cabinet. In order to make up for the lack of first-hand knowledge of the far east in the Foreign Office, Sir John Pratt, a man of long experience in the consular service in China, was attached to the far east department as adviser. Pratt's expertise was much in demand, but the information he provided seldom circulated beyond the far east department, and his status as a member of the consular service restricted the amount of influence it was possible for him to wield.[25]

The head of the far east department was Charles Orde. He had held this post since 1930. Orde could be relied upon for a careful well-balanced account of the issues but his rather pedantic approach was irritating to those outside the Foreign Office who sought solutions to Britain's problems. Inside the Foreign Office Orde seems to have been respected but his unspectacular career suggests that he was not found to be an impressive personality.[26]

Of the senior members of the Foreign Office, the man who displayed most interest in far eastern affairs was Sir Victor Wellesley.[27] By 1933 he was nearing the end of his diplomatic career. He was conscious of the limitations of Britain's position in the far east, convinced of the inevitability of Japanese expansion in China and aware of the threat this presented to Britain's image as an imperial power. When Wellesley retired in 1936, Sir Alexander Cadogan, ambassador in Peking, became deputy undersecretary and, on his return to the Foreign Office, took an active interest in far eastern affairs.[28]

One of the strengths of the Treasury lay in the closeness and continuity of the relationship between the chancellor, Neville Chamberlain, and the energetic permanent under-secretary at the Treasury, Sir Warren Fisher. Chamberlain and Fisher shared the belief that it was idle to arm against a possible challenge from Japan and that Britain's defences in Europe were the first priority. It seems probable that the association between the different foreign secretaries and the Foreign Office was a less easy one. In 1935 Vansittart complained that Simon told him one thing and did another, went behind his back, kept him in the dark and, on occasion, lied to him.[29] The relationship between Hoare and Vansittart had an unhappy outcome for both men.[30]

The Foreign Office felt its view was the 'professional' one which must be allowed to prevail in far eastern policy.[31] This professional view was that the only solution to Britain's difficulty of balancing imperial security against the problem of Japan in China was to try to antagonise neither China nor Japan. To ardent and systematic minds in the Treasury, particularly to Sir Warren Fisher, this looked like a 'do nothing' policy. It seemed to him that the far east department was unduly cautious and he accused its head, whom he described as a pedant ignorant of human nature, of being 'obsessed' with the idea that original sin was monopolised by Japan and of believing that Britain should have no contact with such impiety.[32] Fisher claimed that the 'amateurs' at the Foreign Office were a source of danger when dealing with the complicated issues raised by far eastern policy.[33]

Faced with the problem of protecting a valuable British investment in China in the face of Japan's power and China's weakness, the Treasury advocated discarding the traditional tool of British prestige in the far east, the royal navy, and favoured for reasons of imperial strategy as well as for its commercial advantages, the cultivation of Japanese friendship and a return to something like the alliance days. It was debatable whether the Anglo-Japanese alliance had ever had any practical effect in China[34] but, as seen from 1933, there was the illusion that, in the period before 1921, Anglo-Japanese friendship had provided a means for the protection of British interests in China and for security in the far east. The Treasury argument was based on finance and defence priorities. Britain's greatest danger was seen to be in Europe and from Germany. An alliance with Japan was a means by which Britain might achieve security at home with forces she could afford while at the same time avoiding that nightmare of strategic planners, the war on two fronts.[35] In cabinet, the chancellor of the exchequer was a consistent and persistent exponent of his department's policy for closer ties with Japan. His enthusiasm carried some members some of the time when, for differing reasons, they saw merit in appeasing Japan.[36]

An alternative to cooperation with Japan might have been expected to be cooperation with the United States, but an Anglo-American front was not contemplated by Britain in political or naval matters. The impossibility of acting in concert with the United States had, it was felt, been demonstrated by the Manchurian affair. American policy was suspect in both Foreign Office and Treasury and the foreign secretary voiced the general feeling when he suggested that when Britain did act with the United States she was left with 'the brunt of the work and of the blame'.[37] Though the Republican administration which had steered America through the Manchurian crisis had been replaced by a Democratic administration led by Franklin D. Roosevelt early in 1933, relations between the United States and Japan were regarded as thoroughly bad. There was no point in Britain's incurring Japanese odium by the acquisition of so unhelpful an ally. All the same, although the active cooperation of the United States was neither sought nor desired, it was felt, in the long run, to be impossible to ignore her susceptibilities and the knowledge of American sentimental attachment to China was one of the factors which inhibited the pursuit of a policy of appeasement towards Japan.

In 1933, therefore, a Foreign Office far east expert wrote, 'In the far east our problem may be stated as the problem of correlating our attitude towards America, Japan and China.'[38] He suggested that this problem might be resolved by being considerate but not subservient to Japan, by coordinating British policy with American but refusing to be drawn into intemperate courses, and by being sympathetic to China while making it clear that friendship did not imply surrender of essential British interests or absolve China from responsibility in the domestic and international fields which properly rested upon her shoulders. The potential for conflict in these requirements was apparently greater than the possibility of correlation but the situation was not a new one. The British had, in fact, been aware since 1919 of the need for feats of balance in order to maintain the stability which was important to them in the far east.[39]

INTERNATIONAL TREATY ARRANGEMENTS IN EAST ASIA

From 1922, stability and strategy in the far east had been based on the system of multi-national agreements reached in Washington in that year. These various agreements defined relations between Britain, the United States and Japan and were intended to harmonise the divergent interests of these powers. The two aspects of international relations in the far east, the preservation and maintenance of the territorial *status quo* and the problem of China, which had been of particular concern to the British, were reflected in the treaties.[40] The signatories of the Four Power treaty, Britain, the United States, Japan and France, agreed to respect each other's rights and interests in relation to their insular possessions in the Pacific Ocean. They were required to confer with each other should any threat to their respective rights arise. By the Five Power treaty Britain, the United States, Japan, France and Italy agreed to a proportionate limitation of tonnage on their capital ships. The ratio of 5:5:3 was established between Britain, the United States and Japan and these powers also agreed to maintain the *status quo* in regard to fortifications and naval bases in certain areas in the Pacific. Britain agreed not to build a base east of Singapore and the United States agreed not to fortify the Philippines or Guam. Thus, neither Britain nor the United States had a base within striking distance of Japan whose defensive position in the western Pacific became impregnable by sea at that time. The ban on the development of naval bases on the Philippines and Guam also meant that the American fleet could not operate effectively in the western Pacific and, until Singapore could be completed, the activity of the British fleet in the area had to be distinctly limited.[41] Since little progress had been made on Singapore by 1933, Japan's naval position in the western Pacific was a strong one.

The principles for the conduct of international relations in China were set out in the Nine Power treaty which was signed by Britain, the United States, Japan, France, Italy, Belgium, Holland, Portugal and China. The powers agreed to respect the sovereignty, independence and territorial and administrative integrity of China; to provide the fullest opportunity to China to develop and maintain herself as an effective and stable government; to use their influence for the purpose of equal opportunity for the commerce and industry of all nations through the territory of China; to refrain from taking advantage of conditions in China in order to seek special rights and privileges which would abridge the rights of subjects or citizens of friendly states. This treaty, which was a reflection of China's weakness and acknowledged by implication that China did not have the attributes of sovereignty, involved greater sacrifices for Japan than for any of the other signatories. 'Geographical propinquity' as well as economic and strategic considerations made China more important to her than to any other power. The treaty also reflected the generally-held beliefs about China's enormous economic potential. None of the western powers had either the inclination or the capacity to intervene in China in 1922 so that their pledge to refrain from doing so merely amounted to a recognition of the realities, but all were anxious that the opportunities there should be preserved against the day when China's prosperity would be such that a great market could be opened up. The treaty was there to prevent obstructive action by China or any other power; and the assumption was that China's reconstruction was a matter of international interest. This was not a situation which could be expected to appeal to the Chinese but it was one which suited a power with interests in China which it was incapable of defending. It is not surprising that, in the face of Japan's challenge, preservation of the Nine Power treaty and of the open door became the cornerstone of Britain's China policy in the 1930s.

The attitude adopted by the powers towards China was

reflected in the continued existence after the Washington conference of the so-called unequal treaties. By these, China accorded certain privileges to foreign nationals which were not reciprocally granted to the Chinese. Extraterritorial rights which removed foreign citizens, their property and liabilities, from the jurisdiction of the Chinese government and led these residents in China to claim exemption from Chinese taxes, had been enjoyed by foreigners in China since the mid-nineteenth century. In spite of China's urgent representations, there was no revision of the unequal treaties at Washington, nor was the tariff autonomy which China had lost in the nineteenth century restored to her.[42] While such limitations on China's independence remained, the Chinese could scarcely be expected to find the Washington arrangements satisfying. The contention that, by the Nine Power treaty, China was being offered an opportunity to set her house in order, with its implication that powers other than China were best qualified to judge the nature of China's house-keeping requirements and the standard which this house-keeping must reach before treaty rights could be relinquished, was insulting to Chinese nationalists.

To the exasperation of western observers, China did not seize the opportunity offered in 1922. She did not grow prosperous and strong. The country appeared to be the prey of innumerable war lords, and in the generally unsettled situation anti-foreign feeling grew. This anti-foreign feeling exploded in an incident in Shanghai on 30 May 1925 and its repercussions were felt in a series of outbursts which followed in other parts of China.[43] These led to further demands for treaty revision and ultimately in 1925–6 to a tariff conference at which it was agreed in principle that China's tariff autonomy should be restored in 1929.[44] In spite of further upheavals and continued Chinese dissatisfaction, the framework of the unequal treaties remained, though tariff autonomy was to be restored in 1929–30.

The events of 1925 had made it clear that the Washington formula had not provided China with a stimulus towards stronger political organisation and the establishment of an ordered state in which foreign powers could enjoy the maximum economic benefits. Moreover, the spirit of cooperation which had prompted the powers at Washington no longer survived. Alternatives to the Washington formula had, therefore, to be sought.[45] In terms of economic benefits, it was evident that order in China was more important than the perpetuation of extraterritorial privileges and when, by the end of 1926, it seemed that Chinese nationalism was asserting itself and that the Kuomintang might provide China with order, Britain publicly reaffirmed her support for the legitimate aspirations of the Chinese people. The December memorandum[46] in which this reaffirmation was contained was circulated to all the signatories of the Nine Power treaty. It was not a revaluation of the unequal treaty system, though it was an acknowledgement that this system must ultimately end, nor did it alter the Washington framework. It was, therefore, of little interest to the Chinese. The treaty structures remained in spite of the upheavals in China which continued after the establishment of the Nationalist regime in 1928. During this time the signatories of the Nine Power treaty failed either to act together or to work out individually with China any new system which might assist in the promotion of stability and prosperity in that country. Such was the situation when Japan launched her campaign in Manchuria in September 1931. It was claimed that, by this attack, Japan destroyed the whole structure of international relations built up at the Washington conference, but in fact that structure had existed for some time only as a shell.

REPERCUSSIONS OF THE MANCHURIAN CRISIS

Relationships between the Washington signatories deteriorated during the Manchurian crisis. Most marked was the deterioration in relations between Britain and the United States. A remarkable similarity of concern for the maintenance of good relations with Japan was shown by these two countries during the critical period from 1931 to 1933; but their contacts with each other were less happy. The Manchurian affair demonstrated that Japan could not be stopped from taking action in China if she wished to do so, by the moral force of the disapproval of the world powers. It also suggested that these powers were disinclined to intervene in China themselves. The British resented the American stance, their readiness to advise and moralise and their refusal to act during the crisis; and it seems likely that the lack of accord between Britain and the United States together with the demonstration of Japanese military strength in Manchuria finally undermined the already empty framework of the Washington agreements.

Britain had also to face the fact that an independent and defiant Japan would probably reject naval limitation in the Pacific when the Washington Five Power naval treaty came up for renewal in 1935. This had, for some time, been on the cards. The inferior ratio which had been accepted by Japan in 1922 had always been resented by a group in the Japanese navy. By 1933 this group had gained control of naval affairs in Japan.[47] The many propaganda pamphlets published by the Japanese navy at this time insisted that the ratio must be abolished, that the Japanese need not be afraid of a race to build warships, and that more efficient and economical plans could be made without the treaties.[48] The signs were thus already ominous when the Japanese army's success in Manchuria made a hardening of the navy's attitude most likely. The possibility of uncontrolled naval building was an alarming prospect for the British at a time when their naval establishment was seriously run down, when an increased defence budget was likely to be politically unacceptable and when Britain's relations with the United States were not particularly good. A Japanese naval challenge could only be met by Britain in cooperation with the United States. The consensus necessary for such cooperation did not exist.

A further consequence of Japan's Manchurian successes was her increased activity in China south of the Great Wall. The open door and British investments in the Yangtse valley were felt to be in jeopardy. The British were already aware of a blast of Japanese competition beyond China which was partly the result of the war in Manchuria and the consequent loss of Japan's markets because of Chinese boycotts. The cheapness of Japanese goods made them particularly attractive in world markets. The old textile industry of Lancashire was especially hard hit. The solution of meeting Japanese competition with concessions in China was not attractive; and the only alternative to a world-wide economic struggle seemed to be, from the British point of view, to persuade Japan into some sort of market-sharing arrangement. Failing this, measures of economic retaliation such as tariffs and quotas likely to rouse Japanese hostility and, the Foreign Office feared, likely to have a further deleterious effect on Britain's position in China in particular, were the almost inevitable response to mounting public pressure. The important duties introduced by Britain in 1932 and the tariff agreements reached at the imperial economic conference held in Ottawa that year had in fact been the British response to the upsurge of economic nationalism following the sharpened trade rivalry arising from the depression. The declared aim of the commercial agreements reached between Britain, the respective Dominions and India at Ottawa was, by the lowering or removal of trade barriers between them, to encourage the flow of trade between the various countries of the empire.[49] Coming as they had, during the Manchurian crisis, these measures had been received with considerable hostility in Japan. The imperial economic bloc was regarded as directed against her and the first step towards an economic boycott of Japan. In view of this, the Foreign Office was anxious in 1933 that no new measures of economic retaliation should further exacerbate the already strained Anglo-Japanese relations.

Britain's departure from the principle of free trade, however, put new strains on British governments and the Foreign Office in this post-depression period. Having accepted a specific legal responsibility for the protection of British trade, the government found itself under increasing pressure to use foreign policy specifically for the promotion of trade. The lobbying of British business interests was most active in those areas where the competitive power of British industry had decreased. The far east was one such area. A Foreign Office commentator noted bitterly in 1934: 'If the sun cannot be made to stand in the heavens, businessmen are apt to attribute it to the weak policy of the Foreign Office.'[50]

The weakness of the business lobby interested in the far east was that it was not at all clear about what it wanted the British government to do for it. A 'strong' policy in China which would preserve British interests against Chinese inroads into extraterritoriality and Japanese inroads into British commerce in China was called for. At the same time better relations with Japan in China were demanded in apparent recognition of the fact that Japan's goodwill was essential to the preservation of British trade in China.[51] The outlook of British businessmen was predictably opportunistic and the 'China' lobby was not automatically anti-Japanese.

BRITAIN'S INVESTMENT IN CHINA

Up to 1933, China had been the pivot of international relations in the far east. In fact, the interest taken in China was out of all proportion to the value and volume of trade passing over her borders, or to the total foreign investment in that country.[52] After almost a century of attempted exploitation, only two per cent of the world's trade went to China and her external *per capita* purchases were not more than half those of India. The western powers had always contended that in China's vast territory and huge population there lay an undeveloped market of fabulous potential but in practice there was only a small group of people who had an interest in China or who would consider investing there. This reflected the realities of the situation. China's potential remained unrealised in 1933 and greater profits involving fewer risks could be made elsewhere.[53] The myth of wealth to be found in the orient nevertheless remained.

In 1933, China absorbed 2.5 per cent of Britain's total exports, ranged sixteenth in the list of Britain's customers and held 5.9 per cent of Britain's total foreign holdings in a British investment of approximately £244.2 million pounds.[54] Nearly 77 per cent of this investment was held in Shanghai. Direct business investment as distinct from loans accounted for 81 per cent of the British total. Half of this was in fields directly associated with trade: import, export and general trading, banking and finance, shipping. The remaining half was principally invested in real estate, reflecting business wisdom of an earlier date, with a smaller percentage in manufacturing, public utilities and mining.[55] It was characteristic of the British merchant companies which held the bulk of this investment that they had been started by individuals who had very little capital and made their fortunes by reinvesting profits and so enlarging their business.[56] Of the 19 per cent or £46.4 million of the British investment which was in government loans and in Chinese government railway loans, interest amounting to £12.7 million was in default in 1933 and the Chinese government appeared to be making little effort to meet the demands of creditors. The total investment in China represented less than the British investment in Argentina, for example,[57] and made a proportionally smaller contribution to Britain's balance of payments because such a high percentage of the capital represented real estate and because such a high percentage of the profits tended to be reinvested in China.[58] In spite of this, the concept of the untapped wealth of the orient had so captured public imagination that the investment in China was often described as 'enormous' and there was public, as well as government, concern that it should be safeguarded.

For Japan geographical proximity alone would have made China an important market. As it was, her investment of £233.5 million in China including Manchuria represented 82.9 per cent of her total foreign investment. In normal times China took 20 per cent of Japan's exports and Japan was China's best customer.[59] Clearly Japan's interest in China was far more important to her than was Britain's financially greater interest. The British ambassador in Tokyo went so far as to say that the market of China was a vital necessity to Japan and that she would not allow it to be closed against her without a struggle.[60]

Sixty-three per cent of Japan's investment was in Manchuria so that, superficially, the figures showed a drastic reduction of Japan's share in the foreign investment in China after the severance of Manchuria in 1933. In practice, of course, her control of Manchuria and of the Manchurian section of the Chinese Maritime Customs increased, rather than reduced, her economic interest in the Chinese mainland. Japan's control over Manchuria and its customs organisation and her influence in north China represented a threat to the stability of the Chinese Maritime Customs administration both in terms of the actual reduction in revenue and in relation to the prospects for smuggling through north China and Manchuria. The maintenance of the integrity of the Chinese customs organisation was a basic tenet of British policy. This was partly from motives of immediate self-interest since the important Chinese government loans held in Britain were secured on the customs, but also because the successful operation of the service could be regarded as likely to enhance the prospect of achieving a stable and prosperous China.[61] Japanese cooperation was essential in the prevention of smuggling and of the undermining of the customs service. This could be obtained only if Japan could be persuaded of the value to her of the maintenance of the 'open door' in China.

After 1933 it was recognised that, whether Japan dominated China by force or China and Japan came to an agreement, British interests in China were threatened. British policy had hitherto been based on the assumption that Chinese nationalism was the vital factor to be cultivated with the object of preserving British interests and ensuring for Britain a fair share in the future expansion of the Chinese market. Reasons of prestige as well as the expectation of future commerce on an astronomical scale demanded that the British remained in China but Chinese goodwill was unlikely to save them from total loss if Japan chose to make China a Japanese preserve. Thus there appeared to be sound commercial, as well as strategic, reasons for cooperating with Japan in China and there were indications from 1933 onwards that Japan would favour such a policy of cooperation.[62] There were two reasons for hesitation. Apart from the feeling that Japan might not 'play the game'[63] there was the fact that, in spite of the inflated importance attached to them, British interests in China were not so valuable as to encourage the government to break the deadlock by risking a political gesture which would forfeit Chinese goodwill, cause an outcry at home and entail difficulties with the United States. The reality of the situation was that, given the actual stake in terms of British overseas investment and trade and given Britain's lack of territorial ambition in the area, it emerged that the advantages of sustaining a friendship with China were marginally greater than the long shot of gambling on the appeasement of Japan. This was to lead to a good deal of heart searching on the part of the British government in the next few years especially at times when the advocates of an accommodation with Japan were pressing strongly.

BRITAIN'S PROBLEM

Britain's motivation in her search for a far eastern policy was primarily economic. The British wanted a stable China and an improved Chinese market. They were not prepared to use China as a *quid pro quo* with which to reach an accommodation with Japan, but the protection of China's territorial integrity was not a feasible aspiration for them in the 1930s, and the fact was that Japan was in a position to control Chinese development. Any measure of assistance which Britain offered China could have a reasonable chance of success only if it had the approval of Japan. The problem was to find a scheme with which Japan could be induced to cooperate which at the same time reconciled the interests of China, Japan, and those western powers interested in China. In foreign policy, the British tended to attribute to other powers motives similar to their own. This led them to attribute to Japan a stronger economic motivation in her China policy than was probably the case after 1933.[64] At that time the idea of a Sino-Japanese *entente* was unacceptable to the British even though it offered the prospect of a more stable China, because it increased the chances of an unfavourable market for British goods in China. By 1935, when the world trading situation had improved and economic rivalry was less acute there was, on the one hand, less anxiety about this one presently small market in China, and on the other the feeling that British trade might after all benefit from Sino-Japanese *detente* if this reduced the internal chaos which restricted all commercial expansion in China.[65] It was difficult, however, to find a formula by which to encourage better Sino-Japanese relations since Japan, in her position of strength, needed the services of no honest broker.

The period between 1933 and 1937 found Britain on the defensive, uncertain of Japan's aims and in search of a viable policy in the far east. Her leaders seemed to be trying at different times within this period to contrive a balance between the conflicting interests of China and Japan, to be attracted to 'appeasing' Japan and to be actively supporting China. There could be no question of a confrontation with Japan in China. The problem was to contain Japanese activities there, to convince Japan that there was room for both Britain and Japan in China and to induce in her a frame of mind which would prevent further Japanese assault upon China or British interests in that country. In the last resort, Britain's determination to remain in China was not so much related to the sterling value of her interests there as to the deductions which might be drawn in the empire and around the world from the revelation of her inability to defend these interests.[66] Her concern for the preservation of the *status quo* in China was based on British weakness rather than British ambition. If Japan's ambitions in China could be resisted, not only would Britain's trade and investment there be saved, but the myth of Britain's imperial power might be sustained.

2 BRITISH TRADE AND JAPANESE COMPETITION

Britain's policy was a delicate amalgam of commercial, political and strategic factors. In later chapters the political problems of relations in the far east and the specific strategic problem of naval disarmament will be discussed. But these two problems can best be understood against a background of commercial rivalry with Japan. This rivalry, which affected not just Britain but her empire from Hong Kong through India to west Africa, will be considered in this chapter.

1933 found Japan under pressure in the far east. Her Chinese trade was declining as a result partly of a decline in purchasing power due to silver depreciation and partly of a Chinese boycott of Japanese goods introduced in 1931. The effects of this situation were evident in a number of different ways. The Japanese trade drive for markets outside China, particularly in cotton textiles, was at once apparent in India[1] and caused an outcry there and in Lancashire. British businessmen also complained of the harassment of their activities in Manchuria[2] and Japanese competition was feared in every British colonial market. On the other hand, and quite as ominous from the British point of view, there was evidence from May 1933 of Japanese attempts to achieve a *rapprochement* with China.[3] Japan was, in normal times, China's best customer, and events from 1931 until the Tangku truce put an end to the Manchurian crisis in May 1933, had shown her to be a menacing enemy. A Sino-Japanese *rapprochement* might, therefore, have more appeal to China than British friendship. In 1933 this prospect made the British nervous. While it was possible that a Sino-Japanese *entente* might lead to relatively peaceful industrial expansion, it seemed most probable, in view of the tensions created over Manchuria and the Japanese disappointment with the British attitude at the League, that British interests would suffer.

BRITISH MERCHANTS IN CHINA

In their new vulnerability, British merchants in the far east were apt to regard with increasing aversion the policies of the home government to which they looked for support. The effect of their vehemence was to increase the caution of the Foreign Office. If businessmen believed that it was quite possible to make Japan fall into line in China they would be bound to blame failure to make progress on the weakness and folly of the British government. The result was that British merchants in China felt that Whitehall failed to understand their difficulties. The situation in which British traders found themselves was, of course, a symptom of Britain's economic weakness and, in the far east which had long since been beyond Britain's physical capacity to embrace, the chances of effective action in support of British trade were remote. The problem for the policy-makers in the Foreign Office was that they were apt to be faced with concrete proposals backed by cogent reasons and expressed in forcible terms by other government departments who wished to be seen to be responding to the groups experiencing difficulty. Unless some equally concrete adverse political effect of the action proposed could be demonstrated, it was very difficult for the Foreign Office to stand out. The result was that, at times, it seemed that the control of policy in the far east had drifted out of Foreign Office hands and that its tone was other than that which the Foreign Office had in mind.[4]

From 1926, Britain had expressly disclaimed the idea that the political and economic development of China could only be secured under foreign tutelage and had adhered faithfully to the doctrine of the open door. A politically stable and prosperous China which would provide opportunities for commerce was conceived to be to Britain's advantage. Theoretically, there was no objection to a strong China, but there were dangers in this for Britain since a strong China would represent a challenge to Japan whose power to hurt Britain in China was far greater than Britain's power to hurt her.

The association of British interest in the far east with British investment in China was due, apart from the 'wealth of the orient' syndrome, to the peculiarity of the trading position in China. Foreign trade depended not simply on competitive price and quality but on the immunity from Chinese law of the foreign merchant residing in China. A 'quite extraordinary degree of protection'[5] was provided to the foreign merchant by his home government and the problem since the 1920s had been to maintain these privileges without offending China's rising nationalist spirit. The British government had accepted that in the long term these privileges would have to be surrendered in the interests of commerce, but this day was still regarded as being distant in 1933.

It seems probable that foreign influence as a whole may have inhibited Chinese development though foreign investment played an important part in the economic modernisation of the country.[6] By 1933 industrial development was going ahead in the treaty ports and in Shanghai in particular. Here, the foreign merchant communities enjoyed banking, insurance and shipping facilities and there was the added benefit of low rates of taxation. There was a large foreign element in this phase of China's industrial development. The British were interested in cotton mills and tobacco, the Japanese almost exclusively in textiles, and the Americans in carpet manufacture.[7] After 1929 when countries on the gold standard were suffering from depression, China whose currency was based on silver, experienced mild inflation. The price of silver was falling in terms of gold and Chinese exports were cheap on the world market. It was a situation which encouraged the expansion of Chinese industry and the activities of local Chinese merchants. The situation also attracted foreign merchants into new enterprises. By 1933 a new kind of British merchant could be observed in China. This man appeared to be settled in China for good and his interests were local. He was engaged in such activities as sending Chinese wool to America or selling American locomotives to the Chinese or in developing some local Chinese industry.[8] He probably spent and reinvested his income in China and was not necessarily contributing to the volume of British trade though he enjoyed the privileges of extraterritoriality to the same extent as the banks and the big merchant trading companies whose activities made their contribution to Britain's visible and invisible exports. The interests of the new merchant were quite different from those of the big concerns with spread risks and headquarters in London. It was calculated that the capital of these traders, often engaged in importing and exporting on a small scale, represented under five per cent of the British investment in China.[9] This did not deter such merchants from vociferous complaint in defence of their interests when after 1931 business in China became much less favourable to all concerned. For the locally-based foreign merchant whose total capital was invested in China, the situation was particularly serious and the retention of extraterritorial privileges became relatively more important to him. The big firms could afford to go along with the British government policy designed to maintain Chinese goodwill and to show sympathy with the legitimate aspirations of the Chinese people. For the small trader, threatened by and competing with an increasing number of Chinese merchants in an unfavourable financial climate, this policy was not enough.[10] Complaints from China were particularly loud, perhaps because the situation had once been so favourable. Sir John Pratt, adviser to the far east department at the Foreign Office, had another explanation. He wrote,

The Englishman in general gets on very well with 'natives' so long as they are willing to accept tutelage but when they reach the stage of resenting tutelage – as the Chinese have in recent years – he lacks with few exceptions, the suppleness and patience necessary to make friendly contacts with Chinese business or to deal with the exasperating difficulties of Chinese bureaucracy.[11]

Be that as it may, the policies advocated by the China Association and the British Chamber of Commerce, the established links between British business interests in China and London, were too negative for some of the locally-based residents in Shanghai. They used the British Residents Association formed in 1932 to press for a more militant attitude on the part of the British government in support of their nationals in China. The organisation was successful in gaining a good deal of publicity for 'China questions' in both houses of parliament.[12] The merchants in China wanted a 'strong' policy and, provided their interests were not eroded, were not scrupulous about whether this policy involved support of China or cooperation with Japan in China. The

British ambassador to Japan was surprised, when he visited Shanghai in 1935, to find the British community anti-Chinese and inclined to be pro-Japanese. He said that the British community felt that the government at home would do nothing for them while the Japanese government at least got things done.[13] In contrast with the Japanese policy, British policy, in the eyes of British businessmen in China, seemed to be one of concession and drift.

Clearly in 1933, the whole commercial system in China was under strain. There was evidence on all sides that the Chinese were determined and able to play a leading part in their nation's economic life. The foreign merchant was reluctantly and uneasily adjusting himself to this fact and facing the necessity to cooperate with Chinese enterprises in order to retain a foothold. Japan's success in Manchuria and influence in north China added to the difficulties.

JAPANESE COMPETITION

Unlike other countries which were struggling to retain their export trade or were actually losing it, Japan was making advances in 1932 and 1933. In December 1931, the yen had been devalued and this was followed by a continuing decline in its exchange value which had spectacular effects on Japan's export trade. In those industries such as textiles where, in anticipation of devaluation, large quantities of raw material had been bought up, finished goods could be sold at an extremely low price. Japan's competitive power was further enhanced by the fact that internal prices did not rise so that manufacturers' costs remained steady and a living wage in Japan seemed quite remarkably low when expressed in terms of any other currency. The deadly combination of low wages, good workmanship and favourable exchange meant that Japan offered goods at prices with which no other country could compete. World-wide attention was drawn to Japanese competition because Japan's trade was increasing when world trade was shrinking and because Japanese goods were appearing in markets to which Japan had not hitherto exported. Another new phenomenon was the export of fairly large quantities of manufactured goods to highly industrialised countries and in

Britain and the United States there were complaints about the import of Japanese rubber boots and shoes, electric light bulbs and pottery. In Britain, the complaints of unfair Japanese competition tended to be exaggerated. British and Japanese exports were to a large extent non-competitive but where they did compete British exporters usually suffered so that the threat of Japanese competition and the fear that this roused was enough to cause an outcry.

Except for cotton textiles, there was no evidence in 1933 of a serious decline in British trade in an important industry as a result of Japanese competition. There had been little change in the character or volume of Japanese exports to Britain in the previous decade and the balance of trade remained in Britain's favour. In addition Japan was an important market for the British empire and, excluding India, the balance of trade was substantially in the empire's favour. It could, therefore, be argued that, in any action which led to an economic breach with Japan, the British empire was likely to suffer more than Japan.

One of the most difficult aspects of Japanese competition from the British government's point of view was that it appeared to affect most severely the old and vulnerable Lancashire textile industry at a time when the depression was in any case hitting the area hard. Unemployment in Lancashire, the most densely populated part of the British Isles, presented the government with a social problem which could not be ignored, whether or not the manufacturers deserved sympathy. The government could not ignore the very active Lancashire members of parliament[14] or that well-organised pressure group, the Manchester Chamber of Commerce which found in Japan an obvious scapegoat.[15] The worst United Kingdom losses in the lucrative textile markets of China, India, Egypt and the Dutch East Indies were due to the development of textile industries in India and China.[16] Japan, however, threatened the remaining markets and Lancashire was determined the government should somehow help preserve these.

The hostility felt towards Japan in some British circles in 1933 did not go unreciprocated in Japan. Britain's departure from the gold standard in 1931 had been followed by a ten per cent tariff on all imports and in November 1932, after the imperial economic conference in Ottawa, by a system of imperial preferences. The Japanese interpreted these tariff barriers as hostile and directed against them. The arms embargo instituted by Britain in February 1933 against Japan and China was seen in Japan as a further step in this British plot to organise an economic blockade against them.[17]

The tension in Anglo-Japanese relations caused by economic matters clearly worried the Foreign Office in early 1933, particularly once Japan had announced her intention to depart from the League of Nations. It happened that at that time the Foreign Office found itself under pressure from both the Board of Trade and the India Office for economic retaliation against Japan. The Board of Trade wanted the Anglo-Japanese commercial treaty of 1911 abrogated on behalf of the west African colonies and assured the Foreign Office that if action was not taken at once, this market would be lost to Japan. As a result of the action proposed, the colonies of Sierra Leone, Nigeria, Gold Coast and Gambia would be able to put tariffs on foreign imported goods and give adequate preferences to British cottons.[18] The market in west Africa was relatively small, the figures did not show any substantial increase in arrivals of Japanese goods in 1932[19] and, in the last analysis, the market for British textiles, as for other British exports, was the world, not the colonial market, but for the Board of Trade the abrogation of the treaty for these colonies represented a chance to make a responsive gesture to Lancashire without too seriously damaging Japan's trade and so incurring her wrath.[20] The India Office asked for the abrogation of the Indo-Japanese commercial treaty of 1904 so that effective steps could be taken to stem the flow of Japanese cotton textiles which were undermining the market for locally manufactured cotton.[21]

For the Foreign Office these proposals were an unwelcome addition to the complexities of the far eastern situation at a time when skirmishing with Japan was particularly undesirable. Apparently simultaneous action against them in two parts of the British empire was open to sinister interpretation by the Japanese. On the other hand, action of the kind proposed might be desirable if it sufficiently calmed Lancashire to prevent demands for much wider measures against Japan. The final decision depended, as so often in foreign relations, on weighing domestic advantages against international repercussions.

The cabinet considered the question of Japanese competition and the need to react to it in March 1933. The foreign secretary argued that retaliation against Japan was undesirable while the political atmosphere between Britain and Japan was strained but the protective measures proposed in India and the west African colonies were finally approved.[22] It was stressed that these steps were prompted by commercial rather than political difficulties and the Japanese ambassador in London was told that the government hoped that talks between British and Japanese industrialists on market sharing could be arranged in the near future so that action against Japanese competition in other colonial areas might be avoided.[23]

Japan's textile trade with India was worth 63 million yen and the denunciation of the Indo-Japanese convention on 10 April 1933 was, therefore, a serious matter for her. The action against Japan in the west African colonies was unimportant by comparison but its announcement in May added fuel to the indignation against British commercial practises already being expressed in industrial and business circles in Japan. The *Japan Chronicle* proclaimed,

The erection of tariff barriers in India is a direct product of the Ottowa conference . . . The Indian tariff does not mean a conflict between India and Japan but a conflict between British industry or capital and Japanese industry or capital.[24]

It seemed to be felt in Japan that Britain had seized a moment when the Japanese were out of favour with the rest of the world to deal her a staggering blow. Some Japanese cabinet ministers and the military party including young officers were reported to be interpreting the abrogation as the beginning of an economic boycott inspired by League of Nations policy. Retaliation against imports of Indian raw cotton, British spinning machinery and Australian wool was spoken of in Japan; and, though these may only have been idle threats, they indicated the concern felt at the threatened loss of trade in British possessions but especially of the vitally important Indian market.[25] It seemed that irritation over measures taken to meet commercial competition would aggravate Japanese political relations with the British empire as the Foreign Office had always feared and reports of very strong anti-British feeling in Tokyo increased nervousness in Whitehall. The Foreign Office was unpleasantly aware that, in trade questions, a kind of pin-pricking policy had developed towards Japan and it was suggested by the British embassy in Tokyo that the 'margin of safety' in relations between Britain and Japan had fallen dangerously low.[26] Such forebodings filled some in London with gloom especially as it was felt that further retaliatory duties were inevitable. More realistically, the permanent under-secretary at the Foreign Office demanded to know what was meant by 'grave risks' and 'margin of safety'. As he pointed out, unless the Foreign Office could show that Board of Trade proposals for increased duties against Japan were likely to mean a Japanese attack on Hong Kong or Singapore, its argument would not be very strong and a phrase like 'the margin of safety' would become misleading or meaningless.[27] Thus confronted, the far east department found it hard to give a concrete example of a 'serious consequence' but the 'disastrous effect' that an embittered Japan might have on British interests in the far east was noted by the head of the far east department in the following way,

Japan is making progress towards an understanding with China and she could do us untold harm in that country if she sets herself to attack our trade and vested interests generally; and she could under-mine our position there completely if she chose.[28]

The problem of Japan's position in China emerged as the best reason for advocating caution in defensive action against Japanese competition elsewhere. Some amicable arrangement for the division of markets with Japan was obviously highly desirable from the British point of view.

ANGLO-JAPANESE TALKS

Discussions between British and Japanese industrialists were planned, at Britain's suggestion, to follow negotiations which were taking place between India and Japan for a new commercial treaty. These negotiations began in September 1933. A Lancashire delegation which went to India at that time was unable to win any concessions for British textiles on the Indian market[29] and it quickly became apparent that the agreement reached between India and Japan was likely to dim further the prospects for exports from Lancashire to India.[30] This led the British government to intervene and offer the Indian government a definite guarantee of support for financing the Indian cotton crop so that India would be encouraged to stand out for terms less favourable to the Japanese.[31] This action represented a notable victory for Lancashire's campaign, in parliament and elsewhere, against Japanese competition. The Foreign Office would have favoured greater caution but the chancellor of the exchequer, who advocated the scheme, described it as 'the first round in a fight against Japanese competition in many other articles and many other markets'.[32] There was relief at the Foreign Office when Japan did not reply by breaking off negotiations with India and declining to hold talks with British industrialists.[33]

The fact that Japan, who held all the best cards, should have elected to solve her problems with India by negotiation and compromise led the Foreign Office to hope that she was now somewhat less confident of her economic and political position. The prospects of the Anglo-Japanese discussion on market-sharing were felt to have improved. The British ambassador in Tokyo drew attention to the statement by the Japanese foreign minister, Hirota Koki, in which he referred to the need for Anglo-Japanese friendship and the necessity for Japan to settle trade differences with other countries in the same way as with India. The ambassador thought Japan was anxious about Russia and would, in the trade discussions, be willing to make concessions.[34]

These hopes proved unfounded. The talks began in London at the end of January 1934 and by mid-March had broken down. It was evident that the Japanese government was anxious that there should be friendly agreement over trade problems but no basis for negotiation could be found by British and Japanese industrialists. The British government rejected the idea of making proposals to Japan or pursuing negotiations at governmental level, fearing loss of face in event of failure.[35] It remained, however, a major British interest not to antagonise Japan so that there was firm resistance to the more extreme measures for which some Lancashire members of parliament were pressing. The Japanese ambassador was nevertheless warned that action in the form of quotas and increased tariffs in colonial markets would now be taken to safeguard British trade.[36] Public satisfaction with the news of this communication was reflected by *The Times* which spoke of these protective measures against Japan as a 'necessary step'.[37]

In May 1934 the Foreign Office was conscious that it had been unable to prevent the restrictive commercial practises which it had feared would bring the 'margin of safety' between Britain and Japan dangerously low. Time, however, had diminished the hostility in Britain and Japan which had been generated on both sides by the Manchurian affair and the Foreign Office had been able to delay actions which might have been inflammatory when feelings were running high. The possibilities had not been great but the ring had been held.

British experts in Tokyo and Peking assessing the situation in 1934 agreed that the only commercial settlement likely to be of value was one between governments and they argued that this would involve Britain in the gravest political difficulties for very little economic gain. Recognition of 'Manchukuo'[38] or cooperation with the Japanese in China would simply draw on Britain the odium which already hampered Japan's trade there.[39] If trade benefits were the criteria, apparently the economic advantages of taking the gamble of appeasing Japan in China, the only area outside the British empire where she might have been prepared to discuss terms, would be outweighed by the subsequent political problems in China and elsewhere. In these circumstances the British had to learn, albeit reluctantly, to live with Japanese competition in mid-1934. All the same, concern over Anglo-Japanese relations at the height of the tension caused by trade matters in 1933, resulted in the decision that a review should be made by the far east department of British policy in the far east. Trade matters were the catalyst which stimulated this first post-Manchurian crisis reconsideration of the problem of Japan's position in China and the question of Britain's relations with both China and Japan.

3 BRITAIN'S SEARCH FOR A POLICY

Japan's departure from the League of Nations marked a low point for British far eastern policy. British actions and motives during the Manchurian crisis seemed to have been thoroughly misunderstood. At Geneva, Britain's endeavour had been to follow a policy which was pro-League not anti-Japan. As a result, China appeared to feel that Britain had not protected her from Japan while Japan appeared to feel that Britain had been the mainspring of the League in condemning her. Japan's evident resentment at the British attitude, exacerbated in the months after March 1933 by British measures taken to safeguard her trade against Japanese competition, worried the Foreign Office. It was felt that Anglo-Japanese relations were at a dangerously low ebb, and the inability of the staff of the far east department to define their fears or to state precisely what form they thought Japanese exasperation with Britain might take prompted Sir Robert Vansittart, the permanent under-secretary, in an attempt to identify the problems and establish the dangers, to initiate a review of the changing situation in the far east.[1]

Clearly, thinking in British policy-making circles had moved to a political plane. The commercial problems examined in the last chapter were serious, but it is a fact that states can tolerate a considerable degree of commercial rivalry before it affects their political relations. There were, however, nagging political issues which divided Britain and Japan and coloured the policy of both. The attempts of the Foreign Office, the chiefs of staff and the cabinet to define the issues and set out the aims of British policy in the far east will be examined in this chapter. The special question of naval relations between Britain, Japan and the United States is considered in the next.

The Foreign Office was stimulated in its efforts to establish the aims of British policy in the far east by despatches received in mid-1933 from British representatives in China and Japan. There was general agreement between them that Japan's aim was the domination of China and that the failure of western powers to assist China would lead eventually to the formation of a Sino-Japanese bloc which would admit westerners only on sufferance.[2]

Agreement between Peking and Tokyo was relatively rare. The legation at Peking was headed by Sir Miles Lampson, a genial and energetic minister who was highly thought of in Whitehall. In the eventful years since his appointment in 1926, Lampson had displayed both vigour and skill in important negotiations, the most recent of which was the settlement of hostilities between China and Japan in Shanghai in 1932.[3] Lampson considered the true interests of British policy lay in 'keeping in with China and the Chinese people'.[4] He was succeeded, at the end of 1933, by Sir Alexander Cadogan who, as adviser on League of Nations affairs at the Foreign Office, had impressed Anthony Eden when he was under-secretary at the Foreign Office.[5] While Peking was not in itself a key diplomatic post, its importance in the Foreign Office career structure was demonstrated in the careers of both Lampson and Cadogan. The former left Peking to become High Commissioner in Cairo, while Cadogan went from Peking to become deputy under-secretary and ultimately permanent under-secretary at the Foreign Office.

The British ambassador in Tokyo from 1930 was Sir Francis Lindley. He was described by his American colleague in Tokyo as 'a good stolid Englishman',[6] but during the Manchurian crisis the excited and, it was thought, pro-Japanese tone of his despatches, had been criticised in Whitehall. Lindley retired in 1934, disappointed at not having obtained a 'good European embassy'.[7] He was succeeded by Sir Robert Clive, 'a superb public servant' of agreeable manner and appearance.[8] Both Lindley and Clive relied heavily on the opinion of George (later Sir George) Sansom, commercial counsellor at the embassy. Sansom's knowledge of Japan and the Japanese and his writing on Japanese cultural history had given him an international reputation among orientalists.[9] His views were highly regarded in the Foreign Office where he was acknowledged to be 'the greatest living authority on Japan'.[10] Within the civil service hierarchy, however,

Sansom's status as commercial counsellor was relatively low, and this reduced the weight which might otherwise have been attached to his opinions. The Treasury, for example, dismissed Sansom's comments on the difficulties of dealing with the Japanese government after 1931 as those of a man 'labouring under a sense of grievance against Japan'.[11]

In 1933 there was some difference between Tokyo and Peking as to the extent to which Japan was likely to succeed in dominating China. Lampson was of the opinion that, in the long run, China was 'too big and too tough a morsel for anyone to digest'.[12] The question was, however, what effect even limited Japanese success in China would have on British interest and if, as it was generally agreed, she could not fight Japan in China, what Britain's policy could be. The failure of Britain's representatives in the far east to supply an answer to the question they did not hesitate to pose, made the reappraisal in London all the more important.

Meanwhile, difficult questions about the far east were being raised by the work of other departments. In October 1933 the annual review of the chiefs of staff sub-committee of the Committee of Imperial Defence appeared.[13] This paper was significant as the first review since the ten-year rule had been dropped and as the first comprehensive review for nearly three years. Predictably, it revealed the extent of Britain's vulnerability in a deteriorating international situation. Its conclusions were that the far east remained a potential danger zone, the importance of which from the point of view of imperial defence had in no way diminished; that the defence of British possessions and interests in the far east was the first of Britain's defence commitments, followed by European commitments and the defence of India; that priority in expenditure on defence should be in that order; that the maintenance of Britain's sea communications was the first principle of imperial defence. These conclusions immediately drew other departments, notably the Treasury, to consider far eastern policy.

The stress laid on the importance of the navy and naval deficiencies in relation to the far east, raised particularly sensitive issues. The expense of naval replacement had already caused repeated difficulty between Treasury and Admiralty in 1933.[14] If the need to provide a main fleet in the far east sufficient to meet Japan at her selected moment was, as the review maintained, the navy's greatest commitment, it was logical from the Treasury point of view to seek to slash that expenditure by removing in advance the need for this commitment, and it was natural that nostalgia for the supposed halcyon days of the Anglo-Japanese alliance should be expressed. Preliminary skirmishes in 1933 indicated the line which would be taken in the numerous cabinet discussions of 1934. In November when the Committee of Imperial Defence discussed the report, one of its members, the chancellor of the exchequer, Neville Chamberlain, pointed out the desirability of eliminating certain powers from defence calculations in order to reduce the proportions of the problem Britain faced. France, Italy, and the United States were not considered as potential enemies in 1933, and Chamberlain hoped it might be possible to eliminate Japan as well. He argued that, if it proved possible to improve relations with Japan, it might be possible to reduce the far east in order of priority and so concentrate Britain's limited resources on defence spending in Europe.[15] In a cabinet discussion on the naval programme in the same period, the chancellor drew attention to the extent to which limitation of naval armaments was hampered by the situation in the far east, and referred to the chiefs of staff's paper. He asked the foreign secretary to consider whether anything could be done to improve relations with Japan and commented that he felt that Britain had received no adequate compensation for the termination of the Anglo-Japanese alliance and that her position in the far east had simply been rendered more precarious by the loss of it.[16] These were the kinds of assertion with which the Foreign Office had little sympathy. It hoped to be able to counter them with concrete evidence as a result of the research presently being undertaken.

THE FAR EAST DEPARTMENT'S REPORT

When completed in January 1934, the Foreign Office survey consisted of thirteen formidably detailed papers.[17] The survey as a whole was China-centred. This was partly because naval questions were ignored. These were not, of course, the concern of the far east department[18] but they were an inescapable factor in Anglo-Japanese relations. The observance of a dividing line between the technicalities of strategic planning and diplomatic thinking had the effect not only of leaving a gap in this survey of the situation in the far east, but also of disturbing its balance. The elimination of naval matters altered the character of the problem to be considered.

The view emerged that friendship with China should be regarded as essential. It was affirmed.

If Great Britain is to retain her position and prestige in the Far East she must endeavour to gain and keep the friendship and goodwill of China [. . .] Without the goodwill of China it will not be possible to obtain fair treatment for British trade and enterprise.[19]

The accounts of British and Japanese investment in China made clear the supreme importance to Japan of her economic interest in China and demonstrated the great importance of Japan as China's best customer. This situation was recognised as an important bait to China for the restoration of better relations with Japan. The possibility of a Sino-Japanese *entente* with results detrimental to British interests could not be denied. Britain, it was suggested, might avert this danger by continuing to cultivate good relations with China, meeting her legitimate national aspirations and thereby establishing a moral claim on her sympathies sufficient to prevent such cooperation with Japan taking place. It was, of course, doubtful whether China would allow gratitude to stand in the way of her immediate economic interests. The problem of the future, it was suggested, was to find a formula for international cooperation so that Japan did not become the sole supplier of, and beneficiary from, foreign technical assistance to China.[20] Although the power centre in Japan was acknowledged to be moving from the civilian to the military side, it was suggested that the 'enlightened minority' would not readily abandon their ideas to 'fanatical men, ignorant of all but Asiatic ways'.[21] In this situation Britain's best policy would be to recognise the 'real needs' of the Japanese economy, avoid any appearance of 'deliberate antagonism' and confine her actions within 'essential defensive limits'.[22] The Foreign Office saw no scope for British initiatives or for any drastic policy. British far eastern policy had of necessity to be opportunist.[23] The *status quo* was to be maintained; the problem of Japan's position in China remained. Among those who sought answers to Britain's difficulties in the far east, the policy advocated by the Foreign Office, however expedient, was likely to be found disappointingly negative.

DEFENCE REQUIREMENTS IN THE FAR EAST

While the far east department had been engaged in establishing priorities in its area of immediate concern, the whole field of imperial defence was being reviewed. The cabinet's consideration of the report of the chiefs of staff sub-committee had led to the setting up of a committee to prepare a programme for meeting the worst deficiencies in defence.[24] This committee accepted the priorities laid down by the chiefs of staff which meant that, to a large extent, its interest was focussed on the far east which the chiefs of staff had established as their first defence priority. The Defence Requirements committee, às it was called, was preparing its report at the end of January 1934.

By that time, the news from the far east seemed rather better than it had been at any time since the outbreak of the Manchurian crisis in 1931. The Japanese foreign minister, Hirota Koki, who had taken office in September 1933 was apparently friendly towards Britain, a country of which he had had first-hand experience during a period of service at the Japanese embassy in London. The appointment of Hirota, an experienced diplomat who had been Japan's ambassador to the Soviet Union before becoming foreign minister, had not been regarded as promising by Whitehall, partly because of his early connection with the Genyōsha.[25] A personal and informal message of goodwill from the British foreign secretary to the new Japanese foreign minister was, however, well received by Hirota whose reference at that time to the 'disastrous blunder' of the abrogation of the Anglo-Japanese alliance and of the need to act 'in the spirit of that alliance' was reassuring.[26] In a speech in the Diet in January 1934 Hirota skilfully balanced a firm insistence on Japan's expectations and position with an apparent moderation. He specially referred to the 'traditional friendship' between Japan and Great Britain.[27] The British ambassador reported the impression he had formed in early 1934 that naval and military extremists were on the defensive after the dropping of General Araki, the army minister,[28] and it was felt in the Foreign Office that there was some chance that Japan's most militaristic phase might be over and that the danger of a war through Japanese aggression might have been reduced. There was at the time also a suggestion that for Japan the 'Russian bogey' might again be looming and that this, with United States recognition of the U.S.S.R. and the United States naval building programme, had made Japan anxious to improve relations with Britain.[29] Moreover, in January 1934, it seemed that the Indo-Japanese negotiations were on the point of settlement and that Anglo-Japanese talks between industrialists might reach a successful conclusion.[30] It seemed not unreasonable to hope that Japanese fear of political isolation might drive her back to her first ally as the best available.

It was perhaps logical that the Defence Requirements committee should have taken a rather optimistic view of Anglo-Japanese relations. The far east was accepted as the area of immediate concern as set down by the chiefs of staff and a provisional policy of 'showing a tooth' for the purpose of recovering standing was envisaged. This was, however, to be a preliminary to an 'ultimate policy of accommodation and friendship' since long-range defence plans were to be directed against Germany. The committee noted ominously,

We cannot overlook the danger created by our total inability to defend our interests in the far east. Japan is fully armed both in the material and moral sense. This is not our position.[31]

The fleet, supplies of fuel and resources, the intermediate ports, and the Singapore base, were all judged inadequate to meet a Japanese attack; but since, like the Foreign Office, the committee did not consider there was any immediate danger from Japan this was a less serious consideration than it might have been. The committee recorded the opinion that every advantage should be taken of any opportunity to improve Britain's relations with Japan and reported,

We cannot overstate the importance we attach to getting back, not to an alliance (since that would not be practical politics) but at least to our old terms of cordiality and mutual respect with Japan.[32]

There were obvious contradictions in an argument which suggested that goodwill existed and should on every occasion be cultivated, but that a show of force was necessary, after which even greater efforts for friendship must be made. The differing conclusions of the Foreign Office and the Defence Requirements committee about the degree to which a positive accommodation with Japan might be sought or was necessary, reflected both the difference in the scope of their respective enquiries and the complexity of the problem of designing a policy for the far east. In the more narrowly-focussed Foreign Office survey, British interests in China were central, but in terms of defence requirements, Australia, New Zealand, India and the protection of general trade were of primary concern. The problem was to reconcile commercial interests in China with imperial and commercial interests elsewhere in the area in a policy which Britain could afford. In terms of these wider policy considerations, a policy of friendship and accommodation with Japan assumed more positive importance.

In March 1934 the cabinet was faced with the necessity of making decisions on the recommendations in the Defence Requirements committee's report and this initiated discussion on the whole far eastern question.[33] There was every reason for urgent attention to be paid to defence requirements. Hopes for the success of the disarmament conference at Geneva were fading and Germany, who had withdrawn from the conference in October 1933, had announced plans for rearmament. All the same, the report's five year programme involving the expenditure of £85 million was a 'staggering prospect'[34] which at once put the chancellor of the exchequer on the defensive.

The Treasury view was that Britain could not afford a role in the far east and that a policy of political appeasement towards Japan should be followed so that the area could be eliminated from defence calculations. The idea had undoubted appeal, even for those who were not so enthusiastic over the prospect of financial savings. A *rapprochement* with Japan would offer Britain the prospect of independence of the United States. It had been noted in the Defence Requirement's committee's report,

There is much to be said for the view that our subservience to the United States in past years has been one of the principal factors in the deterioration of our former good relations with Japan and that, before the naval disarmament conference, 1935, we ought thoroughly to reconsider our attitude.[35]

This kind of sentiment widened the appeal of an accommodation with Japan but ignored the Foreign Office objection that Chinese goodwill would be jeopardised by attempts at conciliation. In the final analysis this always proved the stumbling block. Loss of Chinese goodwill could not be justified without assurance of some corresponding benefit from Japan. There were grave doubts that such assurances could be found and in the long run this was to make the government hesitate, given the realities of British financial and military weakness, to risk alienating the United States.

The structure of cabinet discussion on the Defence Requirements committee's report was dictated by a series of questions put before the cabinet by the prime minister. He asked,

(i) Does the cabinet approve the general recommendation that we should try to get back at least to our old terms of cordiality and mutual respect with Japan?
(ii) What does this mean and how can it be done?
(iii) Is this reconcilable with our commercial policy towards Japan?
(iv) What bearing has this on Anglo-American relations?[36]

Predictably, the warmest support for a policy of accommodation and friendship with Japan came from the chancellor. Neville Chamberlain saw no point in the effort and expense of 'showing a tooth' when ultimately the olive branch might have to be extended and in this pointed to the anomaly in the Defence Requirements committee's report. He advocated a bi-lateral pact of non-aggression with Japan, mere discussion about which, he maintained, would soothe Japanese feelings 'ruffled' by the termination of the Anglo-Japanese alliance. An understanding might also improve commercial relations and remove anxieties over Japanese activity in north China. Chamberlain suggested, as a lure to Japan, a positive British detachment from the United States, specifically in the matter of the naval treaties. The rationale was that better relations with Japan would free Britain to carry out defence requirements nearer home more effectively. It was acknowledged that a pact might have to be subject to certain assurances such as Japan's attitude to China but the question of just what assurances it might be possible to obtain on this vital matter was glossed over.[37]

At this cabinet meeting Chamberlain seems to have fired the enthusiasm of a number of members including Sir John Simon, the foreign secretary, who claimed, not altogether accurately, that the Foreign Office survey had 'rather strikingly' confirmed the Defence Requirements committee's report as to the desirability of good relations with Japan. Further support came from the lord chancellor, Lord Sankey, and Sir Bolton Eyres Monsell, first lord of the Admiralty since 1931 and a former naval officer. Although there was some dissent, there was no real argument at this stage and, as the prime minister noted, all were agreed that something would have to be done to improve relations with Japan. The foreign secretary was, therefore, given the task of preparing a definite recommendation for improving Anglo-Japanese relations. This conclusion stimulated Simon and the Foreign Office into the first of the several reviews of Anglo-Japanese relations which Chamberlain was to initiate between March and November 1934.

The foreign secretary chose to set out both sides of the problem of improving Anglo-Japanese relations and produced a paper giving the pros and cons of a non-aggression pact.[38] The form of this paper provided the cabinet with the case against Chamberlain which, apparently, no member had been qualified to present earlier. The pros of a pact were, it was suggested, the comfort it would give Japan as an assurance that Britain would not be an ally of the United States against her, and the faint possibility that this might tend to moderate Japanese naval demands. As against this, Simon weighed the question of violating the government's stated dislike of multiplying pacts; the bad effect on China and Russia who would certainly regard the pact as a demonstration that, as far as Britain was concerned, Japan might have a free hand against them; the offence to the League of Nations Union who would regard it as condoning Japanese action in Manchuria. The leaders of the Conservative party were sensitive to the popularity and propaganda of the League of Nations Union, an effective pressure group for publicising and gathering support for the League. In 1934 it had nearly a million members and it had been severely critical of the government's 'lack of firmness and consistency' during the Manchurian crisis.[39] It was certainly not in the government's interest to rouse the fiery idealists within this organisation.

As this outline makes clear, Simon felt the balance inclined in favour of the cons, but he reminded the cabinet that the Japanese appeared to be as anxious as the British for good relations and the solution of commercial problems. He recommended that a non-aggression pact should be kept in reserve pending the naval negotiations. If at that later date it should be found that Japan might be persuaded to accept a lower ratio in return for a non-aggression pact with Great Britain and possibly also the United States, the proposal might serve a useful purpose.

The idea of linking a political agreement with the naval talks was an attractive one which was to recur but it implied a different and narrower view of the function of a non-aggression pact than that which Chamberlain had had in mind. It reflected, moreover, wishful thinking about the amount of leverage Britain might have with Japan in naval matters. Japanese evidence indicates that by March 1934, there was no chance of the Japanese accepting a lower ratio with or without a non-aggression pact with Britain.[40]

Evidence on the economic aspects of the proposals for closer relations with Japan was supplied by the president of the Board of Trade, Walter Runciman. He had no doubts about the desirability of maintaining the friendliest possible relations with the Japanese and pointed out that there was not much that could be done in the economic sphere either by way of defence or aggression.[41] Everything seemed to point to a policy of 'wait and see' and with this the cabinet shelved Simon's paper[42] and nothing was allowed to leak out about a non-aggression pact.

Meanwhile the Foreign Office was trying to develop its views in line with the cabinet conclusion of 14 March which had asked for a definite recommendation for improving relations with Japan. In a lengthy memorandum which was overtaken by events and was

never actually seen by the cabinet.[43] it was pointed out that the
object of improved relations should be to build up a credit position which could be drawn upon in taking measures to meet trade
competition and in combating the threat of expansion in naval
armaments. These were not in themselves, therefore, matters on
which it was possible to yield to promote friendship, and in any
case, yielding in these matters seemed unlikely to do this. This
apparently left China as the only sphere in which concessions
could be offered as a bargaining counter, but a reversal of policy
there, either by tamely acquiescing in the abandonment of
interests or by partnering Japan in trampling China would, it was
suggested, not be worth the antagonism of the United States, the
ill-will of Russia or the loss of goodwill in China and the rest of
the world. As can be seen, the writers of this memorandum found
no solution for the problem of Japan's position in China. Apart
from offering support should Japan's claim to the mandated
islands be contested, no particular suggestion for improving relations with Japan could be found and the memorandum concluded,

our only course seems to be to continue to cultivate friendly relations from
day to day without taking an exceptional step to demonstrate our desire or
need of them.[44]

In the Foreign Office there was little enthusiasm for the suggestion about the mandates and it was generally agreed that the
impossibility of improving relations with Japan by any positive
step had been demonstrated.

At the Admiralty's request, a significant addition was later
made to this paper. While it made no difference to the conclusion reached, it showed the Admiralty under pressure to
remind the Foreign Office of the importance of British interests in
the far east and of the navy's role in maintaining them. The
Admiralty agreed that Japan was anxious to keep good relations
but asked for an interpolation which would indicate that this
should not be regarded as an excuse for retreat. It read,

The ultimate end in view must be to maintain our interests in the east and the
first essential is that we should not leave it doubtful whether we have the
intention and the ability to do this. Certainty on this point is necessary to

make our friendship appear worth anything to Japan, and to restrain her from adopting a policy hostile towards us.[45]

The Admiralty, in fact, supported the principle of 'showing a tooth' and was anxious that it should be made clear that British strength would be demonstrated whether or not Japan actually constituted a menace to British interests. Altogether, the papers of 1934 agreed that Japan sought good relations with Britain, but at the same time underlined the problem of making any advance on the existing situation. Moreover, the difficulties of policy-making were increased by the naval matters which became an important feature of all foreign policy discussions in 1934.

4 NAVAL QUESTIONS

While the research, reporting and discussion described in the last chapter had been going on, naval questions as they affected the far east, and the naval relationship between Japan, Britain and the United States, remained to be discussed. Naval policy was a major issue for both Britain and Japan in 1934. Decisions had to be made on the future of the Washington and London naval disarmament treaties;[1] and, for both Tokyo and London, the political implications of the renewal of these treaties were at least as important as the technical. The Japanese government could not afford to renew the treaties; the British government could not afford to see them go. Both governments were suspicious of the United States.

Neither British nor Japanese naval men had been happy either with the Washington conference of 1921–2 which had established what was to become the notorious ratio of 5:5:3 between Britain, the United States and Japan in capital ship building, or with the arrangements reached at the London naval conference of 1930 which extended the principle of naval limitation to various categories of auxiliary vessel. As a result of the first conference, the Admiralty, which had been pressing for the resumption of capital ship building, was faced in 1922 with the task of scrapping twenty such vessels and as a result of the second was forced to accept a drastic reduction in cruiser numbers.[2] At Washington the British accepted what amounted to a 'one power standard'. The theory was that naval strength should be great enough to enable the British fleet, wherever situated, to equal any other fleet, wherever situated. With the establishment of this standard, a two-ocean war really ceased to be practicable for the British navy. Since Japan was at the time regarded as the only power likely to threaten British merchant shipping, the one power standard meant in practice, the maintenance of a navy capable of meeting the Japanese navy at its selected moment. In 1922, when Germany was without a navy and was bound by the provisions of the treaty of Versailles, and with the European naval powers limited by the Washington treaty, it seemed that Britain had a sufficient margin of strength for this purpose. In any case, given the climate of opinion which existed in Britain then and in the next decade, it would have been difficult for any government to justify increased naval spending even supposing the British economic position had permitted it. As it was, it became after 1923 an accepted cabinet rule for the purpose of framing defence estimates, that there would be no major wars for ten years.[3] This strengthened the hand of the Treasury in resisting demands for all but limited expenditure on defence. Between 1923 and 1934 there could be rebuilding and re-equipping of the fleet on only a very minor scale and very little progress had been made on the key, but controversial, naval base at Singapore by that time.[4] Both Japan and the United States were more active than Britain in this period in modernising ships and their new ships were larger than those built by Britain.[5] By the early 1930s, British naval experts were of the opinion that naval strength had fallen below the one power standard safety limit, but it was not until the Shanghai episode of 1932 caused the dropping of the ten year rule, and an investigation of defence requirements in the light of this, that it became realistic for the Admiralty to anticipate a thorough programme to repair deficiencies and to plan future naval building. By the time this programme had been drawn up, however, the European situation had so changed that the one power standard, at least in the eyes of naval enthusiasts, seemed scarcely sufficient.[6] Nevertheless, until existing deficiencies were repaired, it was essential that naval limitation vis-à-vis Japan should be retained. Sir Bolton Eyres Monsell, a former naval officer who had become first lord in 1931, with Admiral Sir Ernle Chatfield, who became first sea lord in 1933, began a determined effort in 1934 to make good existing deficiencies and to re-establish the principle that the navy's major role in imperial defence required a two power standard. Their aim was a navy large enough to provide in the far east a force of sufficient strength to ensure security for the empire and its essential interests against Japanese encroachment or attack, to provide also protection for British merchant ships and at the same time to leave sufficient forces in European waters and the Atlantic to give security against the strongest European naval power.[7] They still faced formidable opposition from the Treasury. On the one hand, therefore, they needed to present Japan as a very real danger in order to make the strongest case for a larger and better equipped navy; on the other hand they wanted to retain naval limitation treaties, certainly until the worst deficiencies were repaired and the Singapore base had been completed. Above all, it was desirable to avoid a situation in which British naval weakness tempted Japan to aggression so that British naval deficiency was publicly exposed.

For the Japanese navy, the effect of the Washington conference had been rather different. Divisions within naval ranks which were characteristic of the 1920s dated back to that conference. The Japanese delegation had been led by Admiral Katō Tomosaburō, the navy minister, who had over-ruled Vice-Admiral Katō Kanji, the technical expert accompanying him, and had accepted arrangements which limited naval armament and condemned Japan to an inferior naval ratio in relation to Britain and the United States. Katō Kanji had strenuously opposed the ratio and, in the next decade, he and others in the navy never ceased to fight against a policy of naval disarmament.[8] This faction has been described by Japanese historians as the Kantaiha (fleet group), while those who accepted the arrangements made at Washington and the further limitations which were the result of the London naval conference of 1930, have been called the Jōyakuha (treaty group). In fact, after the death of Admiral Katō Tomosaburō in 1923, the Jōyakuha, which represented the traditionally moderate and pro-British leadership of the Japanese navy gradually lost ground, though it still had sufficient influence over policy to frustrate Katō Kanji, who was, by 1930, chief of naval general staff, in his campaign against the ratio in auxiliary vessels which the London naval treaty imposed upon Japan.[9]

The upshot of the fight in Japan over the London naval treaty was a badly divided navy. Katō Kanji, however, had enhanced his reputation with the Kantaiha which, of course, included plenty of officers frustrated by their poor promotion prospects under this disarmament policy and resentful of traditional leadership.[10] This situation gave Katō Kanji and his deputy, Vice-Admiral Suetsugu, an opportunity to exercise hitherto unprecedented influence over the direction of naval policy. In 1932, Prince Fushimi was installed as chief of naval general staff; and the moderate navy minister, Admiral Okada, was unable to resist his princely authority used, as it was, by Katō Kanji and the Kantaiha to carry out their demands.[11] Career officers in the middle ranks of the navy, moreover, had links with men in right-wing political circles and took part in various 'incidents' which reflected their discontent with the existing state of affairs.[12] Certain moderates were forced into retirement, and these purges in the upper ranks effectively demoralised the treaty group so that, by 1933, restraints on the Kantaiha had disappeared and, as milder counsels were no longer being heard, disagreements within the Japanese navy tended to be within the Kantaiha.

One effect of the success of the Kantaiha was a reduction of interest in technological development as applied to the navy. As a group they tended to be traditionalist and to accept the traditional strategy of big ships and big guns.[13] More revolutionary ideas came in fact from moderates like Admiral Yamamoto who was obsessed with the idea of naval aircraft.[14] In their preoccupation with the removal of the ratio, the Kantaiha tied themselves to a view of naval strategy which was implicit in that ratio. This gave them a particularly inflexible attitude as far as alternative plans for naval disarmament were concerned. Events in Manchuria and the announcement in March 1933 of Japan's intention to leave the League served only to enhance the feeling in the Japanese navy that independence must also be exercised in decisions over naval armament.

From the beginning of 1934, therefore, Japan was flying kites with messages suggesting her unwillingness to accept a lower ratio than that of Britain or the United States.[15] The Japanese navy's nightmare was an Anglo-American front against them in the Pacific but their main practical concern was with the American naval 'threat' there. The announcement in June 1933 of the American naval building programme had shocked Japanese public opinion and further alienated it from the United States.[16]

BRITAIN'S NAVAL PROBLEMS

These different factors were all important when, in early 1934, the Foreign Office began to consider British objectives for the naval conference the following year.[17] It was appreciated that her successful survival after rejecting membership of the League was unlikely to make Japan receptive to restraint in naval matters and that clearly the Washington and London treaties were in jeopardy. Nevertheless, the financial grounds on which the repeated pleas of the chief of naval staff and the first lord for some relief for the parlous condition of the navy had been rejected in earlier years, still held good. It was necessary, therefore, to consider strategy for increasing naval security with the minimum of expenditure and for the Foreign Office this meant, if possible, saving the Washington system from complete disintegration.

From the first it was hoped that Japan's demand for parity could perhaps be satisfied with some face-saving formula granting her equality of status and certain increases in relative naval strength. There was no support in the Foreign Office for the idea of a united front with the United States in an approach to Japan, the experts feeling that, in view of the unsatisfactory attitude of the United States towards Britain on a number of points, it would be a mistake to approach her in advance of all other countries. In any case the necessity of avoiding any stirring of Japanese nationalist sensibilities was stressed and it was felt that an Anglo-American front would probably render Japan 'quite intractable'.[18] It was suggested that, once British objectives for the 1935 conference had been defined, the best course for the British government would be to inform the Americans of its intention to commence informal discussion with the Japanese government in preparation for the 1935 conference and that, before doing so, it would be pleased to hear from them. If no satisfactory reply had been received within a reasonable time, conversations would then be opened with the Japanese government. The foreign secretary agreed to this plan which was to be submitted to the prime minister.[19] At this point, the British received what the Foreign Office interpreted to be an approach from the United States. In their turn, the Americans imagined they had been approached by the British.[20]

Americans and British were, of course, anxious to know each others reaction to Japan's probable stand on the ratio. When, therefore, in an informal conversation at the American embassy in January 1934, Prime Minister MacDonald dropped the idea of a secret exchange of views on the naval situation, Washington approved.[21] The Americans were surprised to hear no more of this idea, which seems to have been MacDonald's own[22] and it was not until March, when the prime minister met Norman Davis, the American delegate to the disarmament conference, at the latter's invitation, that the question of Anglo-American talks was revived.[23] Thus the Americans were under the impression that they were carrying on from the original British approach while the Foreign Office had the impression that the Americans had initiated proceedings.

MacDonald and Davis agreed that an exchange of views between experts would be desirable though MacDonald, who on this occasion had been briefed by the Foreign Office,[24] emphasised that other signatories to the Washington treaty should be informed. Davis stressed that the United States could neither agree to equality with Japan nor consent to any increase in the ratio. MacDonald thought that Britain would not agree to equality but made no categorical promise about her attitude to an increase in the Japanese ratio. According to Davis, MacDonald showed great anxiety about Japan's attitude and activities and indicated that he thought it most important that Britain and the United States should agree to the position they would take with regard to Japan's claims. Davis had great hopes of this conversation and had the impression that the British would be keen to iron out their differences with the United States over the maintenance of naval parity, in order to reach a common understanding with the United States as to Japan's demands for an increased ratio and, he thought, 'even to go further, if we are disposed to do so, for the maintenance of peace and the protection of our respective rights and interests'.[25] Clearly MacDonald, whose record of this meeting is thoroughly non-commital,[26] gave Davis the impression of greater concern about Japan and anxiety to cooperate with the United States than was evident among his advisers at the Foreign Office.

As a result of the conversation between MacDonald and Davis, a meeting between the Foreign Office and Admiralty naval experts and Davis and the American ambassador in London was arranged.[27] There is no American record of this meeting which the British described as 'particularly "hush hush" ',[28] but the British documents indicate that Davis, who appeared to assume that the British would oppose any increase in ratio, suggested that, if Japan would not agree to the existing ratio, Britain and the United States should conclude a treaty and that it should be made plain to Japan that Britain and the United States would increase their fleets as the Japanese did. Davis thought this threat would have a salutary and stimulating effect on Japan. Commenting on this meeting, the Foreign Office naval expert wrote,

There is a tendency on the part of the Americans to get us to pull the chest-nuts out of the fire for them in connection with this question of the Japanese ratio. This our people are not in the least disposed to do, and believe in fact that the more 'solidaire' we and the Americans appear on this question at the present juncture, the more stiff we are likely to find the Japanese when the time arrives to talk to them.[29]

It is thus clear that the British were both a good deal more reluctant to cooperate with the United States and were more cynical of American motives than Davis imagined.

Behind the scenes, the Admiralty was preparing its requirements for the 1935 naval conference and in March, a lengthy memorandum appeared. The chief of naval staff's basic assumption was that minimum security required that,

we should be able to send to the Far East a fleet sufficient to provide 'cover' against the main Japanese fleet; we should have sufficient additional forces behind this shield for the protection of our territories and mercantile marine against attack; at the same time we should be able to retain in European waters a force sufficient to act as a deterrent and to prevent the strongest European naval power from obtaining control of our vital home terminal areas while we can make the necessary redispositions.[30]

In discussion, the chief of naval staff stressed the fact that the British replacement programme could not be postponed in the face of American and Japanese naval building and made it clear that he felt that, if Japan would not accept the existing ratio, there was nothing to be gained by giving in to her demands and that it would be better to be free to build up British strength according

to the situation.[31] A junior minister at the Foreign Office commented that the Admiralty had always had a 'bee in its bonnet'
about Japan but admitted that, if only because of Australian and
Canadian opinion, the Japanese navy could not be ignored.[32]
Any explicit declaration that the government might not be
prepared to send the fleet to the far east in an emergency would
have been exceedingly badly received in the empire and it was
of course one of the Admiralty's most important claims that,
once the fleet was in the far east, the security of the Dominions
against aggression would be assured.

MINISTERIAL DISCUSSIONS

When the cabinet committee set up to consider matters relating
to the naval conference held its first meeting in April,[33] a new
dimension was added to the ministerial discussion which had been
going on since the early part of 1934. For the chancellor of the
exchequer, the committee provided a new platform, if not a new
audience, for his view that an Anglo-Japanese rapprochement
might offer a solution to Britain's far eastern problems. Chamberlain argued in his usual forceful and business-like way that, in the
event of a breakdown of the conference in 1935, public apprehension would be allayed if the government could say that, in
spite of this, a treaty with Japan had been arranged. He believed
it should be possible to reach some agreement with Japan over
China, the only forseeable difficulty between the two countries,
and he felt a solution would be found if Britain's negotiators went
frankly to Japan and asked,

What do you want in China? Is it trade? If so, is there not enough for us
both? We want to do nothing detrimental to your trade with China. What
China needs is development. Can we not leave you free to supply capital in
one area while we are free in another?[34]

Chamberlain argued here that a friendly arrangement with Japan
could provide the solution of commercial difficulties and, in the
friendlier atmosphere created, Britain and Japan might arrive at
some understanding over naval matters. Chamberlain's insistence
on the solution of commercial and naval problems as the primary
aim of good relations with Japan and his focus on China as the

area in which leverage might be found was in line with the most recent conclusions of the Foreign Office[35] but the kind of bold approach here proposed was, of course, his own. This approach would have ignored China's national feeling and was likely to have political repercussions at home and abroad which Chamberlain chose to ignore or perhaps was prepared to risk. It was, however, significant that, in the first ministerial discussion on the naval conference, the problem of Japan's position in China as the stumbling-block to better Anglo–Japanese relations had been identified.

When Chamberlain was not present at meetings of the naval conference committee, there was no ardent advocate of an Anglo–Japanese *entente* among the ministers, but sympathy with Japan's aspirations continued to be shown and the desire not to give the impression of an Anglo–American front was also evident. The belief that Japan 'badly wanted a friend' was expressed even after the pronouncement from Tokyo known as the Amau statement which, as the prime minister pointed out, did not improve the chances of friendliness.[36] Since it was going to be difficult to find agreement over ratios where it seemed likely that Britain might eventually find herself on the side of the United States, it was felt advisable to consult Japan first and to find out her views in order to demonstrate that no Anglo–American front existed and in the hope that this gesture might make Japan more amenable to existing ratio arrangements. After three meetings in April 1934 it was decided by the committee,

(a) that we should not agree to an increase in Japan's ratio without some substantial *quid pro quo.*
(b) that the Foreign Office should consider making as soon as possible an approach to Japan with a view to ascertaining in the most friendly way, her views on the subject of the ratio and that this information should be obtained before entering into preliminary discussion with representatives of the United States of America.[37]

The naval conference committee's discussion of British naval requirements was based on the chief of naval staff's paper of March 1934 to which reference has already been made,[38] and time had been devoted to detailed discussion of cruiser numbers, tonnages and guns.[39] The basic assumption of the report now came under strong criticism from the Treasury in a paper written in the usual vigorous style of Sir Warren Fisher, the permanent secretary.[40] Fisher, who clearly shared many of Chamberlain's views, argued that Britain should settle her own interests without reference to the United States, for whom, he felt, the Admiralty paper had shown too great a consideration. He described a naval agreement between Britain and the United States as a 'complete *non sequitur* from every point of view' and American support of Britain as 'the very last thing upon which we can count'. While Japan could, he admitted, 'scoop not merely such outposts as Hong Kong but the whole of our China investments and trade', given a completed Singapore and an anti-Japanese America, he did not believe that Japan's capacity for endangering British trade routes or India or Australasia would ever assume such proportions as to lay Britain low. Clearly Fisher saw no point in the concept of the fleet as a deterrent in the far east. The Admiralty regarded evidence of readiness and the capacity to send a sufficient fleet to Singapore as the weapon which would prevent 'unreasonable' Japanese action or Japanese aggrandisement at British expense. The security of the empire east of Suez and the maintenance of imperial prestige depended, it was argued, on the navy.[41] It was not so much that Fisher cared for none of these things, but that he argued that an accommodation with Japan would be the most practical way of defending them. In his estimation there was no point in basing war preparations primarily on Japan since the risk of disaster existed nearer home. For him, the empire had no importance without its centre. Britain could not, he pointed out, 'down' Japan at a distance of 10,000 miles and, since even the most optimistic estimates made it clear that Britain could not fight Japan and the strongest European power, Britain had everything to gain and nothing to lose by effecting a genuine and lasting reconciliation with Japan. He advocated, therefore, detachment from the United States, a thorough and lasting accommodation with Japan and the indication to Germany that Britain was prepared to concentrate maximum force in Europe.

Fisher's paper went, with Chamberlain's support,[42] to the ministerial committee on the naval conference and to the ministerial committee on disarmament. The Foreign Office view of it was contained in a letter from Vansittart to Fisher. The Foreign Office had, of course, only recently explored the possibility of improving Anglo-Japanese relations and Vansittart wrote,

The difficulties of effecting a 'thorough and lasting' accommodation with Japan are even with the best will in the world, more formidable than one would at first believe to be the case. It must, I think, be more a matter of attitude and opportunism. It is when we come to the specific methods by which you seek to bring about these events that our troubles begin.[43]

Vansittart pointed out that, while theoretically there need be no worry about the size of the American fleet, the Admiralty was bound to worry about the size of the Japanese fleet built, inevitably, in competition with the American one. This three-cornered competition and its reaction on British building made it difficult leaving the United States to build what she wanted. As he pointed out, reductions in the British navy since the first world war had notoriously been due far more to motives of economy than to subservience to the United States. Vansittart did not deny that every effort must be made to improve Britain's relations with Japan but did not think this should be done by sacrificing American goodwill and doubted, furthermore, whether a deterioration in Anglo-American relations would contribute to peace in the far east. He wrote that it seemed to him that

the necessity of maintaining good relations with China (owing to our great commercial and financial stake in that country) constitutes a fact of much greater difficulty in the way of an Anglo-Japanese *entente* than does the maintenance of reasonably good relations with the United States.[44]

Vansittart expected this problem to become more difficult in the future and his conclusion was that both the United States and Japan should be kept in play. Again, the problem of relations with China had been identified as the obstacle to better relations with Japan; and once again, the Foreign Office had rejected a Treasury demand for action with recommendations which looked suspiciously like a policy of drift.

The situation in Europe having deteriorated further in April with the rejection by the French of a British revised plan for a disarmament agreement which included Germany,[45] it was more than ever important to establish policy for the far east. Part of the problem was, as the prime minister noted, that no-one knew whether Japan would respond to a political approach or what cooperation with her might mean.[46] Some indication of Japanese desiderata as far as China was concerned seemed, however, to have been given in the Amau statement of 17 April.[47] Japan appeared to be demanding as of right to be consulted by other powers over China. The British government's initial reaction to this statement had been to try to play it down since Japan's capacity to hinder development in China was already evident. Pressure from members of parliament and the press, however, forced the government to ask Tokyo for clarification,[48] and the outcry over the episode was still at its height when the Japanese ambassador in Berlin stated publicly that his country was con-vinced that the disparity in naval armaments would have to be removed at the naval conference.[49] The unwelcome publicity which these events brought Japan made the Foreign Office doubtful about the wisdom of first consulting her about the ratio as the naval conference committee had recommended.[50] Of course, Chamberlain would have liked to see the exchange of communications over the Amau statement used to point out to the Japanese that the question of the relative positions of Britain and Japan in China was the only one likely to give rise to difficulty between Britain and Japan and that, if an understanding about this could be reached, military and naval problems would be greatly relieved. Although he had some support for this view from the first lord, Simon's scepticism successfully quashed the sug-gestion. Sir John Simon thought Japan's awareness of her special relationship with China went very deep and that attempts by Japan and Britain to discuss a common *modus vivendi* would be represented as an attempt to partition China. He pointed out that Britain relied on the Nine Power treaty to keep Japan in her proper place in China and it would be difficult to arrange any concession which would be preferential to Britain and Japan as distinct from the other powers. Nevertheless, ministers remained helplessly aware of the importance of good relations with Japan should the naval conference fail and agreed that, in this event, a treaty with her about the Pacific ocean would be necessary.[51]

Foreign Office unease about approaching Japan in her present mood with an enquiry about her views on the ratio led to the foreign secretary strongly recommending that this should not be done.[52] The draft telegram making the preliminary enquiry was, therefore, cancelled by the naval conference committee and the foreign secretary was instead charged with the task of sounding the Japanese ambassador in London in order to find out what the attitude the Japanese government might be likely to take at the forthcoming conference.[53]

The British were ready to enter into preliminary talks with Washington and Tokyo.[54] In reply to Simon's enquiry about the possible attitude of the Japanese government at the conference, the Japanese ambassador said that his government was strongly opposed to extraneous political questions being discussed at the 1935 conference; the introduction of questions relating to China would, he thought, greatly complicate the issues at a conference which should be confined to naval matters. Simon commented drily that the British government was also against complicating matters.[55] There, for the time being, matters rested. It seemed, however, that the possibility of using China as a lever for per-suading Japan to agree to stand on the existing ratio had been anticipated and rejected in Japan.

This outcome was, in any case, in line with the realities as most recently assessed by the Foreign Office. In an attempt to answer the prime minister's query at a ministerial committee meeting in April as to whether Japan would respond to approaches of a political character and what, in terms of China, cooperation with Japan might mean,[56] a memorandum on Anglo-Japanese relations and the question of naval parity had been drawn up. Although relations with Japan were much better than in 1933, a definite approach to her with any hope of concrete results was considered to be surrounded with the utmost difficulty. A Japanese claim to a larger navy seemed inevitable and the only possible offer which Britain might make to induce her to abstain from putting forward such a claim must, it was believed, relate to China and Man-churia. The possibility of any comprehensive cooperation with Japan in China was rejected on the grounds that Japan's methods there were repugnant to western ideas and would not be tolerated by the British public and that in any case cooperation would probably not produce the results the British desired. The utmost that could be done, it was concluded, would be to convince Japan that the justice of her claim not to be excluded from any scheme of economic reconstruction in China was recognised and to make it clear to Japan whenever the opportunity offered, that it was genuinely desired to help her. Persuading China to be friendly or showing readiness to facilitate any reasonable solution of the Manchurian problem were suggested as examples of actions by which British goodwill could be demonstrated to Japan. The best course from every point of view would be that Britain, the United States and Japan should be brought into 'friendly union' and the forthcoming naval negotiations, it was suggested, if 'carefully handled', might conceivably offer the occasion to bring this about.[57] The Foreign Office felt it was impossible to be more precise and even this amount of optimism about the impending conference was difficult to sustain in view of the signs from Japan.

5 BRITAIN, CHINA AND THE AMAU STATEMENT

For Britain, China was a promising market and a political headache. The irritation with which she regarded the political upheavals in China in the 1920s did not remove her interest in seeking ways to stabilise political and economic conditions there. In spite of the inauspicious circumstances, some progress in reconstruction was made before 1933, much of this being carried out with the help of League of Nations organisations.

Cooperation between China and the League began in 1922 with the visit of a member of the health section of the League and a plan for regular cooperation in health matters went into operation after the visit of Dr Rajchman, Director of Health, in 1929. Two years later, at the request of the National government, the director of the Financial and Economic organisation of the League, Sir Arthur Salter, and the director of Transit and Communications, Robert Haas, also went to China with Dr Rajchman, by now a regular visitor. They discussed the possibility of continuous collaboration with technical organisations of the League and gave further advice on finance, public works and health programmes. As a result of their visit, the Chinese government established the National Economic Council for the purpose of planning and coordinating reconstruction projects in China in collaboration with experts sent out by the League.[1] Both Rajchman and Haas paid further visits to China between 1931 and 1933 and League education experts, engineers, agricultural scientists and specialists in the reform of civil administration visited China, made recommendations and submitted lengthy reports.[2] The willingness of China to turn to the League for assistance attracted much attention and, though the achievements of the reconstruction programme were modest, the request for League collaboration was regarded outside China as a hopeful and potentially significant sign. The powers wanted a reconstructed China and development by a disinterested organisation suited them all. From 1930, moreover, the reconstruction programme developed new signifi- cance as an increase in China's purchasing power might go a little way to help solve the world problem of industrial surpluses.

The members of the Lytton commission, writing at the end of 1932, declared the 'vital problem' in China to be the reconstruc- tion and modernisation of the state and they endorsed the idea of further development through the technical organisation of the League and through the National Economic Council. They felt that 'in spite of difficulties delays and failures', considerable progress had been made[3] and their attitude was such as to encourage the Chinese to look to the League for further help in 1933. This was all very well but, once Japan was no longer a member, League activities in China were bound to take on a new, if not hostile, significance for the Japanese. It was hard, especially while boycotts against Japanese goods operated in China,[4] not to see efforts at Chinese reconstruction as being directed at enabling that country better to resist Japan. The possibility that she might be excluded from Chinese reconstruc- tion roused deep suspicion in Japan.

The Chinese, for their part, were trying to establish a new order and a policy of their choice in the increasingly confused framework of international relations in the far east. They seemed, in March 1933, to have an opportunity to play off the powers and to make capital out of the apparent unpopularity of Japan in the west. The Nanking government was, however, divided about how or whether this should be done. Both the United States and Britain were regarded as possible sources of financial aid but aid from either of these sources involved the issue of the consortium. This was the procedure agreed in October 1920 by banking groups in the United Kingdom, Japan, France and the United States, by which all were to share equally in loans made for the purpose of providing China with the capital necessary for de- velopment. Formed ostensibly for China's benefit, the consortium was greatly resented in China.[5] It had made no loan by 1933 but any infringement of the spirit or the letter of the agreement by an individual member could be expected to cause an outcry from the others. The Chinese were also aware that reconstruction could not easily be sustained by any agency in the face of determined Japanese opposition. There was, therefore, logic in seeking a Sino-Japanese *rapprochement* in order to be sure of Japan's support in Chinese reconstruction. The difficulty was, however, to do this without rousing the anti-Japanese forces sedulously cultivated in China between 1931 and 1933. In the end the Chinese government appears to have attempted to obtain help from the west and exclude Japan from participation in the financing of Chinese reconstruction and to reach an accommodation with Japan in 1933. Neither policy met with any marked success.

CHINESE ATTEMPTS TO SECURE BRITISH, AMERICAN AND LEAGUE SUPPORT

In April 1933, T. V. Soong, the highly-regarded, American-educated Chinese minister of finance, left for Europe *via* the United States to attend the world economic conference. It was reported that Soong was in search of a large loan and that he hoped, by personal contact, to see if help was available from the United States. China, he indicated, had lost faith in the League.[6]

It was soon learned that Soong had successfully arranged a loan in the United States now under Roosevelt's Democratic administration.[7] The scheme involved a loan to the Chinese government by the Reconstruction Finance Corporation, an instrument of the United States government, to be spent on wheat and cotton owned indirectly by the American government. The credit of $50 million was to be repaid over three years at an interest of 5 per cent. One-fifth of the total was to be spent on wheat and four-fifths on cotton. The security offered was the excise on certain items which, in 1932, had produced $22 million.[8] The United States government acknowledged that their purpose in granting the loan had been to aid its own national recovery programme,[9] a self-interested attitude totally at variance with the kind of cooperative principles about China urged on the powers by the United States at the time of the establishment of the consortium and when the Washington treaties were signed. It was evident that the only country likely to gain anything out of the loan was the United States which not only was selling otherwise unsaleable cotton and wheat at market price but also was earning a reputation with the Chinese for generosity which, the British were quick to note, might affect future industrial orders.[10] The non-American members of the consortium were in general agreement that, while the loan might not actually infringe consortium rules, it was definitely in breach of their spirit.[11] The claim of the American group in the consortium that the loan was humanitarian in its concept and not therefore subject to consortium rules was regarded as nonsense[12] and reports that the wheat and cotton would be sold for cash at a discount and the proceeds used to purchase aircraft, armaments and industrial machinery from the United States added to apprehension about the loan.[13] It seemed doubtful that it would in any way contribute to China's reconstruction.

The British found themselves in a dilemma as they considered the significance of the American loan to China. Not only did the Foreign Office agree with the objections to it on principle put forward by Sir Charles Addis, head of the British group of the consortium,[14] but it was aware of the serious practical effects such a commodity loan was likely to have on the Indian cotton trade and the Australian wheat trade with China.[15] On the other hand, it was difficult to establish a breach of the Nine Power treaty and the Foreign Office had long been sceptical of the value of maintaining the consortium which they wanted replaced by an agreement which would allow British manufacturers to get orders in China.[16] Protest on either of these grounds seemed, therefore, to be inexpedient. Furthermore, it seemed possible that China, whose currency was based on silver and which had, until recently, benefitted from the low world price of silver, might be in a good position to profit by any revival in world trade and industry. It was desirable that China should, in this event, be encouraged to spend money in Britain.[17] Any objections to the American loan were liable to ·irritate China and, as Soong was known to be interested in obtaining credits for the purchase of British machinery, it was felt on these grounds as well, to be wisest to show forebearance of the wheat and cotton loan. As might have been expected, practical economic considerations finally dictated British policy over this matter.

The episode of the wheat and cotton loan and Soong's impending visit caused considerable discussion of the question of the consortium. The Foreign Office recognised that, should the hoped for revival of trade take place in China, the consortium obligations might well prove a hindrance. It was felt, however, that the time had not yet come for the British to suggest a dissolution. It was recognised that, while Japan was probably not wedded to the consortium, Chinese antagonism to her was so strong that the consortium was a safeguard against other powers gaining a rapid lead over Japan in China. Any attempt to dissolve the consortium was, therefore, likely to be regarded as an attempt to cut the Japanese out and, given the delicate state of relations between Britain and Japan in mid-1933, it was felt that such suspicion could not be incurred.[18] Britain's problem of keeping at once on good terms with the United States, China and Japan, was nicely illustrated by this debate over the wheat and cotton loan and the related issue of the consortium.

T. V. Soong, who had arrived in Britain in June, saw leading figures in the government and financial worlds. He at once developed his ambitious ideas for Chinese reconstruction. In interviews with the foreign secretary, he outlined his plan for a Chinese finance corporation, half the capital of which he hoped to raise outside China, principally in Britain.[19] The purpose of the corporation would be to provide funds for China's development. It appeared to be a device to get rid of the consortium to which the Chinese objected, both because it kept China on leading-strings, and because it included Japan. The British had no objection to the side-tracking of the consortium, but recognised the plan as the 'usual Chinese trick of using other powers to get the better of Japan',[20] whose position was, after all, the crux of the problem. The British did not intend to allow China to use them as a tool for excluding Japan from any share in Chinese reconstruction; and the foreign secretary was unaffected by Soong's account of China's disappointment at Britain's failure to take a more vigorous line against Japan and his claim that, if Britain would cooperate and show her sympathy and support, the United States would be prepared to apply economic pressure against Japan.[21] Since, for the time being at any rate, Japan was all-powerful in the far east, those who controlled the money markets of Europe were unlikely to embark willingly on a course of action liable to infuriate her and the heads of both the British and American consortium groups assured Soong that, until China arranged matters with Japan, she was unlikely to be able to raise money abroad.[22]

At the same time, of course, the British did not want to be shut out from any share in current industrial developments in China so that Soong was listened to with a good deal of sympathy, particularly in the Board of Trade. Orders from China for cotton spinning machinery, rolling stock and river vessels were mentioned as a possibility, provided credit for these could be raised in Britain.[23] The Board of Trade was anxious that advantage should be taken of this trade opportunity and supported the idea of granting China a credit of some kind. There was a great deal of discussion about how this might be done since the Exports Credit department was not designed for providing credit for purchasing bodies abroad.[24] In the event, no definite order was placed, and it seems probable that Soong's suggestions were intended more as a lure than as a serious proposition.

The proposal for an international finance corporation having made no progress, Soong next attempted to set up an advisory committee, the chairman of which would be M. Jean Monnet, a former League of Nations official. There were to be British, French, and Italian, but no Japanese, members of this committee. At first, both Addis and Thomas Lamont, the head of the American consortium, agreed provisionally to serve.[25]

The key to the success of the committee was obviously the Japanese reaction and Lamont was delegated to explain the situation to Matsudaira, the Japanese ambassador in London, who was an old friend. Matsudaira pointed out that the Japanese government was bound to be suspicious of the scheme[26] and this view was put much more forcibly by Nohara Daisuke, the London representative of the Japanese group in the consortium to whom Addis and Lamont wrote. The Japanese group of the consortium suggested that it was inconceivable that the committee as proposed could be 'authoritative and effective' in view of Japan's special position and influence in the far east and rightly regarded the scheme as likely to produce a 'feeling of irritation' in Japan.[27]

The Japanese objections were those of the Foreign Office which successfully urged Addis not to accept office on the committee and was relieved when Lamont too refused to serve.[28] As a result of this lack of support, Soong ultimately shelved the whole idea of the committee although Monnet proceeded to China as arranged.

Soong's deliberate attempts to exclude Japan from his plans to raise funds for China's reconstruction increased general scepticism about Chinese methods and, understandably, roused hostility in Japan. The situation was further exacerbated by Soong's activities in relation to the League. On behalf of the Chinese government, Soong asked for the League's continued collaboration in reconstruction work and the appointment of a technical agent to coordinate League activities in China. A special League committee, consisting of the president of the council and representatives of Germany, Italy, Norway, Czechoslovakia, Spain, China and the United Kingdom, was set up to enable various interested governments to be more directly associated with China's efforts at reconstruction than in the past, and this committee unanimously appointed Dr Rajchman to be the League's technical agent in China for one year.[29]

This appointment was one which filled the British and the Americans with the deepest misgivings.[30] Whitehall officials had no confidence in Rajchman's political judgment or discretion. He was described as a meddler who had 'hurled himself into the fray' of Chinese politics when the Manchurian trouble broke out in 1931[31] and 'saw only through Nanking spectacles'.[32] The Japanese had complained bitterly and, the British felt, justifiably of the activities of this League official. Nevertheless the British were not prepared to object openly to Rajchman's appointment. Their reasons for this reserve were a reflection of their weak position in the far east and the ambivalence of their aims there. Rajchman was reported to be 'hand in glove' with most of the political leaders in Nanking and Soong was known to want him in China. It was considered to be unwise to risk forfeiting Chinese goodwill by maintaining objections to a man who might be a very dangerous enemy.[33] Though there was every sympathy for Japan in this issue, she alone made public her objections to Rajchman.

For the Japanese, the appointment of Rajchman was further

evidence of the anti-Japanese activities of T. V. Soong. The Japanese press attacked the United States and the League for helping China and revived charges against Rajchman for his antipathy to Japan. Japanese officials in Washington made a number of protests against the wheat and cotton loan, the credit from which, it was claimed, would be used to buy arms against Japan. The Japanese maintained that Chiang Kai-shek and his 'group' were being prevented from coming to an agreement with Japan because of the opposition of Soong and his 'group' and that Soong's purpose in obtaining financial support from abroad was to provide the sinews to stiffen Chinese opposition and to make it more difficult for Japan to reach an understanding with her.[34]

By the end of 1933 the problems associated with the reconstruction of China had been delineated. China's reconstruction was a matter for international concern but not a matter for international cooperation. It has indeed been suggested that there had, in fact, been no real international cooperation in China since 1926[35] though the façade of the Nine Power principles had been maintained. Now it was more obvious that it was a matter of arrangements between individual powers and China and the factionalism within the Kuomintang and the chaotic situation in China made matters worse. China was interested in playing off all those powers with an interest in her development and in imposing an international order of her own choice. Bearing in mind always the possible reaction of the Japanese to any change in China, the British, with their ever-present problem of balancing their economic interest in China against their vulnerability in the Pacific and Indian oceans, tried to retain the goodwill of both China and Japan. They were concerned to sustain the international arrangements which condemned unilateral action in China and thus concealed Britain's unwillingness and incapacity to undertake such action in China's interest or her own.

SINO-JAPANESE RELATIONS

While Soong's activities were placing a strain on international arrangements in China the British legation in Peking believed that significant developments in Sino-Japanese relations were taking place in China itself. From the time of the Tangku truce of 1 June 1933, it was suggested, efforts were being made by the Chinese government to get back to good terms with the Japanese.[36] In the autumn of 1933, a rebellion led by the supporters of Marshal Feng Yu-hsiang collapsed and the anti-Japanese minister of foreign affairs, Lo Wen-kan, was, like Soong, away from China. This meant that the balance within the Kuomintang administration in Nanking favoured those who, like the acting minister of foreign affairs and head of the executive yuan, Wang Ching-wei, wanted a *rapprochement* with Japan. Negotiations with the Japanese legation in Peking were accordingly opened by Huang Fu, president of the central political council and governor of Hopei. Proceedings for a settlement of outstanding questions in the north were conducted with the utmost secrecy but were believed to involve customs, communications and frontier problems between Manchukuo and north China. The attitude of the local Chinese in the north towards the Japanese was reported to be friendly but in Nanking counsels remained divided and both Soong and Lo Wen-kan left the administration when they returned to Nanking in November. At this stage, negotiations with the Japanese appeared either to have broken down or to have been broken off and the British concluded that this indicated that, while Chiang Kai-shek and Wang Ching-wei wanted to pursue a policy of conciliation, they could not move too fast for fear of rousing national, and anti-Japanese, sentiment.[37]

No progress had been made in a Sino-Japanese *rapprochement* by the end of 1933 but, by the spring of 1934, it was known that Japan was pressing hard for a settlement of communications questions in the north and was threatening to take action of some kind unless more normal relations between Manchukuo and north China were resumed. Criticism from its opponents, particularly those in south China, impeded the Kuomintang response and a frustrating pattern of response and withdrawal was established. The increasingly delicate position of Huang Fu was believed to have led to his leaving Peking for central China for consultations with Chiang Kai-shek in mid-April 1934.[38] It did prove possible to work out a settlement of the communications issue by June 1934 but before this came about, Japan had seen fit to make her position in China absolutely clear to the rest of the world.

LACK OF PROGRESS IN CHINESE RECONSTRUCTION

Neither the Chinese attempts to achieve a *rapprochement* with Japan nor the reconstruction programme set in train by T. V. Soong had achieved much success by the beginning of 1934. The wheat and cotton loan ran into difficulties and the credit granted to China had to be substantially reduced when it was found that in practice China could not absorb the amount of cotton for which Soong had originally contracted.[39] Continuing fears about the uses to which the loan might be put led to further Japanese protests to the United States in 1934.[40]

The League programme of technical aid to China had some more concrete, if unspectacular, success in health, education, water conservation, and road construction programmes, but the political effect of the League's activities as they developed under Rajchman was regarded by the British as highly undesirable. It was suggested that the League plan for assistance to China looked like a plan for economic reconstruction from which Japan was excluded in breach of the spirit of the Nine Power treaty and financed, at any rate in part, by the proceeds of a loan which was in breach of the spirit of the consortium agreement.[41] It was felt the Japanese had some ground for complaint with regard to the form which League cooperation with China had taken.

At the same time the British were not optimistic about the prospects of the finance corporation which had been formed by Monnet from a combination of the principal Chinese banks. This body was intended to be both a channel and a façade behind which foreign interests could work in China without loss of Chinese 'face'.[42] The Japanese were, however, hostile to the plan which, if it worked, would prevent them from occupying a preferential position in China.[43] The British concluded that the only possibility for China was likely to be a scheme of international cooperation of which Japan approved. It was, however, difficult to see how, in practice, such a scheme could be worked out as long as tension existed between China and Japan.

Clearly the argument led to the desirability of a Sino-Japanese *rapprochement*. On the other hand, the British feared that such a *rapprochement* was likely to be based on Japanese interests and objectives and to be awkward for Britain. The Foreign Office was, therefore, relieved when nothing seemed to be coming of attempts to establish a Sino-Japanese *rapprochement*. The report from Peking that 30 per cent of the Chinese political leaders were in favour of a *rapprochement* with Japan, 50 per cent were apathetic and twenty per cent were relentlessly opposed[44] was received with the comment, 'A Chinese–Japanese rapprochement bodes no good for us and I pray it may be averted as long as possible.'[45] The possibility that China might come to an agreement with Japan on terms unfavourable to British interests was accepted at the Foreign Office as was Japan's key role in the provision of assistance to China. Nevertheless, however undesirable her activity in China, it was considered necessary to remain on friendly terms with Japan since it was felt at the Foreign Office that Britain could not be confident of her ability to sustain the results of any other policy.

JAPAN'S 'AMAU STATEMENT' AND BRITAIN'S COUNTERMOVES

On 18 April 1934, an informal statement given to the Japanese press by Amau Eiji, spokesman for the Japanese ministry of foreign affairs, appeared in the British press.[46] Its content did not surprise the Foreign Office in view of the known facts about reconstruction in China and the political situation there. The Reuter message stated, 'Japan will take positive action if peace and order are disturbed by international cooperation in assisting China. If force is used by others, Japan will resort to force as well.'[47] Japanese press comment included reminders to China that she would not be able to succeed in any reconstruction scheme without enlisting the cooperation of Japan and instanced the American wheat and cotton loan as a case of undesirable assistance used by the Chinese for anti-Japanese propaganda.[48] This fitted in with the Foreign Office idea of the background to the case.

In the absence of a written statement it was, however, difficult to assess the precise meaning of the message. *The Times* correspondent thought that foreign powers were being asked to realise that concerted operations in China, even if designed to give technical assistance, inevitably attained political significance and were likely to end in spheres of influence or international control. He thought that the position could be fairly summed up by saying that

because she is liable to be vitally affected by events in China, Japan asserts that she has the right, as she has the power, to prevent any foreign activities of which she disapproves.[49]

On 20 April, the newspapers carried what *The Times* described as an 'unofficial translation' of the 'unofficial statement'.[50] It was, in fact, a Japanese Foreign Ministry translation of a newspaper report of the verbal statement. This began,

Owing to the special position of Japan in her relations with China, her views and attitudes respecting matters that concern China might not agree in every point with those of foreign nations: but it must be realised that Japan is called upon to exert the utmost effort in carrying out her mission and fulfilling her special responsibilities in East Asia.[51]

The points which followed, while the same in essence as those reported in the original Reuter message appeared, in context, rather less aggressive.[52] The statement, it was felt, merely gave precision and publicity to an attitude of which the Foreign Office was already aware[53] and the press was encouraged to make as little fuss about it as possible.[54] Reports from Washington indicated that the State Department was taking a similar canny line.[55] All the same, as *The Times* noted, in spite of its modest appearance, the statement was the most important declaration of policy in regard to China to be made for many years and readers were reminded that the Japanese saw it as

an epoch making departure whereby Japan abandons her former policy of cooperation with the west in China and inaugurates a policy based on the principle that East Asian affairs should be settled by Japan and China alone.[56]

An equally serious view of the Japanese declaration came to be taken by the head of the far eastern department at the Foreign Office. While he acknowledged that the text of the declaration was somewhat less categorical than the original press summaries and

admitted that it might be possible to minimise the importance of
the statement on the grounds that it did not apply to British
policy, he nevertheless wrote,

the whole tenor of the statement is highly objectionable for it obviously
amounts to warning other powers off action which may be entirely proper
and to reserve liberty of such action to Japan though she is pledged to the
principle of equal rights for all powers in China.[57]

This opinion was shared by Vansittart who had, initially, been
endeavouring to prevent enquirers from making too much of the
incident. By 20 April, however, he informed the foreign secretary
that the 'line' could not be held; that this was 'a question of
considerable gravity'.[58] The seven parliamentary questions put
down for 23 April no doubt influenced Whitehall. Japan was told
'in a most friendly spirit' that the principle of equal rights in
China was guaranteed by the Nine Power treaty to which Japan
was a party and that Britain must, of course, continue to enjoy all
rights in China which were common to all signatories or were
otherwise proper except in so far as these rights were restricted by
agreements such as the consortium or in so far as Japan had
'special rights' recognised by other powers and not shared by
them. The Nine Power treaty gave Japan the right to call attention to any apparent danger to China's peace and integrity but the
British government did not admit the right of Japan to decide
alone whether any particular action promoted such danger and
asked for assurance that the Japanese statement was not intended
in any way to abridge the common rights of other powers in
China or to infringe on Japan's treaty obligations.[59]

The decision to approach Japan was an independent one arising
more out of pressure from parliament and the press than from the
Foreign Office's surprise or indignation at the Japanese attitude.[60]
The Lancashire and Midlands members of parliament, who
featured prominently as parliamentary questioners about the
Amau statement, could be expected to rise indignantly to any
suggestion that Japan might be laying further claim to the
Chinese market. These members had not in April 1934 been
appeased by the introduction of the tariffs and colonial quotas
against Japanese textiles for which they had been agitating for
over a year. The approach to Japan was, therefore, made on the

basis of political pressures and at no stage was a policy of consultation and cooperation with other powers interested in China contemplated. Such, however, was not the impression left with the Americans.[61] Their mistaken interpretation of events seems to have been due in part to carelessness on Simon's part and perhaps to ingenuousness on the part of the American ambassador in London.

On the evening of 20 April, Simon had occasion to see Robert Bingham, the American ambassador, about a matter unconnected with the Japanese statement. During their conversation Simon read Bingham the Tòkyo telegram giving the British ambassador's account of the translation of the Amau statement which had been received at the Foreign Office that day. On this telegram the *démarche* of 23 April, already described, was to be based. According to the American ambassador, Simon

took a most apprehensive view of this Japanese move and said that to meet it successfully he felt close Anglo-American consultation and cooperation was necessary and hoped for his part that once the facts were established there might be an early exchange of views.[62]

As he had promised, Bingham reported the foreign secretary's statement to his government. Washington replied that, not having had either in Tokyo or Washington, any communication from the Japanese government, the State Department had declined to comment on the Japanese Foreign Ministry statement. In the light of what was described as 'Sir John's approach', however, it was indicated that careful consideration would be given to 'any suggestions or proposals which the British government might wish, at an early moment, to make'. Simon was to be informed that the United States, acting for the safeguard of its own interests, was willing to do its part, but no more than its part, in safeguarding the common interest, and would welcome any indication he might be disposed to give of the British government's thoughts and intentions.[63] By the time this cautious telegram arrived from Washington, the British telegram to Tokyo had already been despatched.

Meanwhile, in the far eastern department, the answers to the parliamentary questions about the Amau statement put down for Monday 23 April had been prepared. One of these asked whether the foreign secretary was in communication with the United States to secure concerted action in connection with the Japanese declaration concerning the far east. The Foreign Office minute on this question ran,

We have not communicated with the United States nor have we received any communication from them in this matter [. . .] it would seem desirable that we should approach the Japanese government alone and not in conjunction with the United States or any other power.[64]

The comment of the head of the far eastern department was even more explicit. He noted, 'On all accounts it will be better not to link ourselves with the United States government.'[65] In the event, Simon simply answered this, and the other questions put down, by circulating the telegram which had given the text of the Japanese foreign ministry's translation of the statement and by giving notice of the communication to the Japanese government, the object of which, he explained, was to clarify the position of the British government.[66]

This same information was passed on that day to the Chinese ambassador who called on Simon in a state of acute anxiety about the Amau statement and about the disturbing report of an interview in which the Japanese ambassador in Washington was alleged to have said that Japan would consider it an unfriendly act if those who wanted to deal with China did not consult her first.[67] Simon soothed the ambassador and refused to be drawn on what further action the British were likely to take. He made it clear that nothing had been heard from the United States or any other power.[68] As far as the foreign secretary and the Foreign Office were concerned, British policy was following a consistent and independent line.

This impression of independence was jolted when, on the following day, the American reply to Simon's comments to Bingham was received.[69] Wellesley, the deputy under-secretary, who received this communication was astonished by the suggestion that Simon had indicated that Britain and the United States should cooperate in resisting Japanese pretensions. This was, of course, a far more positive statement than Simon's reported preference for 'consultation and cooperation' and an 'early exchange of views'. It was at once obvious to the American official who had delivered the message that Wellesley was sceptical that Britain would consider any use of threats towards Japan except under provocation of some grave incident and that he was equally doubtful as to how far the United States would go.[70] In his own report of the interview Wellesley wrote of his surprise

at hearing of the suggested cooperation with America since we always try to avoid giving unnecessary umbrage to Japan by taking joint action with the Americans.[71]

Simon's account of his discussion with Bingham was that it had been 'of so informal and limited a character' that he had made no note of it. He remembered telling the ambassador that a version of the declaration had been received from Tokyo and that its claims might not be consistent with the Nine Power treaty. He said that he had indicated that the British would 'naturally be interested to hear the view of the United States government'.[72]

Wellesley was advised to 'undeceive' the Americans as quickly as possible[73] and, at a second interview with the counsellor at the American embassy, he made it plain that the foreign secretary had not had concerted action in mind. The counsellor replied that he had not intended to convey that anything more was intended than an exchange of views and Wellesley accepted this although he felt it did not tally with the offer to consider proposals and to take part in safeguarding common interests contained in the Washington telegram. In a later telephone conversation the counsellor told Wellesley that what he had meant was 'consultation and exchange of views'. This was, of course, the phrase reported by Bingham to Washington, but Wellesley was sure that neither of these expressions had been used by the American in the original interview.[74] Whatever the facts of the conversation between Bingham and Simon which caused this little contretemps, the whole affair became significant for the American analysis of the British government's attitude and actions with regard to the Amau statement. Bingham wrote later,

I cannot but feel that Sir John Simon's personal attitude as expressed to me underwent considerable modification by the time he made his statement to the House of Commons since in his statement he took pains to emphasise that the British government had already made a 'friendly enquiry' at Tokyo (which instruction to the British ambassador in fact had only been drawn up on the previous evening) [. . .] and in response to the question addressed to him regarding cooperation with the United States he was obviously anxious to avoid making any definite answer.[75]

In fact, Bingham's information about the drafting of the message to Tokyo was incorrect and it seems probable that he may have exaggerated the significance of Simon's original conversation, but the impression to be gained from the American documents is, as a result, that a British approach to the United States was made and that British policy then changed. As a consequence of this, the most authoritative account of American policy in this period states that the question of undertaking cooperative measures was

dropped by the British themselves who, in apparent contradiction to their initial stand, decided to act individually and to limit themselves to asking Tokyo for a clarification of the Amau statement with a view to determining, in particular, its relationship to the Nine Power treaty.[76]

It is quite clear, however, that the British attitude as expressed in the cabinet and the Foreign Office was consistently against cooperation with the United States in the far east and that there was, therefore, no 'contradiction' in their independent action on 23 April. If Simon did have other ideas when he spoke to Bingham, they were his own and directly contrary to expressions of opinion in the cabinet and to the already prepared Foreign Office plan for an approach to Japan.

Ironically, the quite different impression that the British gained from this episode and a related report of an interview, in Washington, between the British ambassador and Stanley Hornbeck, head of the far east department in the State Department, was that the Americans, while not actually asking for it, would like some sort of joint policy. Hornbeck described Japanese policy as 'quite extraordinary' and 'something to which other governments could not acquiesce' but made it quite clear that the United States would not take the lead in proposing any action, jointly or otherwise, to other powers. He said, however, that the American government would be most reluctant to repel proposals made to them by others.[77] Foreign Office reaction to this was to instruct the ambassador to make it clear to the State Department that the British government would not favour combined action[78] and to reaffirm to him the need to preserve independence of action.[79]

A similar line was taken by Simon when, on 25 April, he drew the cabinet's attention to the Amau statement. He emphasised that, though the situation was disturbing, there had been no communication with any government other than that of Japan as he was anxious not to give the impression of creating an anti-Japanese bloc. The cabinet approved this attitude.[80]

In the meantime, British efforts to elicit a satisfactory explanation of the Amau statement from the Japanese were not meeting with much success. Sir Francis Lindley, British ambassador in Tokyo, reported that, in a long and friendly conversation, Hirota had explained that the statement issued by the Foreign Ministry spokesman had not been sanctioned beforehand by the Japanese government and had assured him of Japan's support for the Nine Power treaty and the open door.[81] Hirota also referred in confidence to certain activities of a 'doubtful character' in which some powers were engaged in China and pointed out that, while agreeing that all signatories had equal rights under the Nine Power treaty, Japan, being the nearest to China, had most to fear from a conflagration there. In drawing[82] his conclusions about this interview, Lindley commented that the statement would have served a useful purpose if it made China realise that Japan would make serious trouble if China was implicated in schemes of 'assistance' designed to facilitate China's resistance to Japan. He recommended that the incident of the statement be considered closed and noted, 'This attitude on the part of Japan may be as unreasonable as it is unpleasant but we are unable to alter it or to protect China from its effects.'[83]

This was all very well but such frank speaking was not possible in parliament where the government had to face more questions and where a further statement from the foreign secretary was inevitable. The Japanese had not, as *The Times* which sympathised with Japan admitted, entirely corrected the impression that they had seized an inauspicious moment for Britain and the United States to enunciate more comprehensive claims to dominate and control the development of China.[84] Moreover, the essential point of the British message to Tokyo, that Britain could not admit the right of Japan to decide alone whether any particular action endangered the peace and integrity of China, had not been touched on in the foreign minister's answer to Lindley. The question, it was felt, could not be closed with such vague assurances from Japan and it was finally decided to inform Tokyo of the reply to be given in the Commons on 30 April, to point out that the Japanese answer evaded the central issue and to indicate that the matter must be given further consideration.[85]

This move coincided with Lindley's report that Hirota had also given the American ambassador assurances of Japan's determination to uphold the Nine Power treaty. The American ambassador was convinced, and succeeded in converting Lindley to his view, that Hirota did not approve of the statement.[86] Lindley transmitted the text of an official declaration handed to the American ambassador in response to his government's enquiry as to the nature and text of the Japanese statement. The object of this text was declared to be to remove any misunderstandings which might have arisen with regard to the Amau statement. The gist of the new document was that Japan had not infringed and had no intention of infringing China's independence or interests; that Japan had no intention of trespassing on the rights of other powers in China, welcomed *bona fide* commercial activity and subscribed to the open door; that Japan could not remain indifferent to anyone's taking action on any pretext which would be prejudicial to the maintenance of law and order in east Asia for which she, 'if only in view of her geographical position', had most vital concern. She could not, in consequence, afford to have the question of China exploited by any third party which did not take these circumstances into consideration.[87]

The third point of this skilfully worded statement was, in fact, a qualification of the first two and by implication left Japan with the claim to be the sole arbiter of the actions of foreign powers in China. All the same, the Foreign Office found the whole effect reassuring.[88] Since Lindley now pointed out that at the time of his interview on 25 April he had actually drawn the attention of the foreign minister to the unanswered implication but that Hirota had merely laughed as if this was too absurd a claim to be taken seriously,[89] it was felt that there was nothing to be gained by pressing the point further, particularly in view of the statement given to the United States.[90]

The State Department did not release or discuss the Japanese document although it had been made clear by the Japanese that they had no objection to its being given publicity.[91] This meant that the material available for British use in the answers to parliamentary questions rested on the non-confidential part of the conversation between Lindley and Hirota on 25 April and consisted of quite unexceptionable Japanese sentiments about the Nine Power treaty and the open door. If it ever became possible to compare this material with the contents of the Japanese written answer to the Americans, it would seem either that the Japanese explanation to the British had been deliberately less controversial or that there had been a deliberate suppression by the foreign secretary of the controversial aspect of the Japanese explanation.

Simon made his second major statement about the Amau question on 30 April. The first part of this answer to a parliamentary question consisted of a verbatim repetition of part of the telegram drafted by the head of the far east department and despatched to Tokyo on 23 April.[92] The House was told that Ambassador Lindley had been instructed to tell the Japanese minister of foreign affairs apropos the Nine Power treaty that the British government must

continue to enjoy all rights in China which are common to all signatories or otherwise proper, except in so far as their rights were restricted by agreements such as the Consortium agreement or in so far as Japan had special rights recognised by the other powers and not shared by them.[93]

The last part of this sentence roused grave suspicions and was the subject of enquiry by both the Chinese and American embassies. They were assured that the phrase 'special rights' was of no particular significance and referred only to such rights as might be enjoyed by a number of countries including Japan, in connection with loans, railways and so on.[94] The American ambassador attributed the troublesome phraseology to the drafting of a junior in the absence of the head of the far eastern department[95] but the British documents indicate that the head of department, together with Vansittart and Simon, had been concerned in the organisation and wording of this answer.

The second part of Simon's statement to the Commons dealt

with Hirota's reply to the British approach and consisted only of the anodyne sentiments about the Nine Power treaty and the open door, the comments on the objectionable activities of some foreign powers having been confidential. The foreign secretary indicated that the government was now content to leave the question of the Amau statement as it stood.[96] He was not to be let off so lightly.

Simon had agreed to let the matter drop because it was obvious that nothing more specific was likely to be wrung out of Japan. He was aware, as he admitted to the ministerial committee on disarmament, that the government might be exposing itself to some criticism by saying that it was content with the Japanese explanation when it might have been asking the meaning of some of the points raised on the Amau question.[97] As it happened, the government's actions came in for more criticism because of an unexpected American move.

After having done nothing but ask for the exact text of the original statement and an explanation of the circumstances in which it was issued, the Americans, on 29 April, copied the British *démarche*. Their ambassador in Tokyo received 'rush' instructions and called on the minister of foreign affairs on a Sunday evening in order to present an *aide-mémoire*.[98] The ambassador, Joseph Grew, was delighted with this document which he felt was expressed with 'a clarity and moderation' which put his government on precise record 'without giving needless offence'.[99] *The Times* Washington correspondent also congratulated the American government on its quiet reassertion of regard for principle and on the fact that, for the first time since it had come into office, the Roosevelt administration had taken a definite stand on 'matters oriental'.[100]

Whitehall comments on the communication, described as 'hot air',[101] were less complimentary. It was observed that, apart from its wordiness and high-minded sentiments, the American document was making essentially the same points as had the British.[102] It was, however, embarrassing to the Foreign Office to learn that a State Department, spokesman had asserted that the United States and Britain had 'naturally followed parallel lines of action'.[103] The British had, of course, made every effort to avoid giving any such impression. All in all, Anglo-American encounters over the Amau statement served only to confirm the belief that, in the far east, the United States would leave the British to bear the brunt of the action and, if necessary, take most of the blame.

Far more embarrassing than the American *démarche* was, however, the publication in Tokyo of Simon's statement to the Commons, of a summary of the interview on 25 April between Lindley and Hirota, and of the text of the hitherto unpublished Japanese official declaration given to the United States on 27 April. Journalists in Tokyo were informed that the object of the communiqué was to emphasise the third point of the official declaration which was, of course, absent from Simon's statement[104] since it had been incorporated in Hirota's confidential comments to Lindley. Having judged that it would be incorrect to use the text of the reply to Washington before the Americans themselves made it public, Simon and the government found themselves accused of bad faith, both by Japan and in the House of Commons where it was now claimed by M.P.s that there had been a conscious attempt by the government to ignore the disagreeable part of the Japanese statement. Japan had won a trick and had avoided any suggestion of playing off Britain and the United States by publishing first. It was now to be seen that the incident had ended, as *The Times* said, with Japan 'politely but immovably asserting her primacy of interest in developments in China and indicating certain specific foreign activities to which she objects.'[105]

It was easier to protest to Japan against this shabby treatment than it was to satisfy parliament. Questions were put down in the Commons and a motion in the Lords called for more decided and vigorous government policy both in the far east and at the disarmament conference. In order to answer the accusation of having suppressed part of the official Japanese answer, Simon would have to reveal the confidential part of Hirota's conversation with Lindley and, in warning Japan of its wish so to do, the Foreign Office pointed out that the text of the official declaration handed by the Japanese to the American ambassador had not been used because it had not been published by the government of the

United States.[106] Japan's answer to this was that the version handed to the American ambassador was intended also as Hirota's considered reply to the British ambassador and that the omission in the foreign secretary's statement to the Commons of all mention of Japan's special concern for the maintenance of law and order in east Asia had surprised the Japanese.[107] There was really no effective answer that the British could make to these rather questionable tactics.

In the Commons, Simon faced repeated hostile questioning about the significance of the supplementary point in the Japanese declaration given to the Americans and not previously mentioned by him.[108] Similar suspicion of the government's 'mishandling' of what was described as Japan's 'Monroe doctrine for eastern Asia' was expressed in the Lords where both the prime minister and the foreign secretary came in for particular criticism.[109] Suspicions remained and questions continued to be asked until the major foreign affairs debate in the Commons on 18 May. Introducing this, the Labour member, Sir Stafford Cripps, asked,

First. Does this country still stand by the report of the League of Nations of February 1933 and regard Japan's position in Manchuria and Jehol as a breach of the Nine Power treaty?

Secondly. Does this country repudiate its obligations to respect and preserve the territorial integrity and political independence of China including Manchuria under the Nine Power treaty and Article II of the Covenant?

Thirdly. Are the government prepared not to enter into any treaty agreement or understanding with Japan in pursuance of the provisions of Article II of the Nine Power treaty or do they repudiate the article as well?

Lastly. What attitude do the government adopt to the question of security? Are they prepared to sacrifice any part of this country's independence of action or decision in order to attain international security?'[110]

Cripps went on to deal with the question of the far east in some detail but Simon was able to answer his argument and to deal with his questions with relative ease. It is perhaps significant that the foreign secretary and most other speakers in this debate were primarily concerned with the issue of disarmament and the possible breakdown of the disarmament conference, demonstrating that the stir about the Amau statement was peripheral to problems nearer home. Be this as it may, the main drama associated with the Amau statement died down after this debate. Japan had, in fact, sustained her claim to special concern over the activities of other foreign powers in China and if, as was suggested, the Amau declaration was a *ballon d'essai* to test how far these powers would be prepared to go in defence of China,[111] the answer had been fairly unequivocal.

Once the effects of the statement began to be felt and the Japanese government ranged itself behind the policy enunciated, Whitehall debated why it had been made at that particular time. In the Foreign Office which, throughout the crisis, had the satisfaction of feeling its own conscience was clear, there was the impression that it had been touched off by Japan's resentment at the American wheat and cotton loan which might have been used for anti-Japanese purposes; the French, Italian, and American arms shipments to China; the military mission of General Hans Von Seeckt to China; the Chinese building of wireless stations in Inner Mongolia; the activities of Dr Rajchman and suspicion of the report he was due to present to the League; the indiscretion of Monnet in trying to organise finance for China exclusive of Japan. There was also Japan's desire to provide a smokescreen for her activities in north China and the necessity for preparing Japanese public opinion for Japan's stand on the naval negotiations.[112]

The Foreign Office never decided whether the statement was made with Hirota's consent and approval. Its initial reaction had been that the move was intentional and calculated and that the statement probably represented Hirota's views.[113] Hirota's apparently sincere protests that the statement was issued without his knowledge or approval, however, influenced the ambassador in Tokyo and, to some extent, the Foreign Office also.[114] The idea of the statement as an unauthorised outburst appealed to those who wanted to believe that a moderate element existed in Japan, that Hirota represented this group and wanted conciliation of the west. The respected Japanese ambassador in London, who was regarded as a moderate, told British officials that the Amau statement was a bad blunder.[115] Count Makino, minister of the imperial household and adviser to the emperor, told Lindley that the government as a whole had no knowledge of it and Baron Shidehara, a former Japanese foreign minister whose foreign policy had been denounced in Japan as lukewarm, made scathing reference, in conversation with the British ambassador, to the foolishness of Amau's utterance.[116] All such expressions of opinion gave some support for the hope that moderation might in the end prevail in Japanese politics. The publication of the Japanese documents has now made it clear that the statement was, in fact, taken almost verbatim from one of Hirota's instructions to the Japanese legation in Nanking.[117] This fact was actually reported to Washington by the American ambassador in Tokyo[118] but does not appear in the British documents. In any case, the background to the statement and the attribution of blame for the timing of it were, for the British, of more significance than its actual origin.

As was to be expected, the Chinese government tried to make some capital out of Japan's unpopularity. Since no positive action against Japan could be contemplated, the official Chinese reply to the statement was 'moderate and dignified in tone' and the Chinese made it clear to the British minister in Peking that the Japanese statement would be ignored by the government.[119] All the same, they were anxious to know how the British would react if Japan sought to implement her claim and much was made of the threat which this presented to China's sovereignty and integrity.[120] The Chinese minister in London was assiduous in his enquiries about British moves and attitudes and, after one of his visits to the Foreign Office, it was noted rather crossly, 'If the Chinese are dissatisfied with the Japanese declaration, they must say so directly to Tokyo'.[121] Chiang Kai-shek claimed that China's alternatives were to throw in her lot with Japan, to side with Russia against Japan or to seek cooperation with Britain. Unmoved by the threat or the bait in this analysis of the situation, the British minister in China, with the approval of the Foreign Office, made it clear that the British could not assume a definite commitment.[122] The effect of the Amau statement was to make as clear to the Chinese as it had to the Japanese that, however much Britain valued her interest in China, she was not prepared in 1934 to act in its defence.

Within China there was some bitter resentment both of the statement and of the government's lack of reaction to it. In the south there was some stiffening of Canton's attitude to the Nanking government[123] but elsewhere the storm died down quite quickly. One British observer noted,

There is nobody quite so effective at doing nothing noisily as the Chinese and that seems to be all that happened on this occasion and certainly hard words broke no bones.[124]

The Chinese press connected the issuance of the Amau statement with reports that Sino-Japanese relations in north China were about to be cleared up.[125] Meetings between Huang Fu and the political leaders in Nanking had taken place in mid-April and apparently those who wanted a settlement with Japan particularly on the question of restoring communications between China and Manchukuo won the day and Huang Fu was delegated to have talks with the Japanese minister in Shanghai. A meeting took place on 17 April. At this point, it was suggested, Amau, who was regarded in Japan as something of an *enfant terrible*, knowing that western technical assistance to China was about to crumble, in a moment of elation gave out a statement to the press designed to drive home the lesson that no large-scale enterprise could hope to succeed without Japanese blessing.[126] If the Amau statement was the consequence of a thaw in Sino-Japanese relations, it was also a blunder for it made a pro-Japanese stance on the part of the Chinese government harder to justify in Chinese eyes.

In spite of some fears, there was no evidence that British trade in China was adversely affected by Japan's declared stand nor did it gain in any way.[127] The diplomatic effects were more serious. The problem was that the inevitable publicity with which events had been surrounded affected the manoeuvrability which ministers felt they had in dealing with Japan. This, rather than righteous indignation, seems to have been the reason for the cancellation of the approach to Japan with regard to the naval ratio.[128] The effect of the statement on Anglo-Japanese relations was, therefore, to increase the difficulties of those who argued for an accommodation with Japan by underlining the problem of Japan's position in China. The statement also had a deleterious effect on Anglo-Chinese relations because it encouraged the tendency to 'go slow' in controversial issues such as treaty revision where it suited Britain (and the United States) to prevaricate, while further developments in Sino-Japanese relations were awaited.[129]

In the game of international politics Japan, by affirming a position which already existed, effectively demonstrated the incapacity of any western power to do much about resisting Japanese pretensions in China. Summing up the situation, the British chargé d'affaires in Tokyo wrote,

The central point at issue was whether the Japanese government are free, without doing violence to their treaty obligations to take what measures they choose to safeguard their interests in China if they see them menaced, even in defiance of the other signatories of the Nine Power treaty.[130]

As he pointed out, public opinion in Japan had taken this view before the original statement was made and the net result of the exchanges with Britain and the United States was that the Japanese public appeared to be reassured not only that the treaty obligations of the Japanese government would remain inviolate, however far they might be stretched, but also that the British and American governments acquiesced in this view. He felt the view current among Japanese was that, even if their country was not the sole arbiter, she was the final arbiter in any dispute in China. The Japanese public felt their government had gained the advantage. Western doctrines and the phraseology of western diplomacy were out of favour in Japan. On this occasion the Japanese had hardly done lip-service to western principles and the Tokyo embassy felt that 'little would be gained to the cause of peace by further efforts to constrain them for it'.[131] By the time this despatch was received, the Foreign Office was inclined to agree.

6 THE NAVY, THE DOMINIONS AND JAPAN

Ministerial attention was focussed on defence problems in the far east in mid-1934. It was not simply because of the implications of the Amau statement or the proposed talks with Japan and the United States, but because of the whole question of imperial defence which became an issue at that time. It seemed probable that the French rejection of a British plan for a disarmament agreement which would include Germany had delivered its quietus to the ailing disarmament conference.[1] Moreover there was, in April 1934, renewed worry over German rearmament to heighten any discussion of matters relating to defence and security. The Defence Requirements committee had taken Germany as the ultimate and potential enemy and news of the substantial augmentation of German estimates for their three services and of the construction of German bombers,[2] emphasised the growing menace nearer home.

Such factors made decisions on the Defence Requirements committee's report the more urgent.[3] In order to speed the consideration of this lengthy and technical document, the ministerial committee on disarmament took over the task of making recommendations.[4] A series of meetings devoted exclusively to a discussion of the report was then held in May, June and July.

In view of the technicalities involved, it was decided, at Chamberlain's suggestion, to consider the defence requirements proposals in the light of the defence of the country and the safety of British interests all over the world.[5] This meant that the ministerial committee did not get bogged down in detail and incidentally that Chamberlain did not have to justify his theories of what constituted vital British interests and where the danger lay. As discussion of defence requirements progressed in these circumstances, a gulf, not apparent when the idea of a non-aggression pact had first been mooted as a means of insuring

British security in the far east, became evident between what might be described as the 'European menace' and the 'big navy' schools of thought. If Chamberlain was the exponent of the former view, Hankey, the defence expert, chairman of the Defence Requirements committee and secretary to the disarmament committee,[6] was the inspiration of the latter.

Chamberlain's opening exposition of Britain's vital interests at once made clear that, not only did he agree with the importance of getting back to the old terms of 'cordiality and mutual respect' with Japan in order to be able to concentrate on defence against Germany, but that for him this implied not merely a readiness to ignore the feelings of the United States but a whole rethinking of the role of the British navy.[7] His view led logically to a smaller navy concentrated in European waters.

When it had first been mooted in March, Monsell, the first lord, had spoken in favour of a non-aggression pact with Japan.[8] Now, under Chamberlain's pressure and in the interests of the service in whose future and size he had a vested interest, he took an exaggerated view of the menace of Japan. Supported by Hankey who emphasised Britain's defencelessness in the far east and contended that, unless Britain had a fully equipped navy and a properly defended base, Singapore and the whole of the British empire in the far east would fall, Monsell spoke of the 'menace' of Japan as a 'constant factor at all times'.[9] Hankey's assumption that Japan, which the Defence Requirements committee's report had declared to be without aggressive designs at that time, might suddenly go berserk, was at variance with his attitude in the mid-twenties when he had seen Japan not as a threat but rather as a possible defender of British interests in China.[10] After 1933 such a view was not possible for one whose primary interest in the far east was in relation to imperial strategy. The issues were less clear for those who were conscious of commercial and financial factors and, as a result, an ambivalent attitude to Japan in which suspicion of her was combined with a desire to be friendly with her, was not uncommon in the cabinet and in the House of Commons.

As meetings of the ministerial committee on disarmament progressed through May and June 1934, it became evident that there was an unanswerable case for the spending of a considerable sum of money on defence deficiencies. The chancellor of the exchequer, however, believed that, as they stood, the Defence Requirements committee's proposals were unrealistic and impossible to carry out. A reconsideration of priorities was required. It was Chamberlain's opinion that the British public would more readily accept preparations against possible hostilities from Germany than preparations against Japan and his first proposition was that, in the next five years, concentration should be on the defence of the British Isles. In a paper presented to the ministerial committee in June he wrote,

I wish to submit very earnestly that the committee must face facts courageously and realise the impossibility of simultaneous preparation against war with Germany and war with Japan. A choice has to be made between the two and there surely can be no doubt as to which demands priority.[11]

Chamberlain's defence building programme which was based on the function of the air force as a deterrent, would have increased the proposed number of air force squadrons and the proportion of these based at home, would have reduced naval expenditure and would have cut expenditure on the army by half.

This 'solution' to the problem of the national defence requirements involving, as it did, a radical change in defence policy, in particular in the role of the navy, roused considerable opposition. Hankey wrote later that Chamberlain's 'heretical doctrines' about the future of the fleet in the far east caused a 'flutter in many dovecotes', including, of course, Hankey's own.[12]

The preparation of a rebuttal of Chamberlain's arguments fell largely to Hankey. He saw Simon, Eden and Hoare, all of whom he found 'very receptive' to his view of naval defence requirements and upon whom he felt he had 'some influence'.[13] He wrote a lengthy brief for the prime minister and sent it also to Baldwin, Simon, Eden and Monsell.[14] Its arguments became the basis of the position taken by all these ministers at subsequent meetings of the disarmament committee.

Hankey chose to quarrel with Chamberlain not so much on the grounds of the cut in expenditure as on the proportions in which expenditure had been allocated. He was concerned in particular with the priority given the air force over the navy. The situation in the far east was, he maintained, no less menacing in mid-1934 than it had been in November 1933 when the recommendations of the chiefs of staff had been responsible for the setting up of the Defence Requirements committee and he argued that Chamberlain had not only ignored the cabinet and Defence Requirements Committee's decisions on priorities, but that he had produced no real evidence to support his proposition that home defence must be concentrated upon. Hankey pointed out that the cabinet's expressed hope for more cordial relations with Japan had been found impossible to implement and he drew attention to the Defence Requirements committee's view that a *rapprochement* with Japan was more likely to be effected if Britain's interests were seen to be defended. He argued that the Singapore base, which Chamberlain had agreed should be completed, would be devoid of value without a strong mobile navy to defend it; he dwelt on the effect on Australia, New Zealand and Britain's 'valuable far eastern colonies' if the Japanese navy was allowed to expand and a war was then forced on an unprepared British empire. Repairs to the unsound imperial structure must, Hankey declared, include the foundations of the navy 'on which the whole empire depends', must consist of a 'balanced' programme similar to that in the Defence Requirements committee's report and must provide for existing proved danger in the far east and less for future 'indeterminable' dangers in Europe.[15]

In the ministerial committee, the first lord made good use of Hankey's arguments in a 'very effective' rebuttal of the premises on which the chancellor's paper was based.[16] The danger from Japan was, he said, 'hourly' and had indeed intensified in recent years. On this basis he made out the navy's case as Hankey had done and declared himself 'heartbroken', though, in view of the Treasury attitude in the past, he can scarcely have been surprised, to find the whole conception of naval power being challenged at home by the department which provided the funds.[17]

Discussion of defence requirements in the light of Chamberlain's proposals continued in the ministerial committee throughout June and July. Though there was sympathy with the chancellor's financial difficulties it became clear that Chamberlain's contention that there was no evidence that Japan wanted to fight

Britain and that there was serious doubt whether, even if all the proposals were implemented, Britain would be able to tell Japan to keep her hands off China,[18] was no defence against Hankey's effective lobbying[19] and the suggestion that the chancellor's plan would mean the end of the sea power of the British empire.[20] It was decided that the far eastern menace could not be set aside; that the general priorities given by the Defence Requirements committee must be supported; that the naval deficiency programme should be worked out between the Admiralty and the Treasury; and that the naval programme after 1935 could be decided after the naval conference.[21] The result of the discussions of the ministerial committee was, therefore, unsatisfactory both to Chamberlain and the Treasury and to the supporters of a big navy. There, however, the matter rested while parliament was in recess.

ANGLO-AMERICAN NAVAL TALKS

June 1934 had in fact been an unhappy month for the Admiralty and its supporters. The preliminary naval talks with the Americans had begun on 18 June and, as these progressed, the British found the Americans determined on a reduction in tonnage, unforthcoming about the details of their plans, and apparently astonished at increased British requirements in cruiser tonnage.[22] A stalemate had been reached by the end of June and it was finally decided that further talks should be postponed until the Japanese arrived in October. The Americans were bewildered by what they felt was a change in the British attitude since MacDonald had, as they imagined, first broached the subject of naval conversations. They supposed that the French rejection of Britain's disarmament proposals might account for this and there was some unconfirmed suggestion that the British might now be leaning towards an Anglo-Japanese *rapprochement* as the only way to protect their interests in the far east.[23] In any event, the American view was that the 'proper' strategy was to take a 'strong stand' with the British government at the outset.[24] In fact the American position was not one of negotiation. The president made it clear that he wanted a reduction in all armament and no alteration in the ratio and that this did not represent a 'bargaining position' but a 'deep inner conviction'. Moreover, the idea of an alliance however disguised, which might give the British advance assurance that they would not have to deal with the Japanese single-handed, was specifically repudiated by him.[25]

For their part, the British felt that the Americans had failed to grasp that Britain's duties and responsibilities were necessarily greater and more various than those of the United States, and that the stated requirements were based not on desire but realistic need.[26] The American demand for a parity with the British was regarded as being based simply on pride. It seemed to the British that the American plan was probably to let the conversations break down on account of the uncompromising attitude of some other power, probably Japan, and then to work for an Anglo-American understanding under which both countries would adhere to the principle of parity.[27] It was felt to be important to steer a middle course as regards America and Japan but in view of the unsatisfactory nature of the Anglo-American talks the need for a better understanding with the Japanese appeared to be all the more urgent. In this connection, the reassuring attitude of Matsudaira, the Japanese ambassador in London, and his apparent support for the suggestion of a tripartite political *entente* as a means of relieving the fears of Japanese alarmists and assisting in the solution of the American–Japanese ratio difficulty kept British hopes alive in June.[28]

Two conclusions, both considered too risky to include in the official record, came out of the Anglo-American talks. It was agreed that neither side would cease to oppose any increase in the Japanese ratio without first consulting the other and that, should any wider arrangement with other powers prove impossible to reach, agreement to regulate naval construction should be reached between Britain and the United States.[29] It seemed to Warren Fisher that this policy smacked of collusion with the United States and that these arrangements were tantamount to an undertaking that, in the case of differences with Japan, Britain would overtly align herself with the Americans. He at once took issue with the chief of naval staff. Fisher emphasised that Britain's chances of getting permanently on good terms with Japan would be fatally affected and that, by leaving herself in the position of having to stand guard in the far east, Britain would provide Germany with a wonderful opportunity. The *amour propre* of the services must, he wrote, be sacrificed for the maximum effective insurance at home.[30]

The difference in their personal and departmental priorities was reflected in Chatfield's reply to Fisher. 'The all important consideration', he wrote, 'is not the security of this country alone but of imperial defence.' Its 'imperial position' gave Britain its 'great voice in the world'; and it was the navy's function to secure this position without which Britain would become nothing but 'an insignificant island in the North Sea'. Air forces, he argued, could 'spring up overnight' but imperial security, once abandoned, could never be restored. The aim of the naval conference was, he suggested, to ensure Britain's world position and naval prestige and, having won recognition of Britain's requirements, the problems of financing them could be faced.[31] Such an attitude can scarcely have commended itself to the permanent head of the Treasury but, on the other hand, the Anglo-American talks produced no result of comfort to Chatfield and the Admiralty. At the talks, as in the ministerial discussions, neither the 'European menace' nor the 'big navy' philosophies had won general acceptance.

HANKEY'S TOUR OF THE DOMINIONS

London's failure to agree on a naval programme led to the cabinet to decide not to send the Dominions, so vitally interested in future naval policy, a copy of the report of the ministerial committee. It was felt, with some justification, that the failure to deal with the size of the navy might be misunderstood and, in order to avoid this, it was decided that Sir Maurice Hankey should personally convey the general result of the ministerial enquiry to the Dominion prime ministers.[32]

The centennial celebrations of the state of Victoria had been recognised by the commonwealth government of Australia as an opportunity to invite some distinguished persons from Britain, preferably some senior officers who might at the same time be able to advise on matters of regional defence in the antipodes.[33] In February 1934, it had been decided in London that Hankey should be the 'distinguished person' to go.[34] He had, as chairman of the Committee of imperial defence and of the Defence Requirements committee, obvious qualifications for giving the Australians the kind of advice for which they were asking. The acceptance of the Australian invitation led to an invitation from New Zealand[35] and later to the extension of the tour to include South Africa and Canada. It was an opportunity for the British government to inform the Dominions of the 'trend of thought' on defence matters.[36]

Hankey, who remained alarmed by the chancellor's attitude to the navy and its implications for naval strategy in the far east, was due to leave for South Africa in the first week of August. After a 'long and full discussion' in which he told Chamberlain bluntly that he could not recommend the Australian government to spend six million pounds additional to the budget to carry out a scheme on the fundamental basis of which the chancellor appeared to have doubts, Hankey asked for Chamberlain's support for a formula outlining the British position.[37] This formula represented the naval position as the Defence Requirements committee wished to see it and was in line with the desiderata for far eastern defence recommended by the ministerial committee. It stated,

With the object of enabling the fleet to proceed to Singapore in any major emergency in the far east, it is the intention of His Majesty's government in the United Kingdom

1. to complete the first stage of the deficiencies of the Singapore base by 1938.
2. to proceed with plans for the defence of fuelling stations east of Suez.
3. to make good the deficiencies of the navy as financial conditions permit.

The naval construction programme, however, cannot be determined until after the naval conference, 1935.[38]

Hankey felt that he should be able to assure the Australians that Britain would be able to fulfil her part of the bargain, but Chamberlain was not prepared to give him such authority. He agreed, however, that, if Baldwin, as chairman of the ministerial committee, authorised Hankey to use the formula, he would withdraw his opposition. Hankey, therefore, drew up an *aide-mémoire* which he asked Baldwin to confirm, explaining that,

The principle on which all reports have been based has been that there will be a naval base at Singapore sufficiently strongly defended to hold out *until the arrival of the main fleet of capital ships, which thereafter provides the shield to cover the whole of our interests in the south Pacific and Indian Ocean.*[39]

Asking for assurance that this remained valid, Hankey confessed that he could not conceive any alternative system of imperial defence in the far east which was not based on 'the centuries old assumption of sea power'. Any failure on Britain's part to do her share would, Hankey was convinced, break up the empire and he wrote, 'nothing would induce me to be a party to that'. Baldwin signed the *aide mémoire* without question.

Before he left, Hankey wrote to the prime minister that the *aide-mémoire*, which he did not propose to show to the Australians, gave him the 'moral backing' to discharge his task of advising on Dominions' defence.[40] In order to protect himself and the cause of the navy further, he also wrote to Baldwin while he was away, urging that the bearing of naval defence on the preservation and unity of the empire should not be overlooked by the cabinet and warning him against Warren Fisher who, he thought, had 'never been sound about the navy or understood the defence question in the Pacific'.[41]

In fact, even as Hankey set off on his journey, the problem of naval defence in the Pacific had taken on a new complexity as a result of important cabinet changes in Japan. A new government under the moderate Admiral, Okada Keisuke, had been formed. Hirota remained minister of foreign affairs but the appointment of Admiral Osumi as minister of the navy was regarded as likely to increase support for the line so long-advocated by Katō Kanji and Suetsugu, now commander in chief of the combined fleet.[42] The Okada programme published in late July made it clear that little compromise on naval defence matters could be expected[43] and suggested that there was probably little substance in Matsudaira's deduction that a way might be found round the problem of relative naval strengths.

TOWARDS AN ANGLO-JAPANESE *RAPPROCHEMENT*

This new and, from the British point of view, unpromising Japanese government was only just established when the whole issue of a non-aggression pact with Japan was reopened in London with the arrival of a despatch from Sir Robert Clive, the newly appointed British ambassador in Tokyo. This gave Clive's impression of the likely Japanese attitude to the naval conference, and recorded a conversation in connection with this in which foreign minister Hirota declared that Japan would be ready to sign non-aggression pacts with Britain and the United States.[44] London's first reaction to this conversation was, 'If an equality of status declaration and a non-aggression pact would help Japan reduce her ratio demands, why not adopt this approach?'[45] Further confirmation that Japan might be thinking along these lines seemed to be supplied by the information that Japan had perhaps been testing United States reaction to a bilateral pact.[46] It seemed possible that Hirota might be looking for a means to overcome the intransigence of the naval authorities.[47]

Simon's immediate reaction to these shadowy signs was an optimistic one. He accepted that Japan would not agree to an inferior ratio imposed by treaty but thought that if conceded 'equality of status' Japan might make a voluntary declaration of the naval limits she would be prepared to impose on herself. Such a voluntary declaration, he suggested, might be annexed to any treaty. Turning to Hirota's suggestion that Japan would accept a non-aggression pact, Simon wrote,

As regards a 'non-aggression pact', *why not*? We should contract for the whole empire (or perhaps the Dominions should sign separately). What would Japan want in return? Something equivalent to recognition of Manchukuo? A free hand in China would be more difficult. I should like to see the idea of an Anglo-Japanese non-aggression pact worked out on paper. It may be a valuable buffer against Japanese naval liberty. It would please many people, here and in Japan, to have this much of the Anglo-Japanese treaty revived.[48]

Simon's attitude forced the Foreign Office to a further exploration of the whole question of naval policy and an approach to Japan, at the very time when the Japanese cabinet was also reaching decisions on the policy to be adopted at the preliminary naval talks.[49] The Japanese evidence indicates that those in London like Chamberlain and Craigie who favoured an equality of status declaration and a voluntary declaration on tonnages as a means of helping 'moderate elements' in Japan to 'save face' and to overcome extremist elements who wanted no naval treaty at all[50] were working from false premises. By 1934, the so-called moderates of the treaty group in the Japanese navy were no longer a force capable of revival, and the Japanese navy's view that the naval treaties and the ratio must go, was accepted by the cabinet.[51] The concept of a Japanese navy divided between extremists and moderates offered British negotiators some hope, but represented a misinterpretation of the situation.

By and large, a realistic assessment of the possibilities was made in the far eastern department of the Foreign Office. There, the 'gravest doubts' were felt about Japan being willing to make a naval agreement which would be moderate as to figures and tolerably binding.[52] It was suggested that a non-aggression pact might have the effect of giving Japan added confidence in her expansionist tendencies and of hampering Britain in resisting them. Japan could not be given a free hand in China. The clear implication was that any non-aggression pact that Britain might be prepared to conclude with Japan would fail to satisfy her, while the type of pact Japan would like would be too dangerous for Britain to accept. The objections seemed overwhelming and, in view of this, it was recommended that a memorandum should be prepared, saying that the question of a non-aggression pact had again been looked into and found wanting.[53] There was no time to implement this suggestion before Simon received a letter from Chamberlain which revived the issue once more.

During an August holiday in Perthshire, Neville Chamberlain became convinced that 'one of those crucial points in history which test a statesman's capacity and foresight' had been reached.[54] The result of his 'cogitations' was a memorandum on Anglo-Japanese relations and the naval conference, intended for the cabinet, but sent first to Simon as a man whose 'cool and analytical judgment' he valued. This further approach to the problem of Anglo-Japanese relations made it clear that, in spite of the difficulties and objections, Chamberlain clung to what he saw as the overwhelming advantages of a satisfactory agreement with Japan. The ideas expressed in the memorandum were an amalgam of the strategic views and financial facts which had been the basis of his comments on defence requirements and his case, argued earlier, for a non-aggression pact with Japan.

Two things had impressed Chamberlain and confirmed his views. The first of these was Hirota's conversation with Clive,[55] the second was a press report of an apparently semi-official statement of Japan's ideas for the naval conference.[56] This report suggested that Japan's plans included the fixing of total tonnage allotments within which each nation would be free, subject to certain limits of size, to build whatever kinds of craft were considered necessary. Altogether, this news from Japan suggested to Chamberlain that he was 'on the right track' and he argued that the government would deserve the blame of future historians if it neglected even to enquire what were Japan's ideas about a pact. The sacrifice of British interests to American 'browbeating' would never, he said, be repaid and he urged the foreign secretary to stamp his tenure of office with the 'special distinction' of a Simon–Hirota pact.[57]

Chamberlain recommended that conversations should be opened immediately with the object of finding out whether Japan was prepared to make a non-aggression pact with Britain and on what terms she would consider such a pact favourably. If this step was successful and a pact was signed, he suggested that, in view of the difficulty of reaching a mutually satisfactory agreement in a conference of the three naval powers, representatives might find acceptable the idea of adding to it a 'gentleman's agreement' on naval matters. This agreement would fix certain qualitative limits within which each country was free to build, and for the purposes of closer understanding the main outline of their respective naval programmes should be communicated each year by one country to the other. In this way, Chamberlain obviously hoped to introduce some rationale for a flexibility in the naval programme which the Admiralty had so far not allowed and, in addition, his plan would have had the effect of presenting the 1935 naval conference with a *fait accompli*. Chamberlain argued that a concession over the ratio had been made to the Americans who had, nevertheless, failed to make any reciprocal gesture[58] and, therefore, had no grounds for objections should Britain choose this alternative to a naval conference which was evidently doomed to failure.

The questions raised by Chamberlain's memorandum were the subject of Foreign Office papers for the next two months. More objections to a pact with Japan were produced. It was suggested that a non-aggression pact with Britain might encourage Japan to attack Russia. In this event, it was argued, Russia would cease to act as a potential check on Germany which would, thus, be in a stronger position in Europe; moreover, while Japan had to watch Russia, she would not move south but a Japan victorious against Russia might become a real danger to British possessions in east Asia.[59] Though it was clear that Japan was not regarded as an immediate menace, this argument led to the conclusion that a pact might well increase her capacity to become one. A treaty which included safeguards for China was regarded as an impossibility after the April declaration[60] and there was, in any case, the risk that a pact, by revealing Britain's fear of Japan, might encourage the Chinese to attack, and so weaken, the British position in that country.

This material provided Simon with his reply to Chamberlain. A non-aggression pact would not create guarantees which did not already exist through the Four Power and Kellogg pacts and would, therefore, have no practical effect. Its political effect would not simply be to increase the sense of security vis-à-vis Japan but rather to give Japan a free hand in the far east as long as she respected British possessions there. Simon doubted whether an improvement in Anglo-Japanese relations would be worth its price because of its adverse effect on relations with China, the United States, Russia, and the Dutch East Indies, and he suggested that a complete survey would be required if so enormously important a decision was to be taken. Urging that he and Chamberlain should meet before Chamberlain's memorandum was circulated, he concluded,

I feel the force of your remark that if the Japanese really have something to offer we ought to find out what it is, but we shall only be able to judge its value if we have first settled in our own minds as to the comparative weight of these pros and cons.⁶¹

Though the memorandum was not circulated, Simon apparently did not convince Chamberlain. Rather, at the first cabinet meeting of the new session, the foreign secretary drew the attention of ministers to the despatch reporting the Clive–Hirota conversation and stated that, although the Foreign Office felt it improbable that Japan would put forward any feasible proposals, he felt that it would be a great mistake to refrain from further enquiries. If the difficulties of reaching a bilateral pact with Japan could be surmounted, he maintained that the advantages to Britain 'could hardly be over-estimated'.⁶² This was not at all the tone of his argument two weeks earlier when he suggested to Chamberlain that the benefits of a pact would be restricted and unequal. Apparently the foreign secretary had been won back to his original view of the significance of Hirota's remarks to Clive and, by presenting the cabinet with such a positive view of the despatch, Simon was, in fact, forcing a resolution of the continuing debate on the feasibility of a non-aggression pact with Japan.

In the course of his remarks in support of Simon at this cabinet meeting, Chamberlain seemed to have absorbed some of the Foreign Office reservations about a pact. He pointed out that it would have to be more specific than the kind of multilateral agreement not to resort to force to which Japan and Britain were already parties, nor could Japan be given a free hand in China or the Dutch East Indies or be left unchecked against Russia. He suggested that, if, as proposed, the ambassador in Tokyo spoke to Hirota, he would have to indicate that Britain must have assurances that her interests in the far east would not be prejudiced by a pact. The Foreign Office argument in the preceding nine months had seemed to prove conclusively that there was little Britain had to offer Japan and it is, therefore, hard to see how Chamberlain imagined such assurances could be obtained. The cabinet was, however, sufficiently convinced by the evidence to agree that the ambassador should make 'discreet and unofficial' enquiries about what Japan had in mind and what price she might be prepared to pay for a non-aggression pact.⁶³ There was no discussion about the plan's long-range effects, but it is clear from Chamberlain's memorandum and from his remarks at this meeting that, for him, it now represented the means of making a revised naval programme possible. There is no doubt that such a prospect represented a threat to the programme of imperial naval defence outlined in the absent Hankey's *aide-mémoire*, that reassuring 'little bit of paper' without which Hankey had claimed he would have felt he was 'walking on a bog'.[64] It was, however, suggested in this cabinet meeting that Australia and New Zealand would be sympathetic to the kind of pact proposed[65] and Baldwin, whose support had given Hankey the confidence to undertake his task, remained silent.

In a 'long and amicable' conversation with Hirota, the British ambassador had the opportunity to fulfil his instructions. At long last, taking the bull by the horns, he asked the foreign minister exactly what he had in mind when he had mentioned a non-aggression pact in July. Hirota replied that the Japanese were very anxious that in case the naval conference should fail, there should be no break in friendly relations with Britain. He indicated that he would like to see some definite understanding, perhaps in the form of a non-aggression pact, and that he wanted the foreign secretary to know this. Hirota appeared to realise that Britain was bound to consider political reactions in the United States and elsewhere, and that a non-aggression pact was an extremely delicate matter for her. When Clive asked whether the failure of the naval conference was anticipated, Hirota smiled and implied that the Japanese proposals might be acceptable to Britain, but perhaps not to the United States.[66]

It seemed from Hirota's statement that, in his eyes, the value of a non-aggression pact lay rather in its ability to smooth over naval failure than in its capacity to ensure success at the naval conference. A remark he made to Prince Saionji at this time would seem to confirm this impression. When asked whether Japan intended to terminate the naval treaties even if the western countries accepted every demand raised by the Japanese delegation, Hirota replied that the treaties must be abrogated 'no matter how much the other powers agree to our proposals'.[67] Clearly, when Hirota and Chamberlain spoke of non-aggression pacts they had very different purposes in mind.

Uncertain that Hirota really had any definite plan, and unwilling to press him further, Sir Robert Clive suggested that an opportunity to elicit more precise information was likely to present itself in London where the preliminary naval talks with Japan were due to begin on 23 October. It had been Chamberlain's intention that the question of a pact should be decided before the talks began. As a result of Clive's recommendation, however, political questions would inevitably be linked with naval ones.

At the Foreign Office, discussion of a political agreement with Japan continued in early October. In fact, Simon's request that the idea should be worked out on paper was met by a series of memoranda written from a number of different angles. In setting out the advantages and drawbacks of the proposed pact, the far east department concluded that a non-aggression agreement with Japan could be signed only on condition that it involved no disturbance of the Nine Power treaty and that it contained some affirmation by Japan of her intention to respect this treaty. Such reaffirmation was considered necessary to save China's face and to diminish her bitterness against Britain. The pact's value to Japan would be to remove the bogey of Anglo-American cooperation to defeat her in the naval or economic sphere and to ensure safety from outside attack in the event of Russo-Japanese hostilities. Russian resentment could, it was felt, be discounted since the Soviet Union had hardly reached the stage of acting as a make-weight against Germany. In order to prevent the possibility that Japan might see a non-aggression pact as an opportunity to attack the Dutch East Indies, a guarantee that the Four Power treaty would not be denounced was suggested and it was forseen that this guarantee, together with the assurance on the Nine Power treaty, might possibly satisfy American sensitiveness so that she might be persuaded into a tripartite agreement.[68] Clearly the authors of this memorandum, though they did not write off a pact, saw it hedged about with qualifications and difficulties.

Greater difficulties emerged when the pact was considered from the point of view of China policy. Here it was argued that Japan's assurances with regard to the Nine Power treaty and the open door and her promises to abstain from aggression were worth nothing and that in any case they did not guarantee British interests in China. Specific assurances of Japan's willingness to cooperate with Britain in China on controversial questions such as extraterritoriality and the abandonment of her methods of intimidation in China were considered to be essential if an Anglo-Japanese pact was to assist Britain's China policy. Given the importance for Japan of her stake in China, it seemed doubtful that she would be prepared to make such specific assurances. The paper made it clear that, from the point of view of Anglo-Chinese relations, the dangers of a pact were formidable and it was pointed out that Chinese resentment was more likely to be visited upon the British than on the Japanese.[69] Equally formidable arguments were presented when the effect of the pact on future naval limitations was considered.[70]

It had become evident that it was impossible to reconcile the different interests involved. A paper summarising the attitude which might be taken by the Foreign Office, assuming that the government was committed to exploring the possibility of a pact, was written in the hope that this might be a better way than mere negation to emphasise the dangers and difficulties.[71] This paper listed Britain's desiderata as follows: that the pact should not hamper or discourage further multi-lateral naval agreement; that the objective should be either a tri-partite pact or two separate bi-lateral pacts (Britain–Japan, United States–Japan), with Australia and New Zealand associated as parties in either case; that the Nine and Four Power treaties should be reaffirmed; that the treaty should not be regarded as justifying some modification of the naval ratio with Japan; that confidential assurances should, if possible, be obtained from Japan on specific points relating to her policy in China. If Japan responded at all to the British advance, it seemed likely that this impossible list was bound to blight negotiations in the end.

On 8 October the foreign secretary saw the Japanese ambassador in London with the object of finding out whether he had received special instructions, as Hirota had suggested would be the case.[72] Matsudaira, the ambassador, was well liked at the Foreign Office and in diplomatic circles. His aristocratic connections[73] and his considerable experience of western diplomats and diplomacy – he had been ambassador in London since 1928, ambassador in Washington from 1924 to 1928 and the Japanese delegate at a number of international conferences – made it hard to associate him with the intransigence of a Japanese government over which the army and navy seemed to have too much control. Simon felt that he conveyed clearly to Matsudaira that the British wanted to know whether there was anything behind Hirota's expressions of a desire to strengthen Anglo-Japanese friendship and his observation that Japan would be prepared to sign non-aggression pacts with Britain and the United States. He asked what assurances Japan had in mind with regard to questions such as China. The ambassador had no specific information, but he explained to Simon that a special messenger bringing urgent instructions was on his way and that Sugimura Yotaro, recently appointed Japanese ambassador to Rome, had instructions to travel *via* London. He promised to communicate as soon as these two messengers arrived and offered his personal opinion that assurances on the subject of China might reasonably be expected to be part of any new understanding with Japan.

London seems to have had hopes of ambassador Matsudaira's next report. Although Clive's recent telegrams had indicated that, in spite of the protestations of friendship, Japanese action on specific issues was not really guided by a spirit of conciliation,[74] the Foreign Office was not altogether pessimistic. It was known that Yoshida Shigeru, son-in-law of the emperor's adviser, Count Makino, and an experienced diplomat who was well known in London where he had, for a time, been first secretary at the Japanese embassy, was to be sent round embassies to inform Japan's representatives of recent developments in Japanese policy. Some significance was attached to his comment to the commercial counsellor in Tokyo, George Sansom, on the eve of his departure: 'I shall be back soon and hope to bring good news from your country.'[75] It seemed that he could be Matsudaira's 'special messenger'.

On 16 October, the paper on the future of Anglo-Japanese relations, promised by the foreign secretary and the chancellor in cabinet on 25 September, was produced.[76] The tone, arguments and phraseology of this paper owed more to Chamberlain than to the Foreign Office or to the foreign secretary's earlier sceptical rebuttals of the proposal for a pact. All the snags, the effect on China, the United States, Russia and the League of Nations were mentioned, but in each case an optimistic view was taken. Matsudaira's personal belief that Tokyo could give assurances about China was quoted as not unhopeful evidence. The Anglo-Japanese pact, it was suggested, might lead to a tri-partite pact with the United States; might restore the balance if Soviet–Japanese relations became unduly strained; might ultimately lead Japan back into the fold at the League. In short, this paper touched on, but did not really develop, the difficulties. It was by no means the thorough survey which Simon had suggested to Chamberlain would be necessary before a decision could be taken. The cabinet was presented with the best possible case for a pact, based on apologetics rather than well-grounded calculations. The serious doubts of the Foreign Office were not mentioned. Until there was news from Matsudaira, however, there was nothing further to be done, and consideration of the future of Anglo-Japanese relations was postponed until further progress had been made on the naval talks.[77]

On 30 October, Matsudaira called on Simon. Though he had received no further instructions on Japanese policy, he was required to find out and report Simon's views about a pact. He assured the foreign secretary that the Japanese government would welcome any acceptable plan to promote good relations. As Simon pointed out, it was Hirota who had hinted at the proposals for a non-aggression pact and it was for him to explain his ideas. In this impasse, Matsudaira revealed, as the Foreign Office appear to have guessed, that his 'special messenger' was Yoshida, who was due to arrive in London on 11 November. Since no more concrete information was available until that date, the *denouement* was once more deferred. At this meeting, however, the suggestion for a 'gentleman's agreement' on naval matters was put to Matsudaira in confidence and he promised to report the idea to the Japanese foreign minister.[78]

The final stage of the year's debate on reaching an accommodation with Japan began on 19 November when Matsudaira conveyed Japan's reply to Simon's enquiry.[79] Of the non-aggression pact, Hirota said that he had assumed that political matters would be dealt with independently of the naval conference and it was not Japan's intention that they should have been connected. It was useless for Simon to protest that Hirota's original suggestion had been made in connection with the naval conference. Matsudaira then enquired whether, instead of a non-aggression pact the same purpose might not be served if the existing Four Power treaty was extended in future for a given number of years ahead.[80] He emphasised that this was merely one possible method of carrying out the proposal Hirota had in mind. The idea that Britain and Japan might act in concert over matters relating to China was also mentioned.

Since the first of these Japanese suggestions provided no new assurances and the second appeared to ignore the tri-partite arrangements at which Hirota had originally hinted, Simon was understandably disappointed with this reply. To add to the disappointment, Yoshida was now described by Matsudaira as simply an ex-ambassador making a tour of European capitals[81] and the idea of a 'gentleman's agreement' was rejected as a device for retaining the existing ratios. Simon had the feeling that Matsudaira himself was most anxious to bring about an agreement, and the cabinet to which he reported the interview agreed with him that it would be disastrous if negotiations broke down.[82] A further meeting with Matsudaira on 21 November, however, produced no result.[83] Japan had made her position clear. The cards were in her hands and there was nothing to be gained by the pursuit of elusive political goals. It was obviously more important at that stage to concentrate on salvaging something from the naval talks with Japan which were still going on.

THE QUESTION OF BACKSTAGE INFLUENCE

It has been suggested that on the one hand the Dominions and on the other a conspiracy led by Lord Lothian assisted by *The Times*, the *Observer*, General Smuts and a group around the *Round Table* were responsible for the final abandonment of the idea of an agreement with Japan.[84] Certainly ministers were always conscious of what they imagined Dominion opinion to be and were particularly aware of the forcefully expressed views of General Smuts. On the other hand there is no evidence that expected Dominion reaction was more than a secondary factor in formulating policy; both those who wanted an accommodation with Japan and those who opposed them and wanted the maximum expenditure on imperial naval defence, claimed they would have Dominion support. Moreover, it is a mistake to regard the Dominions as having a single view. Their characteristic in common was a reluctance to spend on their own defence. The concept of Anglo-American unity favoured by Smuts was not necessarily an alternative to Anglo-Japanese cooperation acceptable to all the Dominions. It was recognised in London that, for Australia and New Zealand, the Dominions most vulnerable to any deterioration in the situation in the far east, Japan might be a better partner than the United States.[85]

The activities of Lord Lothian were followed with considerable exasperation in the Foreign Office but his pro-American propaganda and his belief in the possibility of effective Anglo-American cooperation were not taken seriously. Commenting on an article by Lord Lothian advocating Anglo-American cooperation in the Pacific which appeared in the *Round Table* in December 1934, Vansittart wrote,

Lord Lothian told me recently and repeatedly that we had a 'tiger in the White House' who would 'do our fighting for us in the Far East'. I replied that I had personally known quite a number of tigers in white houses, and that I still thought hutch might be a safer and more accurate word . . .[86]

Vansittart described recent occasions when 'the present tiger in the white hutch' had 'obstinately kept his tail between his legs' and referred to Lothian as 'not a publicist of any profundity, to put it mildly'.

The pro-Japanese movement was not 'killed' as the result of the work of Smuts and others[87] but rather died down in November 1934 because of Japan's lack of response. This was not an outcome to cause rejoicing in all Dominions. In fact, the uncertainties of British policy in the far east were probably more shrewdly assessed by Dominion ministers than was appreciated in London. Hankey was satisfied that he had succeeded in papering over the cracks and reported that the Australian and New Zealand governments were 'in entire agreement' with the defence requirements policy as explained by him.[88] But after Hankey's visit, Sir John Latham, a former minister for external affairs and leader of an Australian goodwill mission to Japan in 1934, noted,

It would be a good thing if Great Britain had a more definite policy about Oriental affairs and if the Dominions actually knew what that policy was [. . .] Great Britain is quite prepared to say in flowing language what the *objectives* of her policy are – such as cooperation, coordination and friendship etc. etc. with the great nations of the East. Such statements only remind me of the noble candidate who states that he will not be deterred from pursuing at all costs the welfare of the people.[89]

Sir George Pearce, Australian minister of defence, to whom this letter was written agreed 'absolutely' with these remarks.[90] A policy of improved relations with Japan was one which could be expected to receive strong support from Australia and New Zealand,[91] and their attitude certainly did not contribute to the dropping of approaches in 1934.

KEEPING JAPAN IN THE RING

Ministerial preparations for the naval talks with Japan had begun in mid-October. The British expected the Japanese to work for an agreed termination of the existing treaties and for agreement as to new terms. It had been made clear that, while Japan wanted parity with the United States, she understood that Britain might require a larger fleet. The British appreciated this Japanese understanding of their situation but in practice, of course, the Japanese demand meant equality for all because the United States insisted on parity with Britain. The question was, therefore, whether Britain could agree to theoretical or practical equality with Japan. It was obviously a delicate matter of negotiation. A possible Japanese demand for recognition of her right to equality could, it was felt, be conceded if, in fact, Japan did not wish to build to equality but, in the interests of equality of security which, with her world-wide interests, was Britain's main concern, adherence in practice to existing ratios was felt to be necessary. The British were prepared to compromise on quantitative and qualitative naval requirements but, until

Japanese proposals were known, it was impossible for ministers to decide on the line to be taken.[92]

The principal Japanese delegates were ambassador Matsudaira and Admiral Yamamoto Isoroku, a naval officer of whom little was known before his arrival in London and for whom the British came to have considerable admiration. The talks opened on 23 October and it quickly became evident that the Japanese formula involved the establishment of a common upper limit of naval tonnage to be determined by the requirements of the power which had need of the largest navy. Within this limit each country would have the right to build in the manner it deemed fit. The British objected that this would effectively fetter the nation with world-wide responsibilities while giving latitude of movement to countries with lesser responsibilities.[93] The 'common upper limit', however, entailed the abolition of the existing ratios and the Japanese attached the utmost importance to it as a matter of national prestige. They proposed to set up the principle of 'non-aggression and non-menace' by the abolition or reduction of offensive arms. The British objected to the Japanese classification and clearly the division of weapons into offensive and defensive categories was likely to produce endless argument. The only ray of light was that the Japanese seemed prepared, should abolition of certain types of vessel prove impossible, to settle for a reduction in each category of vessel and their proposals for qualitative limitation appeared to be not too far from Britain's own.[94] Encouraged by this, the British felt there was a possibility that, if the question of prestige could be solved, Japan might ultimately accept the idea of a 'gentleman's agreement' or a 'voluntary declaration'. On 30 October, therefore, Simon mentioned to Matsudaira in confidence the idea of an equality of status declaration and a gentleman's agreement as a way of meeting Japan's concern for her prestige and her fear of the United States.[95]

A more detailed formal proposal on the same lines was put to the Japanese delegation in early November. The fundamental principle of equality of status as between parties to a treaty was to be laid down; each party to the treaty would make a separate declaration of its intentions in the matter of naval construction over a specific period of years; provisions in regard to future qualitative limitation in the building programmes would be included in the treaty. It was intended that existing relative strengths would in practice be safe-guarded and, as the Japanese at once pointed out, the proposal amounted to a change as far as the hated ratio was concerned, in form but not in substance.[96]

There was a pause while the Japanese delegation consulted its government about the British proposals. The likelihood was that Japan would denounce the Washington treaty but the British had hopes that a limited agreement might still be possible. It was of particular importance to the British to reach some sort of agreement because it might be the basis upon which to start the arrangement of programmes with the European naval powers, including Germany. The Japanese ambassador, whose job it was to keep such hope alive, gave his opinion that the omens in Tokyo were, on the whole, favourable to the compromise suggested.[97]

While talks with the Japanese were going on, the American delegation, led by Norman Davis, was kept informed. The Americans resented this procedure which put the British in the honest broker's position but the British were determined that there should be no suggestion of a united front against the Japanese and felt their role of 'Jack of both sides' to be particularly difficult when the sides had nothing in common but suspicion and mistrust.[98] The Americans were sceptical of the British compromise programme or of any 'middle course'. It seemed to the British that Davis was not always helpful and that he had 'an inherent capacity for getting hold of the wrong end of the stick'.[99]

Japanese reaction to the British proposals came with Simon's interview with Matsudaira on 19 November. The Japanese government recorded its appreciation of the British efforts to find a way of settlement but could not accept a scheme which did not meet the desire of the Japanese to have actual liberty.[100] A further meeting between Simon and Matsudaira on 21 November was no more fruitful.[101] The British felt that to some extent the Americans were to blame since, on their insistence, it had been suggested that building programmes should be embodied in a contractual form and it was this rigid provision to which Japan had special objection.[102] They had no wish to accept the Japanese rejection as final and continued to discuss ways of 'keeping Japan in the ring'.[103] It was now recognised as inevitable that Japan should denounce the Washington treaties by the end of the year. The usually optimistic Japanese ambassador thought that deadlock had been reached because the British were really up against two separate difficulties. On the one hand, there were the Japanese naval authorities whose sole desire was to increase the size of the fleet both relatively and absolutely and who genuinely feared that Japan was vulnerable to an attack by the United States and, on the other, the army which, while it had little sympathy with the aspirations of the navy, was suspicious of a political pact on the ground that it might hamper the work Japan had to perform in Manchukuo. In addition Matsudaira thought that Tokyo was pessimistic about the chances of agreement between the United States and Japan and gave this as the reason for Hirota's harking back to the idea of an Anglo-Japanese understanding.[104] In the meantime, there was nothing to be gained from British attempts to bargain with Japan.

JAPANESE ABROGATION AND BRITISH REACTION

The British were anxious that the Washington treaties should be abrogated by Japan as late as possible so that talks could continue.[105] To this the Japanese agreed. The British also insisted that the conversations should be described as having been adjourned, rather than terminated as the Americans, anxious that breakdown should be clearly shown to be Japan's responsibility, wanted.[106] Anglo-Japanese technical talks on qualitative limitation continued until 19 December when a joint Anglo-American–Japanese communiqué was issued, announcing the adjournment.[107] The Japanese gave formal notice of termination on 29 December.

In Japan, a delighted Katō Kanji announced that, with the abolition of the Washington treaty, the Japanese navy was reborn.[108] For the Japanese navy and the Japanese government the end of the treaty meant the beginning of a new era of national independence; for the British it meant a position of greater vulnerability. The latter still felt, however, that there were real hopes that, even though the treaty had gone, it might be possible to negotiate programmes of actual construction.[109] From Tokyo it was reported that Hirota had said that, in view of the attitude of the navy and the internal position in Japan, it had been impossible to allow any discretion to the Japanese delegates but that this situation could change in the following year and Japan was most anxious that a conference should be held in 1935.[110] Though this was clearly an offer of 'jam tomorrow', it was an interesting possibility and it seemed that denunciation might quieten down Japan's 'big navy' men. Matsudaira also encouraged the view that the Japanese attitude might be less intransigent in 1935, and he suggested that, when Yamamoto returned to Japan, he might be able to secure agreement to the kind of voluntary limitation the British were proposing.[111] In view of these not unhopeful omens for a successful reopening of negotiations in 1935, it was decided that the timing of a conference with all the Washington signatories would be dependent on the degree of success which Yamamoto had on his return to Japan.[112]

In order that they might be ready for a full conference when the sign from Japan came, the British proceeded to deal with the European naval situation as a matter of urgency and arrangements for naval conversations with France, Italy and Germany were put in train in February 1935.[113] While attention was thus focussed on Europe, there were indications from Japan that some form of political understanding was still being mooted. In March, Matsudaira suggested that Japanese acceptance of British naval proposals would be facilitated if some step could be taken simultaneously to improve the political atmosphere. He said that foreign minister Hirota was now inclined to think in terms of a consultative pact between Britain and Japan with provision for the discussion of outstanding questions between the two countries in all parts of the world. In addition, the Four Power treaty might be extended for a period of years. In reply to the objection that a pact between Britain and Japan might create unnecessary suspicion in the minds of the Americans, Matsudaira expressed the view that his government would be prepared to extend the pact to include other nations and that personally he thought a Japanese–United States–United Kingdom pact would be agreed to.[114] The technical difficulties of a consultative pact were formidable; and discussion of it at the Foreign Office was dropped when it received the disheartening news that Admiral Yamamoto had presented his report but thought that there were 'too many diehards' in the Japanese navy to make it acceptable.[115] Since there was nothing to be gained by pushing Hirota, it was felt at the Foreign Office that the best tactic would be to carry on with the discussions with European powers. Naval talks with Germany were pending and, if an agreement based on qualitative limitation rather than a ratio could be reached, Britain's capacity to negotiate with Japan would be strengthened.

After a year's discussion, it had been possible to reach agreement on neither a political understanding nor a naval agreement with Japan. On the other hand, relations with Japan had remained good throughout the period; and in London the hope persisted that moderate counsels would prevail in Tokyo so that naval agreement, if not political understanding, would be possible in the coming year.

7 THE FEDERATION OF BRITISH INDUSTRIES MISSION TO JAPAN AND MANCHUKUO

The failure to achieve a blueprint for either a political or a naval agreement with Japan did not entirely depress those who favoured the concilitation of Japan as a solution to Britain's problem of maintaining the *status quo* in the far east and developing commercial opportunities there. Indeed, the confidence of those businessmen who, with the Treasury, believed in the possibility of real rewards from an Anglo-Japanese *rapprochement*, received a timely boost with the publication in December 1934 of the report of the Federation of British Industries mission to Japan and Manchukuo, led by Lord Barnby. The members of the mission were convinced that a genuine spirit of friendship towards Britain existed in Japan and that the economic prosperity of the far east which was so important to British interests was dependent upon a good understanding between Britain and Japan.[1] This report was some compensation for the apparent setback to improved relations with Japan given by the Japanese abrogation of the Washington treaty.

The Barnby mission arose out of the fears of British exporters that the continued non-recognition of Manchukuo would result in the loss of this small but potentially valuable and apparently unrestricted market.[2] The trade prospects in the new Manchukuo developing under Japanese tutelage and assisted by Japanese capital and expertise appeared to be better than at any time in the past. The exporters of capital goods, the iron, steel and related industries detected commercial opportunities in Manchukuo and wanted a serious effort to develop trade there.[3] The quota policy, which pressure from Manchester had caused to be imposed on Japanese textiles in colonial markets, caused these groups concern as it was likely to push Japan into retaliatory action in areas which she controlled. The formation, in early 1934, of the Manchuria Petroleum Company, a government monopoly in which Japanese interests held four-fifths of the shares, confirmed these fears.[4] Both Manchukuo and Japan appeared unmoved by British and American protests at this violation of the 'open door' and the tactical position of the western powers was, of course, weakened by the fact that they were not in normal diplomatic relations with Manchukuo. Business reaction to this impasse was to advocate early recognition of Manchukuo and to seek to reinforce business connections in Japan and in the areas under Japanese control. The build-up of public interest and pressure on the question of Manchukuo was reflected in a number of parliamentary questions asked, in April and May 1934, about its political organisation and trade potential.

The foreign trade figures for Manchukuo at the end of 1933 showed that, though Britain's share of the trade was very small, it had increased by 50 per cent during that year.[5] This was a pleasing result and future trade prospects were reported to be good. It was, however, easy to exaggerate them. The opportunities were not brilliant and existed really only for the most dedicated, as the British consul-general in Mukden was concerned to point out. He recognised that there were openings for the sale of capital goods of various kinds, particularly machinery, but, having observed the difficulties of British companies already operating in Manchukuo, he suggested that the most sensible method in future might be for British firms to join with Japanese firms. He thought success in the new conditions was dependent on reorganisation and reorientation and warned that British manufacturers must be prepared for hard work and small profits in Manchukuo. This was a much less rosy picture than seemed to be being built up on the basis of the trade statistics and other information circulating in London, and the consul-general suggested that a semi-official trade delegation might be sent to Manchukuo to study the market.[6]

The idea of a trade mission to Manchukuo was not received with much enthusiasm in the Foreign Office or the Department of Overseas Trade. The Foreign Office was sceptical about the actual opportunities in Manchukuo and was bound to be aware of the political repercussions and complications associated with trading with a country which the League of Nations had forbidden

its members to recognise. While determined that British subjects
had a perfect right to trade freely in Manchukuo,[7] the Foreign
Office was only too conscious that, if difficulties arose as the
result of particular transactions, effective diplomatic action in
defence of British interests was dependent, to a large extent, on
Japanese goodwill.[8] Furthermore, British interests in Manchukuo,
even if expanded under the new regime, would be so clearly
inferior to Britain's 'vast interests' in China that the Foreign
Office thought it unwise to risk too much in Manchukuo if there
was a chance that China might be given offence.[9]

The notion of a trade mission to Manchukuo was, therefore,
not seriously considered until the idea was revived in mid 1934
by an approach to the president of the Board of Trade by Sir
Harry MacGowan, chairman of ICI and a prominent member of
the council of the Federation of British Industries.[10] The
Federation had been inspired to suggest a mission as a result
of the activities of an interesting, if rather devious, character,
A. H. F. Edwardes, formerly of the Chinese maritime customs
and presently financial adviser to the Manchukuo government.[11]
Throughout 1933, Edwardes had worked to publicise Manchukuo
in British business and government circles and had consistently
held out high hopes for trade openings. He maintained that
there would be particularly good opportunities for the British to
gain important orders because the Japanese could not alone
supply the expanding market and because Manchukuo was in
urgent need of foreign capital and currency which Britain and
British trade could supply.[12] His promotion of Manchukuo
evidently impressed both Sir Warren Fisher and Sir Edward
Crowe. In June 1934, in his capacity as a kind of public relations
officer to the Manchukuo government, Edwardes spoke to Guy
Locock, secretary to, and director of, the Federation of British
Industries; and MacGowan's approach to the President of the
Board of Trade followed.

After the collapse of the cotton talks between Japanese and
Lancashire cotton manufacturers in April, the government was
understandably reluctant to countenance an official industrial
mission to Japan and Manchukuo but, in view of the public
interest in Manchukuo, the Board of Trade, the Department of

Overseas Trade and the Foreign Office were prepared to bless an unofficial mission if the Federation of British Industries was prepared to send one. It was recognised that Japan would welcome a mission and in the Foreign Office it was even suggested that, in view of Edwardes's share in the business, Japan might actually be promoting this one.[13]

Working closely with the Department of Overseas Trade, the Federation of British Industries set about organising its team. After a certain amount of difficulty in finding someone to lead the mission it was finally settled that Lord Barnby, a past president of the Federation of British Industries, should head a group consisting of Locock, the Federation's secretary, Sir Charles Seligman, director of Seligman Brothers, bankers, and Julian Piggott, representing the Iron and Steel Federation.[14] It was announced that the mission would study conditions in Manchukuo to ascertain whether British industry could cooperate with local interests in its development and would pay a short visit of courtesy and goodwill to Japan with the object of establishing friendly contact with Japanese industrial and commercial organisations.[15]

Given the indignation which Japan's action in Manchuria and her departure from the League had roused in some circles, it is not surprising that the news of the mission was seen by some as a weakening of British loyalty to the League resolution. The Foreign Office, which expected little from the mission, answered the inevitable strictures by arguing that the government could not be expected to put obstacles in the way of legitimate enterprise which might increase exports and that obstruction would only promote agitation in commercial circles in favour of recognition.[16] Such opportunism which, the Foreign Office had recognised, must characterise its policy in the far east, accorded ill with the idealism which prevailed among supporters of the League.

More immediately disturbing from the Foreign Office point of view was the lack of enthusiasm for the mission among official British representatives in Manchukuo and Japan. The consul-general at Mukden had envisaged a small, strictly commercial mission with a view to securing orders. Both he and the ambassador in Tokyo were dismayed at the character of this mission, particularly in view of the fact that the tricky oil monopoly question was under discussion. They both felt that the proposed visit was likely to increase the difficulties of negotiation. In the oil issue, Japan appeared to be deliberately fostering a situation which would bring home to the powers the inconvenience of non-recognition. It seemed singularly inopportune, therefore, to have chosen this moment to send a mission which was certain to be interpreted in both Manchukuo and Japan as a step towards the recognition they desired.[17] It was, however, too late to retract, the communiqué to China and to the press having gone out, and the spate of rumours had to be endured. Both China and Japan were offered assurances of the non-political character of the mission, which they appear to have received with equal scepticism. The Chinese minister in London deplored the failure to include China, 'the keystone of the arch of Asiatic trade' in the tour:[18]

A mission representative of the heavy industries of England in a single corporate capacity cannot escape having a semi-official status that no ordinary business enterprise could have.[19]

The press in Japan and Manchukuo made the same point by stressing the importance of the Federation of British Industries as the foremost economic organisation in Britain. The individual qualifications of the individual members of the delegation were fully reported.[20]

Certainly the composition of the mission could be interpreted as highly pro-Japanese and likely to be reflecting the official line. Sir Edward Crowe, of the Department of Overseas Trade, was thought to be pro-Japanese and had encouraged the mission. Locock, the driving force behind it, was a former member of the Foreign Office and was known to maintain his contacts there. Seligman was a member of the Exports Advisory Board and was in close touch with the Treasury. Piggott, who had been brought up in Japan, and whose family had maintained its contact with Japan, was hardly an unbiased investigator.[21] Edwardes, who certainly should have been biased and who was, in any case, in close touch with the Treasury, accompanied the mission.

In view of the personnel of the mission and of the contact

which must have existed between Japanese officials and Edwardes, it would have been surprising if the Japanese had not sought to make some political capital out of the mission's visit. The Japanese Foreign Ministry was deeply involved with the commercial bureau in drawing up the mission's programme and, to the annoyance of the British Foreign Office, it was found to have arranged an audience with the emperor.[22] Such an honour was hardly compatible with the mission's unofficial status and was likely to cause comment in China and Britain, but in the far east department, which felt its hand had been forced by the Japanese, it was decided that a bad impression on China had to be risked as a lesser evil than the considerable offence the refusal of an opportunity for an audience with the emperor would give.[23]

The mission left in September and spent four weeks in the far east, eight days of which were spent in the train. It was received in Japan and Manchukuo with the greatest goodwill but all reports indicated that the visit was seen as political in character, with economic aspects entirely secondary. In China it was suggested that Britain hoped, by cooperating with Japan, to revitalise British influence in China,[24] while in Japan an Anglo-Japanese non-aggression pact was rumoured. The British ambassador in Tokyo thought that the visit of the mission had been seized upon by the Japanese as an opportunity to mobilise opinion in Britain and Japan in favour of a new Anglo-Japanese political understanding and regarded the extravagances of the press as being deliberately 'inspired'.[25]

Between two short periods in Japan, the mission paid an eight day visit to Manchukuo. Here, though 'perpetually hurried and fatigued', they made great efforts to get general expressions of hope for the expansion of trade translated into concrete proposals.[26] The ambassador in Tokyo, with whom the Foreign Office was inclined to agree, felt, however, that the Japanese would be prepared to grant commercial advantages, not with the idea of continued industrial and commercial cooperation, but as part of a bargain towards a better political understanding. He doubted if they would be prepared to concede any advantages which could not be secured by ordinary methods.[27] This view was strongly supported by Sansom, the commercial counsellor in Tokyo. He

felt the Japanese were engaged in a deliberate attempt to fabri-
cate an Anglo-Japanese understanding which would deceive the
Federation of British Industries mission. Sansom thought that
the Japanese were feeling a 'cold wind' which was probably the
result of a combination of a fear of facing Russia without a
sympathetic supporter, a desire to separate Britain from the
United States over the question of naval armaments, a wish to
tie British hands in case it should be necessary to take some drastic
action in China together with nervousness over the Japanese
financial situation. 'In their present frame of mind', he wrote, 'the
Japanese conception of friendship is give and take; we give and
they take.'[28] He suggested that, if the Japanese were kept guessing for a while as to the British attitude, they might be disposed
to be more genuinely accommodating.

The Department of Overseas Trade and the Foreign Office
were impressed by Sansom's despatch. It confirmed the opinion,
held in the Foreign Office, that nothing of the slightest value was
to be gained from Japan, except as the result of firmness.[29]
Such a pessimistic view of the prospects for Anglo-Japanese
cooperation and such a cynical account of Japanese motivation
were not, of course, what many others, particularly some
members of the Treasury, wanted to hear. The letter was sent to
the prime minister, the lord privy seal and to the chancellor of the
exchequer who noted that he was not impressed.[30] Warren
Fisher, having made his own detailed criticisms of it, promptly
sent the letter to Edwardes for his opinion. Needless to say,
Edwardes attacked Sansom's view which he described as 'distorted'. He maintained that Japan's offer of commercial favours
was no 'trap' and urged that there was a danger in 'keeping
Japan guessing'.[31]

The mission left Japan on 26 October amid a spate of rumours
and distortions in the Japanese press. Both Barnby and Seligman
were credited with stating that they were in favour of a revival of
the Anglo-Japanese alliance and, though Clive admitted that the
mission had made an excellent impression, he felt that in political
matters its members were often beyond their depth and that these
rumours were probably not without foundation.[32] The result was
that a number of influential Japanese believed that Britain was on

the verge of making new advances to Japan. Tentative manoeuvres were, as we saw in the last chapter, under way, but these were closely tied to the naval conversations and were unrelated to the activities of the trade delegation in Japan.

Meanwhile, the mission's hopes for concrete proposals were high. They reported that they had obtained a 'definite assurance' that offers of business on a 'substantial scale' would be made to British industry[33] and expected to carry off a coup in the form of a big trade deal in which the Mitsubishi company, prodded by the Japanese government, would buy in 1935 not less than 20,000 tons of various steel products for use in Manchukuo.[34] This promise, which turned out to be the whole harvest of the mission, was destined to come to nothing. As the Foreign Office had predicted, once it was evident that the mission had failed to offer any important political concessions to the Japanese, it was left 'like some western Madame Butterfly waiting interminably at its Midland lattice for the Japanese Pinkerton'.[35] This outcome was no less than the embassy in Tokyo had feared, and their immediate concern, shared by the consul-general at Mukden, was that the members of the mission would be deluded by Japanese cordiality and hollow promises into agitation for a political agreement with Japan.[36]

That there were grounds for such fears was at once evident when the members of the mission reached home. Locock wrote promptly to Sir Horace Wilson, chief industrial adviser to the government,

I think that a very small advance on our part would have a great effect. Incidentally if Japan thought that Great Britain was prepared for a friendly understanding, it would do a great deal to bring the military round to our side, and they are the real rulers of Japan.[37]

He claimed that Japan's vice-minister of commerce and the head of the commercial bureau of the Foreign Ministry contended that an Anglo-Japanese *rapprochement* would enable their government to force Japanese industry to come to a reasonable arrangement with British industry and would make it possible for Britain and Japan to cooperate in a policy with regard to China. He summed up with his impression that, 'the solution of our trade difficulties will depend on the political relationship between the two countries'.[38] In contrast to this assertion, Foreign Office opinion was that there was no evidence that improvement in the political atmosphere resulted in better terms commercially. Sir Victor Wellesley, deputy under-secretary at the Foreign Office, saw Locock and did his best to convince him of this but feared, correctly, that he had failed to make much impression.[39]

On 13 December, a conference took place at the Treasury at which Fisher, Vansittart, Wilson, Crowe and Orde, the head of the far east department at the Foreign Office, met members of the mission.[40] As the Foreign Office had expected, the mission's thesis was that great commercial benefits were to be expected from some sort of political understanding, the general argument being that, if Britain did not in some sense ally herself with Japan by coming, for example, to some agreement for mutual consulta-tion over policy in China, the British would be squeezed out by Japanese jealousy. Though precise details could not be given, its members assured the meeting that Japan was anxious for a political agreement and would give commercial advantages in return for one. Further, they suggested that Japan was prepared to act in China in the interests of the Chinese and wanted coopera-tion and mutual consultation with Britain in this. The indica-tions that Germany was wooing Japan and the threat of the prospect of a possible agreement between them were noted with alarm by Fisher.

Vansittart and Orde presented the alternative Foreign Office side of the case, in terms of the difficulties a renewal of the alliance might have for Anglo-American, Anglo-Canadian and Anglo-Chinese relations. The discussion made it clear that the members of the mission and Fisher were not worried about the first two of these,[41] but the Foreign Office argument must have had some impact because, although there was no withdrawal of the mission's advocacy of some political understanding, Lord Barnby finally endorsed, as crystallising the mission's ideas, a suggestion of Sir Horace Wilson's about 'sounding Japan as to the conclusion of a multi-lateral agreement between powers ready to cooperate in measures to rehabilitate China'.[42] The test of sincerity, Wilson suggested, should be willingness to lend money to rehabilitate China. The Foreign Office doubted whether there would be any future in this suggestion, the matter having been, after all, thoroughly canvassed in the preceding months, but the mission was temporarily satisfied with this appearance of support for its general theme.

The report came out in December and was well received in Japan where it was compared favourably with the Lytton report.[43] The Foreign Office found it superficial and rather simplistic but, on the whole, less gloomy and more constructive than had been feared might be the case.[44] Sansom, who found it a 'slovenly document, containing some rather inexcusable blunders', considered there were serious objections in practice to most, if not all, of the proposals for solving Anglo-Japanese trade problems.[45]

Here the matter might have rested but, at the beginning of the new year, the head of the far eastern department heard on the departmental grapevine that Sir Horace Wilson had suggested to Walter Runciman, president of the Board of Trade, that a letter from Locock should be printed and circulated to the cabinet.[46] As has been seen, the Foreign Office, guided by the ambassador and the commercial counsellor in Tokyo, took a completely different view of the probability of commercial benefits arising out of a political understanding, from that of Locock and the Federation of British Industries. This view had not been circulated but the far eastern department was now determined that it should. In giving his support to the plan, Vansittart noted that he wanted this done particularly because there were 'tendencies about' which might cause some to take the amateur rather than the professional view, especially if they happened only to read the amateur.[47] He had no doubt of the superior authority of the professional view.

Vansittart probably spoke with feeling because he had, only a few days before, been endeavouring to cope with the results of the outspoken expression of the amateur point of view. Not surprisingly, the Russians had, from its inception, taken a great interest in the Federation of British Industries mission and in the reports of its members' advocacy of a renewal of the Anglo-Japanese alliance. Rumours of a loan for the exploitation of Manchukuo, which would be financed by Seligman's and

Baring's banks, led Ivan Maisky, the Russian ambassador in London, to sound first Robert Boothby, a member of parliament who supported close relations with Russia,[48] and then to consult the foreign secretary.[49] Apparently convinced by neither conversation, he then approached Vansittart with whom he had two separate conversations, on 13 and 19 December.[50] He was assured that the mission was private and commercial and that the Foreign Office knew nothing of the rumoured loan. A few hours after sending away a still doubting Maisky, Vansittart learned that the ambassador's suspicions were the result of unguarded and emphatic opinions in favour of an Anglo-Japanese alliance and the division of China into commercial spheres of interests expressed, in Maisky's hearing, by two well-known members of parliament who were both under-secretaries of state.[51]

This revelation sparked off a discussion in the Foreign Office where the head of the northern department deplored the pro-Japanese policy advocated by members of the mission. He wrote,

I find it difficult to understand how anyone in his senses could advocate any policy which would strengthen Japan politically, commercially or financially; but I have found that such a policy is advocated in very high quarters, particularly in the Treasury.[52]

This writer felt that Britain could not preach the gospel of the *status quo* in Europe if she could not show that it was also being upheld in the far east. The Treasury, of course, maintained that it was financially and physically impossible for Britain to uphold the *status quo* in both areas and this belief was the basis of the attitude to which objection was here being taken. Vansittart saw the Soviet ambassador once more and asked him to report to his government that 'no responsible person in the country' could hold views of the kind which had been expressed to Maisky[53] – a comment which clearly placed under-secretaries of state among the lower orders.

No sooner had the Russians been pacified than the Foreign Office was faced with the danger that the cabinet would be exposed to a similarly one-sided view. Obviously the Federation of British Industries/Treasury case had to be answered and, as Wilson did not like a suggestion that Locock's letter and one from Sansom should be embodied in one paper,[54] two separate

papers were printed and were circulated simultaneously. The
Foreign Office paper consisted of a memo by the foreign secretary
circulating a despatch from the ambassador in Tokyo which
included Sansom's comments on Anglo-Japanese relations from
the economic point of view. A memorandum, 'The Political
Aspects of Trade Rivalry or cooperation with Japan in China',
written by the head of the far eastern department with the
possibility of propaganda by the members of the Federation of
British Industries mission in mind, was added to the paper. Its
conclusion was that no commercial advantage was to be gained
from a political understanding with Japan. The Board of Trade
paper consisted of Locock's letter to Wilson with a covering note
by the president of the Board of Trade[55] who wrote that the
impressions of Lord Barnby and his colleagues, who had had
unique opportunities to meet leading men in Japan and Manchukuo, were worth noting. He added,

The mission hold very strongly the view that Japan is bound to be the
dominating force in the Far East; they believe that (realising that a formal
alliance is impracticable, at any rate for the moment) Japan desires an
understanding with us – an understanding which might begin with cooperation as regards China.[56]

Locock's letter, which formed the bulk of this paper, recorded
the mission's belief in the increasing importance of Japan's role
in the far east and in the need for an Anglo-Japanese understanding. Such an understanding was essential, it was claimed, to
provide security for the British position in the far east, to solve
the problem of Anglo-Japanese trade competition and to improve
British trade relations in China. A positive improvement in
Sino-Japanese relations described as 'the greatest guarantee of
peace in the far east', was felt likely to be one of the most important results of an Anglo-Japanese understanding. The mission
was convinced that Japan, perturbed by her isolation, desired
friendly cooperation with Britain.[57]

Such beliefs in the commercial benefits likely to arise, notably
in China, from a political understanding with Japan, represented
a specific challenge to the Foreign Office point of view. The
Foreign Office had already considered in some detail the problem
of China as a stumbling block to a better understanding between

Britain and Japan without any resolution to the problem suggesting itself. In his introduction to this latest presentation of the
Foreign Office view of Anglo-Japanese relations, Simon paid a
tribute to Sansom, whose memorandum formed the basis of the
argument on this occasion:

He has thirty years experience of Japan and is generally acknowledged to be
the greatest living authority on that country. I have no hesitation in considering that his opinion must be the authoritative one.[58]

Sansom pointed out that, on the surface, the problem appeared to
be a simple one

1. The United Kingdom desires relief from the pressure of Japanese competition.
2. Japan desires relief from pressure of world-wide disapproval of her
   policies.
3. Can any bargain be made on this basis?[59]

Sansom concluded that no bargain was possible because experience showed that, while the Japanese government might take
action to restrict exports in order to forestall or diminish tariff
action, it was unlikely to adopt a long-term policy of voluntary
restriction. He considered that it could be taken for granted
that, unless the government as a whole was convinced that it
would, on balance, be advantageous to Japan, the ministry of
commerce would be neither willing nor able to force on trade and
industry, controls of the scope required to afford any substantial
relief to British industry. Sansom doubted whether such economic
advantages as Japan would be prepared to grant in return for the
political support which she wanted would justify 'mortgaging'
for good or ill Britain's political future in the far east. He did not
believe that cooperation with Japan in China would diminish
Japanese pressure on other markets and increase the outlets for
British goods in China and Japan. Quoting Sir Frederick
Whyte, political adviser to the Nationalist government from
1929 to 1932, he wrote,

When I hear British businessmen in Shanghai say, 'if we back Japan she will
pull the chestnuts out of the fire for us,' my only answer is that when the
operation is complete there will be no British chestnuts left.[60]

Sansom urged that the British should not attempt to make a

bargain without being able to assess fairly accurately the value, in terms of trade, of Japan's assurances.

The gist of the argument in the memorandum which formed the second part of the Foreign Office paper was that, for reasons of self-preservation and livelihood, Japan must seek to be the dominating influence in China; that it would be unwise to identify Britain with Japan in China since it was impossible to trade in a hostile market, particularly when Britain could not compete with Japan at the cheap end of the market; that these considerations did not preclude a policy of general friendliness with Japan though such friendliness or, indeed, a binding agreement with Japan was unlikely to help China towards greater prosperity.[61] These sentiments, as the writer of this memorandum realised, were unlikely to appeal to those who wanted positive action to solve Britain's complex problems in the far east. Predictably, Warren Fisher, a man for action, dismissed this paper as 'a revised version of the Book of Lamentations' and its author as 'a pedantic ass'.[62]

Before the cabinet meeting on 16 January 1935 at which the two papers were to be considered, the Treasury took some care to prepare the chancellor's brief. Doubts were cast on Sansom's objectivity and his assessment of the Japanese political scene; and it was recommended that the cabinet's attention should be drawn to the paper, 'The Future of Anglo-Japanese Relations', which had been circulated jointly by the chancellor of the exchequer and the foreign secretary and had been shelved in October 1934 while the naval talks were in progress.[63] It was suggested that it was now essential to have the matter thoroughly considered by a suitably composed committee which should include the chancellor and the president of the Board of Trade who, it was noted, was being given the same advice by Sir Horace Wilson. The silver policy of the United States government, which was having alarming repercussions in China, had increased the Treasury's sense of urgency. Chinese finance was a matter of concern to both Britain and Japan and the Treasury felt that immediate consultations were vital. In the opinion of the Treasury, Japan had 'already indicated that what she wants from us most of all is that we should consult together with a view to some common policy vis-à-vis China.'[64] An approach which would gain Japan's 'confidence and goodwill' was felt to be called for rather than the 'obvious distaste for close and friendly relations' which, it was implied, was being shown in the Foreign Office.

Further arguments for the chancellor were supplied by Fisher who had his own source of information on the far east in the form of material supplied by Edwardes, the adviser to the Manchukuo government. The files contain a number of examples of Edwardes's work and, given that the Treasury was so critical of Sansom's credentials, the espousal of the opinions of a man whose record was both less distinguished and less reliable and who, as an employee of the Manchukuo government was scarcely disinterested, can only be explained by the fact that in the matter of Anglo-Japanese relations, Edwardes's interests and those of the Treasury coincided. On this occasion, Edwardes argued that Japan wanted an economically strong China, was seeking British cooperation in Chinese reconstruction, was prepared to cooperate in tri-partite action with the United States and would even like to return to the League of Nations. He concluded that there could be no harm in trying a policy of cooperation with Japan and reconstruction in China but that it was in a policy of 'continual drift' that danger lay.[65] The Treasury comment on this conclusion was,

It seems quite clear that if we were to adopt the sort of attitude indicated in the Foreign Office memorandum and allow things to drift, the results might be incalculable. If we refuse to consult and cooperate with Japan (bringing in America of course) and China sinks into economic chaos, an isolated Japan may take military measures there, and whether she does so or not, what is to happen to our vast trading interests and our employment at home?[66]

These sentiments were, of course, calculated to appeal to the anxieties of the chancellor of the exchequer. The truth was, however, that the problems of cooperation with Japan and the rehabilitation of China had been thoroughly canvassed in 1934 and the interests of the two far eastern powers had been found to be irreconcilable. Further, it was misleading to talk of Britain's vast trading interest in China. Though the investment was considerable, actual trade with China represented only two per cent of Britain's overseas trade.[67] The loss of the China market was, therefore, unlikely to throw vast numbers out of work but this kind of argument with its strong emotional appeal was, of course, good material for a cabinet meeting.

The introduction of the silver issue and its effect on the Chinese economy gave a dimension to discussion of Anglo-Japanese relations which, by its very nature, gave the Treasury an advantage over the Foreign Office and at the same time rendered less pertinent the straightforward Japan-centred commercial arguments which were the basis of the Federation of British Industries' case. When the cabinet considered the Foreign Office and Board of Trade papers on Anglo-Japanese relations, the well-briefed chancellor had no difficulty in taking the initiative. He explained that the American silver policy had had a serious effect on Chinese finances and might make conversations with both Japan and the United States necessary. Supported by an equally well-briefed president of the Board of Trade, he suggested the establishment of a committee to consider the problem.[68] The cabinet gave the foreign secretary the task of deciding how the question could best be handled and, after discussions with the prime minister, the president of the Board of Trade and the chancellor, he recommended that the question of Anglo-Japanese relations be further reserved, while the chancellor considered whether some means could be found of bringing assistance to China in its present exceptionally difficult financial situation. This was agreed and the cabinet decided that, when the subject was taken up again, the joint paper of the foreign secretary and the chancellor of the exchequer, 'The Future of Anglo-Japanese Relations', should be considered with the two most recent papers from the Board of Trade and the Foreign Office.[69] This was a further turn in the Treasury's favour for the revived joint paper followed what might loosely be called the Treasury pro-Japanese line.

As the centre of interest in far eastern affairs shifted to Chinese finance, the Federation of British Industries mission and its report which had initiated this stage of the controversy between the Foreign Office and the Treasury, sank into oblivion. Letters from the Foreign Office to the British representatives in Peking and Tokyo relating the events which had led to the issue, in January, of the two cabinet papers on Anglo-Japanese relations concluded,

Here, for the moment, the matter rests, I doubt whether the prospect of commercial advantage will bulk large in future discussions of possible political arrangements with Japan.[70]

The members of the Federation mission came to feel they had been cold-shouldered but, in fact, events had overtaken them and interest in their particular thesis was lost in the much wider problem of saving the Chinese currency and British investment in China.

8 BRITAIN, CHINA AND THE SILVER PROBLEM

Throughout 1934, the Chinese economic position deteriorated steadily. China was the only large country whose currency remained on a silver standard and from 1931 the world price of silver had been rising with correspondingly adverse effects on China's exports.[1] Early in 1934, the group in the United States congress which represented the silver producing states, put forward schemes to raise the price of silver still further and in June the American Silver Purchase Act became law. This act authorised the secretary of the Treasury to buy silver at home and abroad with the object of having and maintaining one quarter of United States monetary stocks in silver. A rise in the price of silver and deepening depression in China followed this act.[2] It became very profitable to export silver from China for sale in London or New York because the Shanghai exchange did not rise to exact parity with silver abroad owing to China's unfavourable balance of payments and fears of the government imposition of an embargo on the export of silver. Silver was draining out of China and the United States was deaf to Chinese complaints. In October 1934, therefore, the government imposed a heavy export tax on silver. Now, if silver was to be exported at a profit, it had to be smuggled and a flourishing smuggling industry promptly began.[3]

This effort to stop the outflow of silver was only one aspect of the Chinese government's effort to prevent the collapse of the currency. The London money market was explored for a loan. In September 1934, Sir Frederick Maze, inspector general of the Chinese customs, was the agent in what he was later to describe as a 'fantastic and ridiculous scheme' to borrow the astronomical sum of £150 million.[4] The second secretary at the Treasury described the Chinese project as 'a mere essay in the completely impracticable if not the completely mad, and I should say that wherever it puts up its head, a cold douche would be very advisable'.[5]

From the British point of view there were two special considerations involved in any loan to China. Restrictions on foreign loans had been introduced in 1933. Only loans calculated to be of direct benefit to British industry or required to increase the sterling assets of a country within the sterling block and so minimise fluctuations in exchange were exempt from the chancellor's embargo.[6] Unless a Chinese scheme was linked with a practical scheme of currency reform or with the necessary purchase of material from Britain, there would be no case for agreeing to the export of capital involved. This was, in fact, the basis on which Maze was refused.[7] Furthermore, the issue of a loan to China involved the Chinese consortium. Its members were always ready to complain jealously of any infringement of the spirit of the agreement, and the American wheat and cotton loan had only recently caused a stir.

The fate of the Chinese currency was important to Britain, not simply because of British investment in that country but also because of China's close link with the trade and with the currency of Hong Kong which was also based on silver. The British minister in China found himself pressed, on the one hand, by the Foreign Office for analyses of the Chinese financial situation and, on the other, by the British banks and business interests in China to use his good offices with the British government to facilitate their plans for assisting the Chinese government.[8] Such requests involved a technical knowledge which diplomats did not necessarily possess and some of the schemes sent forward and apparently supported by Sir Alexander Cadogan, the minister, were suspected by the Treasury to be designed to further the interests of the banks rather than the Chinese government.[9] The situation generated sympathy for the minister. Difficult questions were arising in connection with the silver problem and, as it seemed possible that the government might at any time be required to give advice as a matter of urgency, Neville Chamberlain, the chancellor of the exchequer, proposed in December 1934 that a small inter-departmental committee, made up of

Treasury and Foreign Office officials and a representative of the Bank of England, should be set up.[10]

By the time this committee met in mid-December several other loan schemes had been mooted and dropped, and China had made further representations to the United States but, after a brief success, had failed to get the price of silver stabilised.[11] Then came the news that the Chinese minister of finance, Dr Kung, had placed T. V. Soong in charge of arrangements for the relief of China's financial situation.[12] There was hope that Soong, whose financial ability was not doubted, might be responsible for a better thought out plan. At the end of December 1934 Soong put up a new proposal for a loan of £20 million for the rehabilitation of China to be made by the consortium. One half of it was to be brought to China for the reduction of the internal debt, thus releasing customs funds as security for the loan, the other half was to be utilised to pay instalments on the Chinese government's obligations abroad, thus eliminating the demand for foreign currencies and keeping the exchange steady.[13]

Soong's proposal was considered early in 1935 together with a request from Sassoon's bank, a private company with important interests in Hong Kong and Shanghai, for permission to issue a loan of £5 million as an advance on the larger loan.[14] It was agreed that a small loan would be of no use but that a constructive loan for the rehabilitation of China was another matter. Montagu Norman, governor of the Bank of England, said 'the pot was boiling over in China', that a 'very serious crash was imminent' and that this would be far more serious for British than for Japanese or American interests. Norman agreed with Sir Warren Fisher, who thought that the Japanese might be sounded forthwith, keeping American interests informed, but, whether or not the Americans would contribute, the British should be prepared to go ahead with the Japanese and make a constructive loan to China.[15] A Foreign Office representative who suggested that Japan might want some political concession as regards Manchuria or Shanghai as the price for any help she might give, was crushed by Fisher who referred to Foreign Office 'mistrust' of Japan. The feeling was that any loan or credit must form part of a reasonable scheme of currency reform, including a link with sterling and a fixed rate of exchange to correct the balance of payments. This would necessitate a takeover of the silver reserves of the note-issuing banks in China as security for a sterling credit in London. This credit would be liquidated by the sale of silver commandeered from the banks.[16] In practice, this meant that the rehabilitation of China's currency could not be effected without the agreement of the United States to buy the silver and, of course, there was some doubt whether the United States would readily assist China to adopt a sterling standard. Thus, whether or not Fisher was prepared to acknowledge it, United States concurrence in currency reorganisation was as crucial as that of Japan and there was, therefore, no possibility of acting with Japan alone on technical, as well as political, grounds.

Soong's plan did not involve currency reform but rather borrowing to make it possible to return to a free silver standard. This was felt by the chancellor's inter-departmental China committee[17] to be unsound policy since it seemed that China would within twelve months be faced with the same difficulties aggravated by an additional load of external debt. The loan was, therefore, refused on the grounds that it did not fall within the categories for which consideration had been promised by the chancellor.[18]

BRITISH PROPOSALS FOR CHINA

The timing of this refusal coincided with the cabinet's discussion of Anglo-Japanese relations stimulated by the Federation of British Industries mission's claim that Japan wanted an understanding with Britain, and that this understanding might begin with cooperation over China.[19] This view was, as we have seen, supported by the Board of Trade and the Treasury. The Chinese currency crisis appeared to make the matter even more urgent. The Treasury claimed China was about to sink into economic chaos; that refusal to cooperate with Japan would encourage Japanese military action; that vast British trading interests, the loss of which would increase unemployment at home, were at stake.[20] The Foreign Office did not believe that cooperation with Japan in China would, as the Federation of British Industries hoped, reduce Japanese pressure on other markets or increase outlets for British goods in China or Manchukuo. Moreover, any policy which would lead China to identify Britain with Japanese policy there, seemed likely to rouse Chinese hostility and to lead to a reduction rather than an expansion in British trade.[21] As far as currency reform was concerned, the Foreign Office felt that it was unlikely in the existing circumstances that the United States or France would lend money to China. This would leave Britain advancing towards currency reform and rehabilitation in China in cooperation with Japan. Quite apart from the outcry this seemed likely to cause in the United States, such action was bound to rouse the hostility of Russia which might then fall into German arms, thereby upsetting the *status quo* in Europe.[22]

When in January 1935, the cabinet considered these issues, they had no paper on the American silver policy and its effect on China, the relevance and serious implications of which were suggested by the chancellor.[23] Further discussion of the issues was therefore deferred until the chancellor produced, at the request of the foreign secretary, a paper on the silver position in China.[24] By the time this appeared in February, the cabinet, faced with no less than four papers on Anglo-Japanese relations and the problems of the far east, referred the whole question to a newly created cabinet committee on Anglo-Japanese political and economic relations.[25] In this way, the Federation of British Industries' attempt to lobby the government in favour of positive cooperation with Japan became merged in the more immediate crisis of the Chinese currency, and cabinet consideration of far eastern matters ceased meantime.

The unsuccessful Chinese loan applications provided the necessary lead into the question of the Chinese currency and both the foreign secretary and the permanent secretary of the Treasury saw the political opportunity in the situation. Their reactions were characteristic and different. Simon prepared a memorandum in which he argued that the key to a satisfactory far eastern policy was agreement between China and Japan; that an agreement which amounted to *de facto* recognition of Manchukuo by China might provide Japan with an adequate *quid pro quo* for cooperation in China and recognition of Chinese integrity

south of the Great Wall; that the silver question might provide a
lever to overcome Chinese opposition; that new multilateral
arrangements based on agreement between China and the
powers concerned would be valuable to Britain and the United
States and might even lead to a situation in which the United
States, Japan and Britain could reach agreement over naval
construction programmes.[26] In contrast to Simon's rather acad-
emic and correct approach, Fisher took action. He reported that
in a private conversation with Matsudaira, the Japanese ambassador, he had said that the Treasury must refuse the latest
Chinese proposal for a loan, but that he thought that it offered a
good opportunity 'for us all to put our heads together' and in
particular for the British and the Japanese to work together,
though it would be understood that the Americans and perhaps
others would have to be given the opportunity of joining in.
Matsudaira had said that he personally agreed with Fisher.[27]
Craigie, the Foreign Office negotiator at the recent naval talks
with the Japanese, had been present at this meeting between
Matsudaira and Fisher[28] and, as a result of this conversation and
a further private talk he had with Fisher, tackled the 'pundits of
the far eastern department of the Foreign Office' and, according
to Fisher, persuaded them to recommend to the foreign secretary
that 'the present abortive loan should be taken as an opportunity
for getting together with Japanese, and, of course, also with the
Americans, and possibly others'.[29]

The chancellor himself took a distinctly alarmist view of the
financial and economic position of China, envisaging the possibility of complete collapse. He thought, however, that there was
evidence that the Japanese government was equally aware of the
dangers of the situation and suggested that this provided a
convenient opening for approaches to the Japanese and also to
the United States and French governments to explain and discuss
the most recent Chinese proposal. Joint four-power consideration of the problem would, he suggested, follow in London. He
warned of the grave consequences of a purely negative policy of
watching the economic disintegration of China.[30]

In a memorandum supporting the chancellor's view, Warren
Fisher pointed out that there was a danger that the 'existing

drift' in China might become an external question, affecting the peace of the Pacific. The growth of communism, due to a steady increase in the forces of disorder, could, he thought, lead to anti-foreign outbreaks similar to the Boxer rising and might, like that rising, provoke foreign intervention. He also pointed out that civil war, to which China was perpetually a prey, resulted in a falling off of trade and this alone might compel Japan, to whom the China market was so vital, to take unilateral action. He reminded the cabinet of the trade opportunities a rehabilitated China might offer all countries, and suggested conditions under which a loan to China might be possible. He emphasised that under no circumstances could a loan be made to China unless it included arrangements in regard to defaults on the existing railway loans and unless there were provisions for the strict control of expenditure and over revenues accruing for interest and amortisation of the loan. Without these the money would only be misspent and disappear. He thought the powers would have to make it clear that Chiang Kai-shek and the central government had their support. If American participation could be assured, a modification of their silver policy, a key factor, seemed likely to follow. Fisher, therefore, advocated opening discussion about the recent loan proposals for China and the broader question of China's financial rehabilitation either through the Japanese and American ambassadors in London or through a conference of representatives of the consortium powers. If then it were agreed that the governments would do all in their power to encourage the provision of suitable financial aid for China subject to the adoption of reforms, some British and foreign banks might put up a limited amount of money to carry the Chinese government on until full-scale reconstruction proposals had been worked out.[31]

Chamberlain and his Treasury colleagues seemed not to appreciate that, however great her need, China would not willingly accept foreign control. It was all very well to suggest, as Chamberlain did, that international control of budgetary and economic arrangements would be a prerequisite condition of any large-scale assistance to China and that participation of the Chinese authorities in any joint endeavour was essential, but the imposition of one was bound to exclude the other. China was certain, justifiably enough, to resent her future being decided at a conference from which, Chamberlain and Fisher both seemed to suggest, she was excluded. In any case, such a conference might only reveal that nothing could be effected by joint action. The Foreign Office feared that, once Britain had conceded that she approved of the principle of rehabilitation in China, she would then find it difficult to protest if Japan declared that she was prepared to tackle the job alone.[32] For this reason, the Foreign Office wanted a more cautious approach than that advocated by Chamberlain and Fisher. In the view of the far east department, the chief aim of British policy should be a general *détente* in the far east which, it was hoped, would not only assist China in her economic difficulties but might make it possible to reach agreement on the naval negotiations, concerning which preliminary talks had just been broken off.[33]

The result of Treasury hopes and Foreign Office fears was, as might have been expected, a compromise. The action taken was also affected by reports of Japanese suspicions arising out of the rumours of Sino-British negotiations[34] and of reports that efforts were being made by the Japanese in China to bring about a *rapprochement*.[35] As a first step, telegrams were sent off to Tokyo, Washington and Peking, informing the governments concerned that Britain proposed to consult them with a view to ascertaining whether they were willing to cooperate in considering the best method of overcoming China's financial difficulties in agreement with China, from whom suggestions and observations were now being asked.[36] The British hope was that the silver problem, instead of breeding suspicion, might be used to bring about a *détente* in the far east; but inside the Foreign Office the prospects for international cooperation in the general rehabilitation of China were considered to be poor.[37]

The initial Japanese response to the approach appeared to be satisfactory. Willingness to cooperate in considering the best means of helping China was indicated.[38] The American reaction was more complicated. In early February, the Americans had, in fact, received a request for the purchase of silver and a loan of $100 million to be used to link Chinese currency with the dollar.[39] The United States Treasury and State departments had disagreed over the policy to be adopted with regard to this request, the Treasury favouring unilateral action to assist China, and the State department favouring international action not dissimilar to that which the British were now advocating.⁴⁰ The State department was, therefore, delighted that the British had taken the initiative. 'Let them play the part of broker and explore the possibility of bringing the powers into line', wrote the under-secretary of state.⁴¹ The British recognised that, in spite of their expressions of anxiety to help China, the Americans were hoping to manoeuvre them into making proposals and were determined, at this stage, that these must come from China herself.⁴²

Chinese reaction to the British advance was half-hearted in spite of special approaches to Chiang Kai-shek and Wang Ching-wei, president of the executive yuan, who were known to favour friendly relations with Japan.⁴³ It was indicated that China would welcome the British opening discussions with the United States, Japan and France,⁴⁴ but Soong had no concrete proposals to make and the minister of finance merely spoke vaguely of currency reform and of how much the benefit of British advice in formulating plans would be appreciated.⁴⁵ This unsatisfactory response appears to have been a reflection, not of the Chinese government's lack of ideas, but of its determination not to cooperate with any group of powers which included Japan. Although plans for currency reform apparently existed at this time, the Chinese were determined not to divulge details because of the British efforts to secure international cooperation to assist China.⁴⁶ The vagueness of the Chinese response concealed this attitude which left little scope for the use of the currency crisis either to bring about a Sino-Japanese *détente* or to draw Japan into cooperation with other powers in China.

Although the British wanted to avoid the responsibility for proposals to assist China, the Treasury suggested that the Chinese minister of finance might be encouraged to ask the British to arrange for a mission to visit China.⁴⁷ Fisher's enthusiasm for such an idea now carried matters out of Foreign Office hands. From the original Treasury suggestion there grew the idea that each of the consortium countries should send a financial mission to China. Within a few days Fisher had, without the knowledge of the Foreign Office,[48] seen Matsudaira, Atherton, counsellor at the American embassy and the French financial attaché and had explained that, since the subject of Chinese currency was too technical for an ordinary diplomatic mission, the British had decided to send a man to China who understood the principles of banking. In doing so, he said, the expectation was that a similar type of man would go from Japan, the United States and France. These experts would be in close touch with their missions which would be in close touch with one another. The experts would examine the currency, financial and economic position, and would make recommendations. Fisher thought that, given the American silver policy, no relief would be found possible, except by linking the Chinese currency with some external standard. Britain, he said, wanted to avoid doing anything without the knowledge of her 'collaborators', Japan, the United States and France.[49] The effect of by-passing the normal diplomatic procedures was that Britain's 'collaborators' heard about the mission project before the British minister in China learned that he was to be provided with expert financial advice. Cadogan was understandably sour.[50]

A further effect of this positive approach was to make less significant the production of concrete proposals by China. Cadogan was informed that, in the absence of further developments, progress must wait until a financial expert was added to his staff and perhaps to other legations.[51] The result was that China produced no proposals herself and had high hopes of the mission.[52] The Treasury appeared to have taken charge of far eastern policy and the Foreign Office was understandably concerned.[53] This concern was increased by the fact that the flurry of action in March was followed by an embarrassing pause during which it became clear that no other government was likely to send an expert. April lengthened into May, still no announcement had been made, and the Foreign Office felt that the Treasury policy was making the British look a little ridiculous.[54]

BRITISH MERCHANTS AND A 'STRONG POLICY'

In spite of the scepticism with which the financial mission was being regarded in the Foreign Office, pressure at home would have made it exceedingly difficult to make a case for withdrawing the plan, even supposing Treasury pride had permitted this to be done. It happened that a number of factors combined in the first six months of 1935 to produce particularly active lobbying by British firms interested in China.

At a discussion of the problems of the China market at which Foreign Office, Department of Overseas Trade and business representatives were present, the president of the Board of Trade had, in May 1934, asked the businessmen present to act as an informal committee for the purpose of examining the trade position in China and of making suggestions for increasing the volume of British trade with that country. The implications of the Amau statement of April 1934 were very much in the minds of all of them at that time.[55] A report was produced by this city China committee in July 1934 and it contained the suggestion that Louis Beale, the commercial counsellor in Shanghai, should be brought home for a period to provide first-hand information about China as an export market and to tour the provinces promoting interest in the China trade.[56] The Department of Overseas Trade thought that Beale was unlikely to have much success in this task but recalled him in order to placate the critics and to demonstrate that Britain had not lost her interest in trading in China.[57]

Beale arrived in London in October 1934. He was an enthusiastic propagandist for the China market. In his opinion the proper response to Amau was to increase British activity and investment in China.[58] and his encouraging account of the possibilities of greatly increased British trade in China impressed the chancellor of the exchequer.[59] Beale's presence in London at the beginning of 1935 as tangible evidence of the government's interest in the expansion of trade brought increased pressure on the Board of Trade, the Department of Overseas Trade, the Foreign Office and the Treasury, from representatives of the big companies which traded in the far east and had headquarters in London. All traders in China were feeling the adverse effects of the silver crisis on their business interests in that country and, aware as they were of the exceptional risks of the China trade, were unwilling to participate in its further expansion unless they could be sure that government backing in the form of some sort of 'strong' policy would be forthcoming. The 'admirably spirited' policy of commercial expansion which Beale advocated suggested to business men that the government might be susceptible to pressure for the kind of support for which they were looking.[60]

The Foreign Office detected an increase in this agitation for a 'positive' policy with the arrival in London, in early 1935, of W. J. and J. H. Keswick, directors of Jardine Matheson and Company, the largest and oldest British concern trading in the far east.[61] The opinions of W. J. Keswick were well known to the Foreign Office and the Board of Trade. He believed that British firms and British interests were 'drifting' in China and had reached the point where they must go forward or out. He had told Walter Runciman, president of the Board of Trade, that British merchants could not be progressive unless they had the government behind them and was evidently somewhat envious of the 'very definite' Japanese policy which was to 'slap the Chinese and shake hands afterwards'.[62]

The British minister in Peking also reported the Keswicks' opinions. To him they declared themselves not only reluctant to carry on their business unless they could be assured of a 'stronger' policy on the part of the British government, but also determined not to carry on, should extraterritoriality disappear. The stronger policy advocated seemed to the ambassador to be a 'gunboat' policy, the dangers of which he hastened to point out.[63] If they did not receive more support, the Keswicks explained, Jardines planned either to admit some large Japanese enterprise such as Mitsui to a share in their company's activities as a preliminary to liquidating the whole business and selling out, or else to arrange some Chinese participation. Cadogan gathered they had been discussing with T. V. Soong the possibility of taking him into partnership. Foreign Office comments on these revelations were critical of the Keswicks and merchants like them who, it was felt, had failed to adapt to the demands of the new situation created by China's determination to modernise her institutions and to keep the economic development of the country in her own hands.[64] Nevertheless, all agreed that it would be a misfortune if

Jardines were to 'clear out of China', as the Keswicks appeared to be threatening, and that the company should be encouraged to stay by the assurance that Chinese participation on a minority basis would not deprive it of the support of the British government.[65] In March 1935 when the Keswick brothers arrived in London, they were given this assurance at a meeting with Foreign Office and Department of Overseas Trade representatives.

Instead of comforting the business world, this attempt to reassure Jardines seems to have stimulated other British firms to participate in expressions of their shared discontents. The Foreign Office soon learned of deputations to the Department of Overseas Trade, the governor of the Bank of England, the chancellor of the exchequer and the president of the Board of Trade. A note left with the chancellor by a deputation representing four of the most important companies was typical. A two-fold crisis caused by China's currency and finance problems and by the threat to British interests posed by the increasing freedom of Japan in China and Manchuria was declared to be evident. An assurance of protection for British interests in China and Manchuria in the future and a stiffening of British policy which would indicate to the world that Britain's commercial position in the far east would be maintained, were asked for. The list of ten proposals put forward included requests for the transfer of the British legation to Nanking and its elevation to embassy status, an initiative on the currency crisis, a stand on treaty attrition, a recognition that cooperation with Japan was essential, and various steps which would demonstrate Britain's determination on equality of treatment in China.[66]

Until the Treasury announced the name of its financial expert it was difficult to respond to the complaints of the business community and, as the weeks passed without tangible evidence of the government's response, an important meeting was called by Sir Harry MacGowan who had been chairman of the city China committee, set up in 1934. This meeting revealed the continuing anxiety of British businessmen about the effects of the American silver policy in China, continuing criticism of the 'inactivity' of government and some conviction of the need overtly to support Chiang Kai-shek.[67] The fruit of this meeting was a memorandum which became known as the MacGowan memorandum. It was signed by twenty representatives of firms trading in China. One of its co-authors explained that nearly all British interests in China were losing money and this, plus the apparent success of Japan in creating an oil monopoly in Manchuria to the exclusion of important British interests there, had produced something like a panic. British businessmen, it was claimed, were not only unwilling to venture further in the China market but would gradually close down, unless some encouragement was received. There was a feeling among businessmen in the far east that the government at home regarded this area as of minor importance and not worth backing.[68]

The MacGowan memorandum was in fact a more detailed and sophisticated version of the note which had been left with the chancellor in April. It declared that, unless Britain took a firm stand, her interests in the far east and her power to participate in the potential expansion of the Chinese market would be gravely weakened. A British initiative over Chinese currency reform was called for, lest the case go by default to Japan, and the other concrete recommendation discernable among the verbiage was the familiar one dealing with the status and site of the British legation in China. The general theme of the document was a call for a restatement of British aims and policy in one comprehensive claim of 'equality of treatment' in China.[69]

There was no great sympathy for the complaints and fears of this China lobby in either the Foreign Office or the legation in Peking. The MacGowan memorandum was regarded as reflective of the mental condition of men mystified by the fact that their concerns in China were not flourishing. Companies which had made fortunes from China's submissiveness and the favourable trading situation before 1914 had not, it was felt, faced up to the implication of modern developments and had failed to adapt themselves. The British minister in Peking thought that it would be difficult to substantiate the merchants' claim that Japan had actually encroached on British interests in China and pointed out that Chinese encroachment on British rights, of which the companies also complained, was approved by implication in British policy established since 1926.[70]

The chancellor of the exchequer showed greater sympathy for the merchants' plight. Chamberlain was impressed by the critical trading position which the companies disclosed and encouraged by the account given by them of the business opportunities which, in better circumstances, might be grasped in China.[71] The Treasury view was that, with the existing state of world trade and the consequent depression in Britain's textile and heavy industries, it was out of the question to contemplate being pushed out of the existing market in China or being deprived of a share in the potential market which existed there. Quite apart from the question of safeguarding investments in China, there was the question of trade and employment at home. The chancellor and the president of the Board of Trade recorded their view that a 'critical turning point' might well have been reached in China and prepared recommendations for the committee on political and economic relations with Japan.[72]

The Foreign Office regarded the depression of British firms trading in China as mainly psychological and, as a morale-raising gesture, arranged for a small deputation to be seen by the foreign secretary.[73] This lack of sympathy for the merchant community was not, however, the result of a lack of appreciation of the situation in China. It was generally understood to be a good deal more complex than the comments of the chancellor suggested. On the one hand, there was Japanese commercial competition which could be said to be the business of British firms trading in China. On the other, there was growing Chinese competition which involved both the British business community and the British government since inevitably the vexed question of extraterritoriality raised its head. Over all there loomed the spectre of Japan's Asiatic policy which raised for the British government every sort of question and was not to be solved by such phrases as 'the stiffening of British policy' or 'active diplomacy'.[74]

The chancellor and the president of the Board of Trade supported the recommendations of the MacGowan memorandum with regard to British representation in China and, at its second meeting in May 1935, the cabinet committee on political and economic relations with Japan decided to go ahead with the proposals to change its status and the site of the British legation in China.[75] Chamberlain described this as the kind of definite action which would make British intentions clear. Simon saw the deputation of businessmen at the end of May and was able to report the decision to them in confidence. This concrete evidence of the government's evident attention to their recommendations apparently silenced the critics of the Foreign Office and the government, at least in Simon's presence.[76] In fact, the decision to raise the status of the British legation was precipitated as much by Japan's announcement of her intention to raise the status of her mission in China[77] as by the views expressed by the Treasury, the Board of Trade or businessmen. By whatever route it was reached, however, the decision was bound to moderate pressure for a stronger policy in China. The plan to send a financial expert to China, when it was known, would further alleviate the situation. In June the long-awaited announcement was made. Sir Frederick Leith Ross, chief economic adviser to His Majesty's government, was to be sent to China. He was, as the astonished Foreign Office commented, a really 'big gun'.[78]

9 THE LEITH ROSS MISSION

Sir Frederick Leith Ross, the Treasury's distinguished expert who was to investigate China's currency difficulties, was described at the time as a 'tenacious and sometimes impulsive person [...] not the sort to take attacks lying down'.[1] These were the qualities of a trouble-shooter, not a diplomat. It remained to be seen whether they were appropriate for the involved political situation and the subtle politics of East Asia. Leith Ross's entourage included Edmund Hall Patch, a Treasury official who had been financial adviser in Siam, and Cyril Rogers, a central banking expert on the staff of the Bank of England.[2]

The fact that Leith Ross could not be spared until August subdued Chinese jubilation at this singular expression of the British government's concern for them.[3] Leith Ross used the two months before his departure for interviews with banking and financial interests in the City and for exploring the views of businessmen interested in the China trade. The Manchester Chamber of Commerce took the opportunity to put forward the Lancashire view that the government was not giving China or the cotton industry the attention they deserved.[4] Another group representing prominent members of the China Association in London and the big London-based firms trading in China urged that nothing could be achieved without the support of Chiang Kai-shek and that Leith Ross must make his first task that of gaining the generalissimo's confidence.[5] Leith Ross's energy, his experience and his seniority in the civil service, created the impression in non-governmental circles in London that his mission must have more than the narrow aim of investigating China's financial situation, that it must signify the government's intention to have a more definite policy in China and that Leith Ross's report must contribute to the shaping of that policy.[6] This

148

impression raised the hopes of those in Britain and China who wanted a firmer British policy designed to improve their trading position in China.

It was decided in the Treasury that Leith Ross should have talks with Japanese politicians and officials on the way to China and, this being so, it seemed advisable to suggest a meeting with American officials as well, particularly as American purchase of silver was crucial to any currency plan. When an approach was made to Washington, Henry Morgenthau, secretary of the Treasury, made it clear that nothing short of a meeting with the chancellor of the exchequer would be contemplated by him.[7] Leith Ross therefore travelled across Canada and made no contact with the officials of the United States.

The American attitude of indifference to the idea of a financial mission did not worry the British and suited the Japanese. As the British ambassador in Tokyo pointed out, there was a good chance that the Japanese army which had recently been 'showing its teeth'[8] might welcome financial chaos in China as an excuse for another forward movement and would, in this event, pursue its own way, followed at a discreet distance by foreign minister Hirota. All the same, though it seemed that Japan was likely to resist any attempt at international financial assistance to China, the ambassador believed that joint Anglo-Japanese assistance might be favoured and suggested that this might be in China's best interest.[9] There was, of course, the problem of persuading the Chinese that this was so.

It was equally impossible, before Leith Ross left, to abandon all hope of international cooperation or to suggest purely Anglo-Japanese cooperation which might be interpreted as a sign of British anxiety and weakness. The eagerness of the Treasury in March to acknowledge a crisis seemed likely to have caused the British to drift into a dangerous position. Any suggestion that Britain was aiding Japan in her policy of spoilation in China would have met with an outcry not just from the League of Nations Union but from that section of the business lobby which favoured supporting Chiang Kai-shek.

Leith Ross appears to have been given no written instructions. It was agreed, however, that China should be urged to abandon silver and issue a note payable in foreign currency, particularly sterling, and that, in order to inspire confidence in such an issue, China could be reasonably expected to ask for assistance to strengthen her foreign exchange reserves. The governor of the Bank of England favoured a suggestion that, as part of a deal about Manchukuo, a loan for China could be arranged on the security of the Manchukuo revenues. A loan of £10 million would be issued in London, 50 per cent of the service being guaranteed by the British and 50 per cent by Japan (these percentages to be varied if other powers came in). The loan would be technically a loan to the Manchukuo government, which would get round the consortium difficulty, but the proceeds would be paid to China as an indemnity for the loss of Manchukuo.[10] The chancellor of the exchequer and the foreign secretary discussed this plan and Chamberlain wrote to Leith Ross,

We find ourselves in complete agreement that we should like it proceeded with and if possible developed into a practicable scheme. Assuming that the necessary consents could be obtained, we should feel every confidence in putting the proposed guarantee before parliament.[11]

The Foreign Office doubted whether either China or Japan would see sufficient advantage in the scheme to induce them to cooperate, but found it ingenious and recognized that the regularisation of the international status of Manchukuo would relieve the department of many difficulties. Sooner or later, it was felt, recognition would have to come and recognition through China offered the most respectable way. In any case it was too late by the time that the Foreign Office saw it to voice doubts about the plan because Leith Ross was already on his way and the newly appointed foreign secretary, Sir Samuel Hoare, specifically requested that the Foreign Office eschew a 'negative and over-critical' attitude towards the Treasury. He asked for 'sympathy and impartiality' for any proposals Leith Ross should make.[12] The Treasury was not, therefore, to be deterred from attempting the rehabilitation of China, but it was a thankless task which the wits of the Foreign Office described as 'trying to pin apple jelly to the wall'.[13]

    Leith Ross's aspirations were, in fact, rather grander than the

Foreign Office knew. He hoped to be instrumental in bringing about a 'treaty of peace and good understanding' between the Chinese government and the Japanese and Manchukuo governments. By this treaty reciprocal undertakings were to be made by China, Japan and Manchukuo to abstain from intervention in one another's political administration; China was to recognise the effective independence of Manchukuo; the Manchukuo government was to undertake to pay China a thirty years annuity or tribute representing the appropriate proportions of the obligations charged on the Chinese customs and salt revenues as at 1932; the Japanese government was to release, for the general purposes of the Chinese government, the Japanese share of the Boxer indemnity in respect of the last four years held at the Yokohama Specie bank and was in future to renounce all further indemnity payments. It would be understood that the Japanese would use every endeavour to support the Nanking government; that recognition of the Manchukuo government by the Nanking government would be followed by British recognition; that the treaty would be notified to the League for registration. The Foreign Office did not see this plan which was composed by Leith Ross on his way to Tokyo. In view of the lack of Japanese response, Leith Ross put nothing of this in writing and indicated to the Treasury that the plan should be 'put on the shelf'.[14]

LEITH ROSS IN JAPAN

Leith Ross arrived in Japan in early September. Because of his career in the world of international finance, he had the advantage of knowing a number of Japanese politicians and officials. He had met Hirota, the foreign minister, at the Hague conference in 1929, and Tsushima Juichi, the vice minister of finance, had been a member of the preparatory committee of the world economic conference in 1933 and had frequently been in London.[15] Takahashi Korekiyo, 'the grand old man of Japanese finance', was finance minister for the seventh time at the age of eighty-one, and though Leith Ross had talks with him, it was with Tsushima that he apparently had his most friendly discussions. It was on Tsushima that Leith Ross tried out the idea of a loan based on

Manchukuo. It evidently came as a complete surprise to him. Tsushima thought that, if China would recognise Manchukuo much could be done to save her face and a generous settlement could be made on purely financial questions. He did not, however, believe that China would recognise Manchukuo until after the great powers had done so. Moreover, he thought that Japanese public opinion would be difficult to persuade that recognition was worth paying for, and thought that this would certainly be the view of the army of which he was clearly apprehensive.[16] Leith Ross did not find Hirota, and the vice minister of foreign affairs, Shigemitsu Mamoru, as easy to talk to as he did Tsushima and therefore he did no more than hint at the idea of the loan based on Manchukuo to them.[17] He found, however, that all the Japanese politicians and officials that he met agreed that the recognition of Manchukuo by the great powers had ceased to be a matter of importance, though they were of the opinion that recognition by China might well be in China's own interests and it seemed apparent that they might not be so indifferent to Chinese recognition. Leith Ross explained the conditions which the British regarded as essential for a loan to China. These included adequate security, assurance as to the future administration of the customs under a British inspector-general, a satisfactory scheme of stabilisation and control of the proceeds of a loan to ensure proper use, reform of the Central Bank with a British adviser for the bank, reform of the budget and some settlement of outstanding railway defaults.[18] The Japanese displayed no ill-will to the British project but Leith Ross found them doubtful of the extent to which China really was facing disaster and unconvinced of the wisdom of giving her any help.[19]

Leith Ross carried with him a letter from the king to the emperor of Japan. The idea of such a letter had been Leith Ross's own and was one with which the king expressed himself pleased to cooperate.[20] The chancellor of the exchequer was enthusiastic about the project for which there was very half-hearted support in the Foreign Office. A draft was, nevertheless, prepared. The king expressed the hope that the emperor would regard Leith Ross's mission with benevolence and his desire that, through it, friendly relations between Britain and Japan should

be strengthened. He declared his policy in the far east, as elsewhere, to be

to promote a good understanding between the nations which will restore the
basis of confidence for the trading activities on which both our people
depend.[21]

Since both Britain and Japan had important interests in China,
the king expressed his hope that the representatives of both
countries might be inspired by a desire for consultation and
collaboration. In its expression of economic interest as the goal of
policy, the letter is interesting. It was not an approach which at
that time had similar appeal in Japan. The change in outlook
towards international affairs which had marked Japanese foreign
policy since the Manchurian Incident, included the down-
grading of the pursuit of economic interests as a national goal.[22]
There was, however, a tendency among British ministers and
civil servants in the 1930s to assume that other nations sought
peaceful economic cooperation as keenly as did the British.[23]
Certainly Leith Ross felt that, when he learned about the letter to
the emperor, Hirota was influenced to be more amicable and
forthcoming. His expectations that the letter would be a 'valuable
help' in bringing the Japanese 'off the fence'[24] into cooperation in
Chinese financial rehabilitation were not, however, fulfilled. The
letter was graciously received but it altered nothing. The Japanese
attitude remained non-committal up to the end of Leith Ross's
visit.

LEITH ROSS IN CHINA

In China, Leith Ross found Soong, Kung and Wang Ching-wei
anxious to obtain a loan but convinced that Chinese public
opinion would not tolerate recognition of Manchukuo, particularly as the Japanese government did not appear to be willing to
make any concession in return for recognition.[25] Thus the myth,
held in some British business and financial circles, that mere
mention of recognition would make the Japanese more amenable
and would improve the whole position in the far east, was at once
disposed of. Clearly, recognition of Manchukuo was not to be a
way round the consortium difficulty nor had Leith Ross's

representations had the desired effect of bringing China and Japan closer together. There was no wish to put pressure on China to recognise because, with the Abyssinian crisis newly on their hands, the Foreign Office was afraid of becoming involved in another drama at Geneva and with the League's supporters at home. Stimulated by an enquiry from the Chinese embassy in London as to whether the British government backed Leith Ross's recommendation to the Nanking government to recognise Manchukuo,[26] Vansittart suggested that Leith Ross should be told at once to drop the idea which, he felt, would 'cut no ice' but rather would lead into 'deep waters'.[27] The Treasury, however, refused to agree to such a categorical instruction[28] so that Leith Ross was simply informed of the Chinese *démarche* and reminded of the danger of pressing China to recognise.[29] Such deadlocks between Treasury and Foreign Office were to be common while Leith Ross remained in China.

Before Leith Ross arrived, the Chinese had worked out a programme for stabilisation of the currency which was not very different from that which had been sketched in London, and Leith Ross reported that they were prepared to launch a scheme along these lines provided they could get a loan of £10 million. The Chinese claimed to have an arrangement with the United States government by which the latter would buy unlimited quantities of silver at current market prices. If this was so, Leith Ross felt they had an ample cushion and that a loan would be 'more for window dressing and for budget cover' than for exchange needs. The real difficulties, he pointed out, were the 'corruption, nepotism and inefficiency' of the Chinese administration on the one hand and the Japanese political situation on the other.[30] It seemed unlikely that, whether or not the Japanese Ministry of Finance wished to cooperate, it would be able to do so because of the attitude of the Kwantung army. There seemed little prospect for the better understanding between China and Japan which had been envisaged in London but Leith Ross recommended that, rather than do nothing, the British government should risk the £10 million involved and that the currency reform should be immediately initiated. An improvement in economic conditions would, he argued, do more than anything else to strengthen the Nanking government in the Yangtse valley, the area of greatest interest to the British.[31]

It seemed to the men in the Foreign Office that Leith Ross had 'fallen under the China spell'.[32] From the Foreign Office point of view, the most important function of the mission had been to improve Sino-Japanese relations, but Leith Ross appeared to be ignoring this. He had accepted the Chinese assurances at their face value and, worse still, he apparently felt that China's rehabilitation might be effected by British efforts alone, even in the face of Japanese opposition. In reply to a question from Kung as to whether Britain would go on alone if others refused to participate in a loan, Leith Ross said that London would first have to be consulted but expressed the opinion that Britain could not allow others to veto a scheme which she thought reasonable.[33] Leith Ross was an extremely experienced and confident negotiator, but Soong and Kung were equally shrewd. They wanted no international loan.[34] Having won this admission from Leith Ross, they appear to have concentrated on getting a purely British loan. They led Leith Ross along a dangerous path which included, at their recommendation, a failure to take Japan fully into his confidence.

As the parties concentrated on the technical task of currency reform, there was a tendency for the main object of British policy, 'cordial relations' between China and Japan and a 'friendly settlement' of the 'outstanding difficulties' through international cooperation,[35] to be lost sight of. The Foreign Office felt it knew much more of China than the Treasury and was aware that the Japanese could not be prevented, if they so wished, from destroying the government Leith Ross was trying to bolster up. But it was difficult to maintain stubborn opposition, once the first consideration became a currency scheme which the Treasury found technically sound. The Treasury was also obsessed, to a degree which the Foreign Office found unreasonable, with the thought of the loss of prestige which would result from the return of the mission without any practical achievement. Their widely differing estimates of the situation made it hard for the Foreign Office and Treasury to agree on the instructions to be sent to Leith Ross and, as days lengthened into weeks, Leith Ross became more insistent in his assurances to London that the general outlines of the scheme were 'plain sailing' and that approval to go ahead must be given to prevent a collapse.[36] Finally, the technical details were approved, subject to a definite contract with an adequate time limit being signed with the United States Treasury for the purchase of silver and to the assurance that a long-term loan could be subscribed in Shanghai. A final decision, however, was to be deferred until the views of the British ambassador in Peking were known and Leith Ross made a further visit to Japan, whose cooperation London regarded as essential.[37]

The British ambassador in China was in a difficult position. It was as hard for him as it was for the Foreign Office to stand out against the views of a financial expert of such eminence. He was also under pressure from a revitalised British business community in China who imagined they were at last witnessing a 'stronger policy' on the part of the British government.[38] Though he saw no prospect of a better Sino-Japanese understanding and believed that the Amau statement remained a fairly accurate statement of the Japanese attitude, Cadogan did not seek to dissent from Leith Ross's view that others should not be allowed to veto a scheme which the British thought reasonable. This singleness of view from the experts in the far east made it impossible to resist Treasury enthusiasm for a scheme which was based largely on Chinese promises and which the Foreign Office regarded as having only an outside chance of producing a stable currency and corresponding benefits to British trade. The rather fatalistic feeling in the Foreign Office was that, having gone so far, it was better to go ahead and hope for the best.[39]

While such a decision was no doubt expedient, it weakened the capacity of the Foreign Office to check the Treasury in the future. Leith Ross soon reported that the Chinese were prepared to go ahead without any guarantee of silver purchase from the United States and suggested it was most inadvisable for him to return to Japan since there might be leaks to the press which would jeopardise the whole position. It was suggested too that the question of the future administration of the Chinese customs should be arranged privately and not made a condition of the loan so that a fight with Japan on this issue might be avoided meantime.[40] The British conditions were being whittled away by the Chinese and because any suggestion of retreat had become so obnoxious to the Treasury, there seemed every chance that these Chinese 'super crook' tactics would succeed.[41] When the ambassador in Tokyo saw these terms, he urged that Japan must be kept fully informed and warned that a hostile reception to a loan to China was to be expected.[42] Fisher's reaction was, 'I have very little opinion of Clive's judgment at any time and it is not improved by his childish jealousy of Leith Ross.'[43]

It was small wonder that the Foreign Office felt the Treasury was getting them into a 'rare mess'.[44] After constantly urging a more friendly attitude towards Japan, the Treasury seemed blindly determined on a policy which was in contradiction of all their previous ideas. The uniqueness of the Leith Ross mission and the action now proposed suggested that a 'forward' policy was being adopted by Britain towards China. Such a policy was incompatible with a *détente* in the far east and continued good relations with Japan and, furthermore, the United States seemed likely to be affronted by it. Vansittart protested:

I must express my apprehension as to the contradictory policy which the Treasury are now pursuing, and my strong feeling that His Majesty's Government would be very wise to review the whole situation most carefully before they commit themselves further [. . .] I have never known a case where matters were improved by going further on a bad line. Retreat is humiliating and has *moral* consequences, often grave ones, but it is at least safer than perseverance which may bring unpleasant *material* consequences.[45]

As a result of Foreign Office apprehension, the foreign secretary saw the chancellor. The latter accepted the Foreign Office view that it was dangerous to proceed with a loan in the face of Japanese opposition; agreed that, until both the Japanese and American governments had been fully informed by the Chinese government, no final decision about a loan could be made; consented to the Foreign Office wish that Clive should inform the Japanese government in general terms of the British proposals and explained that, in opposing this course in the past, the Treasury had had in mind the risk of a double negotiation starting, one in Tokyo and the other in China.[46] As this comment indicates, the Treasury felt that the mission in China was their affair. The foreign secretary assured the chancellor that the Foreign Office no less than the Treasury was opposed to double negotiation but wanted to make it clear in Tokyo that the British were not going behind Japan's back.

The instructions based on this interview made it clear that, if the Chinese wanted British help, they must reconcile themselves to informing other governments of the details of the scheme.[47] Their arrival in China produced an immediate reaction. It seems evident that the Chinese had been postponing the operation of the currency scheme without a loan, pending a favourable reply from London. Once it was apparent that this would not be immediately forthcoming, action began. On 1 November Soong told Leith Ross and the British ambassador that the nationalisation of silver and a very high export tax, which would make the legal export of silver at a profit impossible, were to be announced. All holders would be required to exchange silver for notes of the government banks which would become sole legal tender. The profit on the silver so acquired would pass to the state. Soong asked Leith Ross to use his influence with the British banks in China to persuade them to accept the requirements.[48] On the day after this conversation, the Chinese government reached an agreement for the purchase of one million ounces of silver by the United States government. The proceeds of the sale were to be used for the stabilisation of the currency. A Chinese request for a loan was turned down by the United States.[49]

The British banks in China were prepared to accept the Chinese requirements, provided they could be protected from demands for silver on the part of depositors and, after a meeting in London between the Foreign Office, Treasury and bank officials, it was agreed that the Chinese request could be met by the issue in China of a King's Regulation. This would protect banks from claims for payment in silver and would make the provisions of the Chinese law binding on British subjects.[50] The Chinese announcement of the currency reform was made on Sunday 3 November, for release to the press the following day and, on that day, the British ambassador in Peking issued the necessary regulation. The speed with which this regulation followed the Chinese announcement was taken as an indication that the British had had prior consultation with the Chinese. In spite of Leith Ross's denial of this, the Americans and the Japanese were profoundly suspicious. It seems possible that it suited the Chinese that the Americans and Japanese should be left with this impression. Leith Ross was a convenient scapegoat in the face of Japanese hostility to Chinese currency reform and, moreover, if the British could be publicly associated with the reform, they would have a vested interest in its success. This was likely to increase China's chance of obtaining a loan from them.

As a first step in the currency reform, the silver in the banks in China had to be acquired by the central bank of China. At once there was trouble with the Japanese banks. They did not want to exchange their silver for paper dollars, considering either that it should be bought at world prices or that they should be able to export it. All the non-British banks agreed with them and, not surprisingly, this caused the attitude of the British banks to stiffen.[51] This was very disappointing to Leith Ross whose concern for the success of the currency scheme must have pleased the Chinese. Fearful that the 'good impression' gained by the prompt issue of the King's Regulation would be weakened if it were not followed by the surrender of the silver, he suggested that the banks should be content with a written undertaking that the Chinese central bank would extend to them any more favourable treatment subsequently accorded to other foreign banks. Unlike the bank representatives, he had no doubt that the Chinese would honour such an agreement.[52] The Treasury had no doubts either and wanted Leith Ross to intervene personally and arrange some sort of contract between the banks and the central government.[53] Of course, the Foreign Office objected. If the British pushed forward to surrender their silver and found other banks, foreign or Chinese, failed to follow suit, they would look particularly foolish. The news that the Chinese banks at Hankow, Tientsin and Canton would not hand over their silver to Shanghai and that sub-treasuries of the central bank would, therefore, be set up in these places, was evidence that the government could not succeed in centralising silver reserves.[54] The Foreign Office favoured doing nothing and keeping the situation fluid. This did not appeal to the Treasury, but after some acrimony it was agreed that, before

British banks could be called on to hand over their silver reserves, information as to the extent to which the Chinese themselves were obeying the law would have to be supplied.[55]

The Foreign Office had won a stay on the question of the silver reserves but the problem of the loan remained. Leith Ross wanted it to support the currency in the manner of his original plan and claimed that the grant of a loan would give Britain the opportunity to recover prestige and improve conditions for British investors and traders by taking a lead in the reconstruction of China. Supported by the ambassador in Peking, he maintained that the withholding of a loan because of Japanese objections would irreparably damage British prestige in the eyes of both the Chinese government and of the British community in China. If the Japanese ambassador in China failed to endorse the scheme, Leith Ross suggested that he should re-visit Tokyo to explain the details further and, if the Japanese should still refuse to cooperate, they should be told that, in any case, the British government proposed to approve British banks floating a loan. Such firmness, he contended, was necessary to prevent the Japanese receiving the impression that Japanese policy in China could be pursued heedless of British interests.[56]

Aware, as it was, that the Japanese could with impunity disregard British interests because they were without the material backing which would have impressed the Kwantung army, the Foreign Office was derisive of Leith Ross's argument[57] but their position was again weakened from an unexpected quarter. The British ambassador in Tokyo also came out in support of a loan to China as the lesser of the evils facing Britain, even though a hostile press campaign and the suspicions of the Japanese military and Japanese bankers suggested that one of the consequences of continuance with the loan proposal was likely to be an immediate tightening of the Japanese grip on north China.[58] Britain could make the loan and risk being £10 million poorer if the scheme was torpedoed by the Japanese or suffer the humiliation of beating a retreat. The Foreign Office favoured a graceful backing out and, in an effort to persuade the Treasury to accept this line, devised an honourable method of retreat. It was suggested that Leith Ross should continue to discuss the proposed loan with the Chinese

North China

government but should confine his attention to non-political matters such as past railway defaults and should indicate that the Chinese government must provide concrete evidence of good faith by the initiation of the reform of railway administration and of proposals for payment to the bondholders in the three most important loans in default. This approach would provide the opportunity to move over to the Japanese position that China could only be saved by self help and the discussions and arrangements would all take time, which would allow excitement to die down.[59]

JAPANESE MOVES IN NORTH CHINA

The attractions of retreat were enhanced by indications that the reorganisation of the administration of north China was impending under Japanese influence. The Tangku truce signed by Japan and China in 1933 had established a neutralised zone south of Jehol, now the Manchukuo frontier, between that frontier and the Great Wall.[60] The advantages of this for Japan were that it improved Manchukuo's defences and enabled the Japanese army to hold Peking and the north China plain under threat. In May 1935 incidents in the neutralised zone led the Japanese to claim Chinese violations of the Tangku truce, and a series of demands was presented to the Chinese authorities in the area by the Kwantung army. These appeared to have been put forward independently of the government in Tokyo whose policy of Sino-Japanese reconciliation the Kwantung army was known to suspect.[61] The army's demands aimed at the elimination of Chinese military forces in the north and the replacement of officials disapproved of by the Japanese by others more favourably regarded. The Chinese were warned that, if these demands were not met, it might be necessary to extend the demilitarised zone to include Peking and Tientsin.[62] At the time, the British ambassador in Tokyo had the impression that Hirota had been upset by the sudden threats and demands of the Japanese army in north China but that the Japanese army was so powerful that, outwardly and in the press, the minister of foreign affairs preferred to endorse all they did.[63] By the end of June, the Chinese had met the Japanese requirements by carrying out purges of officials in the Hopei and Chahar political provincial councils and the Peking political and military councils. The Japanese alleged that these steps were taken in conformity with agreements which they called the Ho–Umetsu and Ching–Doihara agreements, but the Chinese denied that any such official agreements had been concluded.[64] It seemed probable that the Kwantung army's moves were designed as a first step to create an economic bloc between north China, Manchukuo and Japan. This was a direct threat to Nanking's financial position since such a bloc would be the final blow to the already deteriorating customs service in the area. Moreover it was bound to increase the opportunities for smuggling into and from north China.

The problem of smuggling, which was not a new one in China,

had been growing worse since 1933.[65] British merchants complained of the activities of Chinese smugglers who, with Japanese
connivance, operated between Dairen and the Shantung and
Hopei coasts and along the Great Wall. By 1934 the British
Chamber of Commerce in Tientsin reported that, in certain
commodities, it was no longer possible to do business by legitimate trade.[66] Japanese support for illicit trade in north China
indicated a radically different attitude to the customs service
which was the financial basis of the Nanking regime, from that
held by the British. Japanese success in north China demonstrated
that neither China nor the western powers was likely to prevent
the extension of Japanese political and economic influence in that
area.

In September 1935 a message from Japan announced that the
Ministries of Foreign Affairs, War and Marine had at last agreed
on the policy to be adopted towards China. This policy was to
consist of political and economic cooperation between Japan,
China and Manchukuo, with special reference to north China,
joint defence against sovietisation and the complete suppression
of all anti-Japanese and anti-Manchukuo activities.[67] This could
not be seen as a new China policy but it offered scope for aggressive tactics by the Japanese army in China and the apparent
determination to enforce the policy was ominous for British
interests there. In October conferences on the subject of the
army's policy towards China were held by Japanese army officers
in Dairen, Shanghai and Tientsin. These were followed by statements which made clear the army's determination to eliminate all
resistance to Japanese penetration in north China. The Chinese
ambassador in Tokyo was also officially informed by Hirota of
Japan's three point programme.[68]

The tension created by these events was just beginning to die
down when the new currency measures were announced. The
Japanese army was incensed by China's failure to consult Japan
in advance, by the economic threat to their plans which the
currency control represented, and by the presence of Leith Ross
who appeared to outside observers to be the moving spirit behind
the Chinese measures. A series of fresh demands was presented to
the Chinese and the aim of the Japanese army now appeared to be

the economic severance of north China from the central government. A new government having fiscal autonomy and control over customs and salt revenues was proposed for the five northern provinces of Hopei, Chahar, Suiyuan, Shansi and Shantung.[69] If the Japanese succeeded in nullifying the new customs regulations so far as they applied to north China, the loan situation and the stability of the new currency would be gravely prejudiced. Further, it could be expected that smuggling from the northern provinces into central China would be able to proceed without impediment, thus striking at the heart of Britain's trading area.[70] British interests in China seemed to be seriously threatened and the Foreign Office felt that the Leith Ross mission and the Abyssinian crisis had both contributed to the timing of this Japanese forward movement.[71] There was a certain irony in the thought that Leith Ross's labours might ultimately be responsible in part for the disintegration of China and the extinction of British interests there.

The full Japanese plan for north China was not implemented. Local negotiations were suspended by the Chinese who proposed that negotiations between China and Japan with a view to promoting friendly relations should take place between the Japanese ambassador in China and Chiang Kai-shek himself.[72] The Kwantung army was thus baulked in their major coup but brought off a minor one with the establishment on 24 November of an autonomous area and a puppet government under the style of 'The East Hopei Anti-Communist Autonomous Council'.[73] The position was highly charged with dangerous possibilities and the Foreign Office was highly embarrassed by Leith Ross's reported statement that he had not met a single Chinese who supported the autonomy movement in the north or who believed that there was any desire among the masses in north China for autonomy.[74] Such political ineptitude by the British financial adviser in China merely gave grounds for Hirota's comment to the British ambassador in Tokyo that his hopes for a betterment of Anglo-Japanese relations and a settlement of Sino-Japanese problems by peaceful means had been dashed by the Leith Ross mission; that the fact that Leith Ross was such a well-known figure had encouraged the anti-Japanese element in Nanking and that Leith

Ross's movements and utterances left no doubt that he was involved in the thick of Chinese party politics.[75] The Foreign Office was further embarrassed by Chinese feelers as to whether Britain or any other power was likely to help her against Japanese activity in north China.[76] There could be no response but there was felt to be a danger that China might turn to the League. This might have been very awkward when the League and Europe were preoccupied with the Abyssinian crisis. Not without reason, the Foreign Office urged that every effort must be made to get back to the original basis of 'frank and friendly cooperation with Japan'.[77]

STALEMATE BETWEEN FOREIGN OFFICE AND TREASURY

Over a period of nearly four weeks in November 1935, the Foreign Office and the Treasury argued about the loan and the question of Leith Ross's future. Once more the foreign secretary saw the chancellor in order to put the political objections to Leith Ross's staying in China. The chancellor saw merit in the Foreign Office insistence on preliminary conditions for withdrawal such as the settlement of railway defaults, agreement on a British adviser for the Central Bank of China and for a perpetuation of the system by which a British national was inspector general of the Chinese customs, before a loan was granted. He was also obviously opposed to any action which might force a crisis with the Japanese but clung stubbornly to the hope that things might, after a lapse of time, quieten down sufficiently for a loan to be granted without provoking a crisis with the Japanese.[78] Finally, instructions which in effect suspended Leith Ross's actions in China were issued. He was told that technical questions in connection with a loan should not be pursued, that he should stay on in China, and that a decision as to whether he should revisit Japan was postponed.[79]

Forced out of the limelight and prevented from taking any effective action, Leith Ross, understandably enough, grew restless. He admitted that there was very little chance of Japanese opinion being modified and in his turn applied himself to schemes which would make it possible for him to be recalled without too much loss of face.[80] The Foreign Office would, of course, have been delighted for 'this gallant hero of a lost cause' to be brought home 'behind a smokescreen'[81] but, because the Treasury was in-volved, the mechanics of arranging this took time. Delay was also due to the fact that Leith Ross's request for recall coincided with the opening of the naval conference when it was felt to be especially important that good relations with Japan should be maintained. Then came the crisis over the Hoare–Laval pact. The repercussions of this attempt to make a deal with Mussolini over Abyssinia brought Eden to the foreign secretaryship and caused the premature recall of Cadogan from Peking.[82] Though every-thing pointed to Leith Ross's recall, after a month of discussion between senior civil servants and the ministers involved, the Treasury won the round. Leith Ross was requested to stay in China and to pursue questions of budget and central bank reform and railway loans defaults. Hope was expressed that with 'time and patience' the Japanese attitude might become more helpful.[83] There was no reason to suppose this might be so. Chiang Kai-shek had apparently been seeking to produce a *détente* with Japan and had, in December 1935, given twelve of the major posts to men educated in Japan but Cadogan reported gloomily,

The dispute with Japan is paralysing all the functions of government [. . .] Before this menace all else fades into relative unimportance: communists, floods, currency chaos, financial stringency, breakdown of rural economy – all issues of the first magnitude – take second place and are, indeed, rendered the more intractible by reason of the Japanese menace.[84]

In early January 1936, the British banks in China having established that all the non-British foreign banks except the Japanese, were prepared to hand over their silver, did so too.[85] This meant that, even in Leith Ross's estimation, the currency had ample backing. Instead of relaxing and contenting himself with the honourable work he was doing in connection with rail-way defaults,[86] Leith Ross reverted to the question of a loan. He now suggested that, if the Japanese government would neither participate in a loan nor make it clear that it had no objection to a British loan, it should be warned that its attitude must have serious repercussions on Japanese credit in London and that, in his report, Leith Ross would make it clear that Japan alone had been responsible for the failure to implement a full scheme of currency reform. This threat, he thought, might influence Japanese civilians to control the military.[87] The Leith Ross papers show that, in reviving this suggestion, Leith Ross was much influenced by events in north China. He argued that, if Britain was not going to be placed in a position where she must either fight Japan or 'haul down the flag', she must make every effort to prevent the situation deteriorating further, with or without the support of other powers.[88] He wanted a firm decision either to make a loan or to recall him. The Foreign Office did not believe that Britain's role as an international money market could be used as an effective threat to Japan, nor did it believe that the Kwantung army could easily be controlled from Tokyo. It seemed that Leith Ross had still not absorbed the fact that Britain could not take a strong line and the Foreign Office was appalled by the idea of a public pillorying of Japan.[89] More than ever it wanted to slide out gracefully and shelve the question of a loan. The deputy under-secretary noted,

All this is the result of allowing our far eastern policy to drift into the hands of the Treasury. It is very dangerous. I have always sympathised with Sir F. Leith Ross for being sent out on a wild goose chase. It is high time he came home for as long as this bull remains in the China shop there is no knowing how much political crockery may be broken.[90]

As the Foreign Office repeatedly pointed out, the Treasury, by pursuing or giving countenance to the policy of a loan to China, was entangled in a complete contradiction. The effect of the policy was the opposite from its intention of keeping on the best possible terms with Japan. Nevertheless it remained hard for the Foreign Office to make a good case against the Treasury while the ambassador in Peking appeared to support Leith Ross. The new foreign secretary made representations to Neville Chamberlain but evidently had no wish to risk further upsetting relations between Treasury and Foreign Office over Leith Ross. The question of a loan to China, and of Leith Ross's future, remained undecided in the first months of 1936, and the victim of this joint, but uncoordinated, effort of Treasury and Foreign Office to solve the far eastern problem remained on Chinese soil stranded and irritable.

10 SET-BACKS FOR BRITAIN'S POLICY-MAKERS

When he was asked in March 1935 to define British far eastern policy, Wellesley replied that its goal was as much as might be obtainable in the way of a *détente* between Japan and her Pacific neighbours, and prosperity for China. More specifically, he said, Britain wanted to wean Japan gently and unobtrusively from her jealous lone-handed attitude to an international frame of mind, and to create an atmosphere which would make a satisfactory naval agreement possible. The Chinese currency crisis was described as providing Britain with an opportunity to launch her boat tentatively in 'wider waters' in a manner which seemed unlikely to offend China or cause resentment in Japan.[1] By the end of 1935 it was clear that this voyage was fraught with snags and unlikely to produce the rewards Britain sought. British far eastern policy was always in its fundamentals dependent on her general policy and, as 1935 wore on, a number of important events in Europe had their inevitable repercussions on thinking about the far east in general and about the Leith Ross mission in particular. By the end of 1935 the mission was apparently aground in China.

With a certain feeling of inevitability the cabinet had, in June, accepted an agreement allowing Germany a navy limited to 35 per cent of that of Britain.[2] The British negotiators considered that they had no choice but to accept this arrangement and the Admiralty believed that, provided Britain was not called upon to fight Germany and Japan simultaneously without allies, the 35 per cent ratio was acceptable on strategic grounds. It was calculated that, with France as an ally undertaking responsibilities in European waters, the British fleet should be able to defend Britain's empire in the east.[3] The proviso was that the existing naval ratio with Japan should be maintained. The Anglo-German naval treaty, therefore, made the British doubly determined to

try to preserve naval limitation and anxious specifically to preserve the Washington ratios. Clearly the assumption was that
Germany and Japan could not at the same time be appeased in
their naval relationship with Britain. Nevertheless the situation in
the far east was judged in July 1935 by the Defence Requirements
committee to be no less serious than it had been when the committee reported in February 1934 and the committee urged in
1935 that, given Britain's inability to face a war in Europe or the
far east, appeasement of Japan was of no less importance than
appeasement of Germany.[4] There was, therefore, a contradiction
between the desire to hold Japan to a ratio she was known to
resent and the need on over-all strategic grounds to placate her.

The effect of wider policy considerations on events and attitudes in the far east became the more significant as the Italo-
Abyssinian crisis brought home new lessons to the strategists.
The assumption that there would always be a period when lack of
war preparation could be made good was shown to be invalid
when it seemed possible that Britain might, as a member of the
League, be plunged into a war at very little notice. Further, the
crisis caused a deterioration in Anglo-Italian relations. If Italian
friendship could no longer be relied upon, a more powerful
British naval force would be required in the Mediterranean, particularly in the event of Britain's being engaged in hostilities in
the far east, when it would be essential to maintain lines of communication through the Suez canal. By the end of 1935, a number
of vessels had already been withdrawn from the far east for
service in the Mediterranean, leaving Japan, if she cared to
exercise it, with complete freedom to carry out her expansionist
policy as and when she pleased.[5] In a letter to Vansittart, Hankey
expressed his anxiety. He wrote,

I have watched with growing dismay the strength of the lead we have taken
and are still taking against Italy [. . .] I think we may be going to see the
results in the Far East almost at once. Owing to our weakness, combined with
the concentration in the Mediterranean of a large proportion of what
strength we still have, both we and the League are just as powerless in the
Far East as we were in 1932 and 1933.[6]

The Foreign Office was well aware that Britain had 'poor weapons
in her armoury' with which to face Japan or Germany[7] but the

difference in its attitude to these two countries in 1935 was that, while it was believed that there was no choice but to accept German naval requirements, the Foreign Office appears to have believed that Japan might be bluffing. The longer the calling of that bluff was left, the more risky the situation was likely to become. Japan should not be allowed to think that Britain had lost interest in the far east and a bold front was a better approach than one with 'hat in hand'.[8] Moreover, it could be argued that a resolute attitude before the naval conference was essential so that Japan did not gain the impression she might get her own way and thus upset the knife-edged naval position established by the Anglo-German naval treaty.

LONDON NAVAL CONFERENCE 1935–6

All these factors increased British anxiety about Japan's attitude to the naval conference to be held in December 1935 and made that conference crucial for future British defence planning. Ambassador Matsudaira returned to Japan in October 1935 and it was hoped that he would be able to explain Britain's naval proposals to the Japanese government and to promote an agreement.[9] Admiral Katō Kanji, the persistent advocate of Japanese naval equality, retired in November and it had been suggested to Sir Robert Clive by Japan's vice-minister of foreign affairs that a more accommodating view might then prevail in Japanese naval circles.[10] By the time the naval conference opened, however, it was clear that the British government had been clutching at straws. The Japanese position had in no way changed. Agreement on both qualitative and quantitative naval limitation was demanded and Japan would not be content with one without the other. The British idea of a qualitative limitation by declaring naval programmes in advance remained unacceptable to the Japanese.

The conference opened on 9 December and the early sessions were, in view of the Japanese attitude, devoted to the consideration of quantitative limitation. The Japanese made a detailed explanation of their proposal for a common upper limit. This limit, they explained, should be fixed as low as possible. Offensive arms should be reduced to a minimum in favour of essentially defensive weapons so as to facilitate defence and make attack difficult. Qualitative limitation without quantitative limitation, they maintained, would give unfair results, would be a means for retaining superiorities and would tend to stimulate rather than check a quantitative race in naval construction. The object of their scheme was, they claimed, to reduce armaments as much as possible and to attain a state of 'non-aggression and non-menace'.[11] The British delegation maintained, and the Americans agreed, that equality of security was as far as possible attained by the Washington treaty arrangements and argued that equality of navies would mean the end of equality of security. In a private and secret meeting with the British delegation, the Japanese admitted the special vulnerability of the British empire on account of its geographical distribution and indicated that there might be adjustments in the common upper limit so that the relative vulnerability of the powers could be accounted for. They denied that a fresh set of ratios would by this means eventually be substituted for those of Washington and, as discussion progressed, it became clear that they had not really worked out how adjustments would be made.[12] Furthermore, they made it clear that Japanese opinion demanded that Japan should have parity with the United States so there was no chance of gaining American approval of this idea of a common upper limit 'with knobs on'.[13]

Since the Japanese plan received support from no other delegation, deadlock was avoided after a week by turning to the examination of the British proposal for a qualitative limitation by voluntary and unilateral declaration of building programmes. The atmosphere in the discussions was friendly throughout but there was no sign of a change in the Japanese attitude before the talks adjourned on 20 December.

While the conference was in session, the Japanese negotiators repeatedly used the phrase 'non-aggression and non-menace' to describe the character of the naval policy which they urged upon other delegations. This phrase suggested to Norman Davis, leader of the American delegation, that Japan would ultimately make a proposal for some kind of non-aggression pact.[14] At the same time the British ambassador in Tokyo reported that Hirota had said that, if no general agreement could be reached, he considered a political understanding between Britain, Japan and the United States essential.[15] A non-aggression pact was not actually mentioned but Hirota evidently had this in mind. It seemed to the ambassador that Hirota, whose policy was, he thought, 'good relations with all countries and definitely pacifist',[16] realised that the uncompromising attitude of Japan's navy made Japanese, British and American naval views quite incompatible and reverted to the idea of a political understanding between the three powers. The *ball on d'essai* had, Clive felt, been launched in a deliberately casual manner so that Hirota's face would be saved, should there be no reaction from Whitehall.

An agreement in the political field lost much of its value from the British point of view if it did not serve to bring Japan into a naval treaty. But since it was desirable to avoid the disastrous effects of a collapse of the naval conference and since the hope that a political *détente* might enhance the credit of civilians in the Japanese government at the expense of the militarists remained, particularly in the mind of Craigie, the Foreign Office naval negotiator,[17] a non-aggression pact with Japan was once more considered at the Foreign Office. A skilled and experienced negotiator in naval matters, Craigie was not an expert on far eastern political affairs. His close relations with Sir Warren Fisher suggest, moreover, that he shared the head of the Treasury's derisive view of what Craigie himself described as 'the pundits of the far east department'.[18] Craigie's rather simplistic assessment of the Japanese political situation was not widely shared in the Foreign Office service by those who had a more specialised knowledge than he. In his speech in June 1935 which was described as 'excellent' by the head of the far east department, Christopher Chancellor, Reuter's manager in the far east, had said that he did not think there was in Japan anything so simple as a distinction between militarists and civilians. He maintained that the difference of opinion in Japan was about time and method and that Japanese foreign policy was definitely a national one.[19] Similar sentiments were being expressed at that time by Sansom, the commercial counsellor in Tokyo.[20] Both the head of the far east department and Wellesley, the deputy under-secretary, accepted these views and both were extremely sceptical about the prospects for a pact. If, however, the naval agreement was of paramount importance, they were prepared to allow the exploration of possibilities to go ahead and, if, as rumour suggested, a Sino-Japanese pact was in the offing, a number of British and American objections to a non-aggression pact with Japan might be overcome. It could also be argued that the usual reservations to preserve the Nine Power treaty and safeguard British interests in China might be omitted to make the political proposal as palatable as possible to the Japanese. Wellesley cynically pointed out that the reservations were in any case of little real value because Britain had no intention of allowing herself to be dragged into a war to save China from Japan, except at the behest of the League and on a collective basis. Thus the risk of rousing Chinese antipathy might be worth taking in the interests of a 'higher purpose', naval agreement.[21]

The British ambassador in Tokyo was informed that there was no chance of the Japanese plan being accepted by the naval conference and that the only alternative to breakdown might be the conclusion of pacts which would give Japan such additional security in the political field as would compensate for her failure to secure equality in naval armaments. The key question was, of course, whether the Japanese foreign minister favoured a political understanding as a substitute for a naval treaty or as a means ultimately of securing such agreement. The ambassador was asked for his appreciation of the situation.[22]

In order that the Japanese delegation in London should not get the impression that the British were going behind their backs, Craigie had a private conversation with Nagai Matsuo, member of the Japanese delegation.[23] Expressing a purely personal opinion, Craigie said that the 'political' method of finding a way round the difficulties confronting the conference had not been exhausted. He reminded Nagai of the conversations with Matsudaira in 1934 about the possibility of a political understanding and explained that, while he was in no way speaking officially, he was wondering whether the question of a political understanding should not be explored a little further, particularly in view of the reports that Japan and China were trying to arrange an amicable settlement of their differences. Nagai's response to Craigie's feeler was not discouraging but he expressed his doubts about the willingness of the United States to enter into such an arrangement.[24] Undaunted, Craigie next spoke to Norman Davis and asked whether he had thought any more about the possibility of some political understanding with Japan as a means of preventing her from completely breaking from the conference. Davis said that he had discussed the matter with Roosevelt but had found him doubtful about the wisdom of such a course in view of Japan's attitude to China. Craigie pointed out that Sino-Japanese relations seemed to be better and argued that, if a Sino-Japanese agreement were reached, the whole situation would be changed. While Davis agreed with this contention and thought that the question of future action in the political sphere might be considered, he said that the American delegation felt the best course for the present would be to let the Japanese government realise that, should the Japanese leave the conference, the discussions would continue between the other four powers with a view to concluding a qualitative naval agreement between them.[25] Davis was thus advocating calling Japan's supposed bluff. Craigie had doubts about the wisdom of such action which he thought might simply confirm Japan's isolationist tendencies.

Matters had gone no further than these personal moves by Craigie when the ambassador in Tokyo sent his assessment of the situation. His view, which had the support of his naval attaché, was that the Japanese navy was absolutely determined to have a free hand and would accept no compromise over their proposal for a common upper limit. Clive felt that this uncompromising attitude by the navy had caused Hirota to revert to the idea of a political understanding between the three Pacific powers and he doubted whether the foreign minister had thought the matter out in detail. The talk of a political understanding had, Clive said, been more in the nature of a pious hope than an offer. The embassy in Tokyo felt certain that the Japanese government would not give any guarantees regarding China but considered that the Japanese were at the same time determined to avoid hostilities there.[26] It seemed, on the basis of this information, that a political agreement with Japan could not be regarded as likely either to lead to Japan's participation in some naval compromise arrangement or to improve or guarantee Britain's position in China.

To Anthony Eden, the new foreign secretary, the chances of bringing Japan and the United States into some political understanding with Britain seemed remote but, when the American ambassador brought under-secretary of state, William Phillips, to the Foreign Office to meet Eden, Craigie was asked to attend the meeting to explain the possibility of a political understanding with Japan. Craigie emphasised that a political understanding must be regarded as an aid to, and not a substitute for, a naval agreement and made the point that a political pact would be more feasible if, as seemed possible, Japan and China were to come to terms. Craigie suggested that either a non-aggression or a consultative pact might then be possible. Phillips did not think his government would consider a non-aggression pact with Japan, nor was he enthusiastic about a consultative pact. He made it clear that there could be no question of the United States doing anything which would look as if China was being abandoned to her fate.[27] Phillips could be regarded as expressing the State Department's view and his attitude apparently confirmed the view of the American ambassador in Tokyo who, in a conversation with Clive, had said that in his opinion one difficulty in the way of a political understanding with Japan was that no one in the State Department could visualise the future from a broader standpoint. The department as a whole, he said, was tied to the letter of existing but really defunct treaties. Ambassador Grew thought there was a possibility that the American government might consider a political agreement if it would make it easier for Japan to accept the principle of the existing ratio. He said that the president, who had always been a big navy man, would never yield about the necessity for American naval superiority to Japan but might take a broader view than the State Department about some sort of political understanding.[28] The British ambassador in Washington was not so sanguine. He reported his belief that neither Roosevelt's administration nor American public opinion was ready to take any action which would imply that Japan's actions had ceased to be condemned. He thought any suggestion for a political pact in the far east would be full of potential danger at the American polls.[29]

Events in London had already tended to confirm this pessimistic view. In a conversation with the foreign secretary on 10 January, Davis said that he was confident that it would not be possible for the United States to enter into a non-aggression pact with the United Kingdom and Japan. Such action would, he said, be regarded by the American public as condoning Japanese aggression in Manchukuo. These comments effectively quashed any further discussion. The foreign secretary wrote of the pact, 'I don't think we can make any further headway on this at present. I would consider a political agreement if the United States would come in and as the price of a naval agreement.'[30]

The idea of a political pact with Japan had once again collapsed. The Japanese delegates withdrew from the naval conference when it reassembled on 13 January. If the idea of a political pact was to be revived at all, it could only be when the moment came to establish some *modus vivendi* between Japan and the powers which eventually entered into a naval agreement. Even then, supposing Japan was interested in establishing such a link, the rigid attitude of the United States was likely to make matters difficult. There was no bitterness attached to Japan's withdrawal, however, and the first lord told the cabinet that he still did not despair of eventually bringing Japan into some kind of qualitative agreement. If this was possible, the strategic situation, while dangerous, was not desperate. The cabinet was reminded, evidently by the chancellor, that Leith Ross had been sent to China to convince Japan of Britain's sincere desire for friendly cooperation and, it was alleged, 'this distinguished civil servant' was trusted and liked by both China and Japan.[31] Press reports from Japan might have made the cabinet sceptical of this last claim but they were told, nevertheless, that Leith Ross was thought by some to be the only man who might bring off an agreement between China and Japan, and that it was hoped that he would stay in the far east for some time longer.[32]

This statement rather misrepresented the case and suggested that the Leith Ross mission was to be regarded as a full-scale diplomatic mission, a role which had not hitherto been claimed for it. Surprisingly, this interpretation of events went unchallenged, even by the foreign secretary, whose department, like Leith Ross himself, longed to see the mission ended. Leith Ross's negotiations had not, for reasons which were not altogether his fault, developed the aspect of an attempt to conciliate Japan and to bring her into an agreement with China. In fact, Britain appeared in China to be embarked on a forward policy which challenged Japan. This was particularly dangerous given the situation in Europe and Japan's avowed determination to build up her navy now that the shackles of the Washington treaty had been dropped.

JAPAN REVISITED, 1936

On 7 February 1936 Clive, the ambassador in Tokyo, reported an approach by Matsudaira, former Japanese ambassador in London and now resident in Tokyo. Matsudaira claimed that the misunderstanding by the Japanese foreign ministry and the Japanese military of the Leith Ross mission was now allayed and that the Japanese would be glad to see Leith Ross.[33] Matsudaira proposed that he should send a message to Leith Ross saying that he hoped the latter would be able to visit Japan. In this way Leith Ross's visit to Japan could be made to look unofficial. Clive thought that this move might have been inspired by the Japanese minister for foreign affairs who probably wanted to raise wider questions of Anglo-Japanese commercial relations and he also thought that the Japanese army was feeling anxious about the unsettled state of Soviet-Japanese relations and did not want, therefore, to antagonise Britain.[34] Japanese archives add another explanation for the timing of this manoeuvre. In a letter written at the end of January, Christopher Chancellor, Reuter's manager in Shanghai, had protested to Amau, the Japanese foreign ministry spokesman, about Japanese hostility to Leith Ross. He suggested, as a means of breaking down the atmosphere of misunderstanding and suspicion which had arisen, that Leith Ross should be asked to make a further visit to Japan.[35] Amau's reply to this letter was rather non-committal[36] but Matsudaira's approach followed a week later and a draft of the letter Matsudaira eventually wrote to Leith Ross is in the Japanese files.

It seemed to Clive that it was useless to expect a more official invitation than the letter Matsudaira proposed sending and he favoured its acceptance.[37] Leith Ross, however, was against going to Japan unless there was a much more definite prospect of securing Japanese cooperation in China[38] and the Foreign Office was inclined to agree with him. It was felt to be most unlikely that Japanese opposition really was disappearing and it seemed much more likely that this move was prompted by a desire to escape blame for having prevented the loan to China.[39] Matsudaira's approach was, however, followed by one from the Japanese vice minister for foreign affairs who expressed the hope that Leith Ross would visit Japan. He made it clear that Japan would not participate in a loan to China but said that the Japanese attitude to Britain had improved due to relief at being out of the naval conference since January. This had, he said, calmed the navy and might even make it possible for Japan to adhere to any agreement made by the remaining powers.[40] Such a hint was not to be ignored. The importance of eventually securing Japanese accession to a naval agreement was a new factor in the calculation of whether or not Leith Ross should return to Tokyo.

For his part, Leith Ross was still not anxious to go, especially after the 26 February Incident took place. This mutiny in the Japanese army was the climax of a struggle between factions within the army. On 26 February, young officers of the First Division stationed in Tokyo led 1,400 troops into the streets; they attacked government offices and assassinated a number of government ministers and some members of the imperial household. After three days order was restored. The leaders of the rebellion were executed and a number of generals were purged. The outcome of the mutiny was the elimination of the so-called Imperial Way faction by what is known as the Control faction.[41] With the triumph of the Control faction civilian influence in Japanese politics could be expected to decline. Both Leith Ross and Clive felt that the political situation after 26 February was an excellent reason for declining Matsudaira's invitation. They were no match for the single-minded chancellor of the exchequer.

Chamberlain declared that a visit to Japan was essential and that it would merely be deferred by the Japanese political situation. He clung to the hope that a loan might still be possible and instructed that Leith Ross should remain in China to hearten the British business community and prevent loss of Japanese respect which would result from an overt admission of weakness. He considered that Leith Ross should reply to Matsudaira that he was likely to be staying in China for some time but that if frank and friendly talks would be of advantage, he would be pleased to accept Matsudaira's invitation.[42] Leith Ross protested that there was little hope of an improvement in Sino-Japanese relations, that political rather than financial action was now needed in China, and that for many months to come his mission could have no function except to watch financial developments, a task which might as well be done by the commercial counsellor. He thought that a statement could be issued and the mission withdrawn without any adverse effect on opinion in China.[43] The Foreign Office agreed with him. The formation of Hirota's government after the 26 February Incident made it clear that Japanese policy was to be more subject to military influence than before, and the most recent reports indicated that the Chinese central government was giving greater attention to the possibility of offering armed resistance to the Japanese. This increased the risk that money lent to China would be used to bolster military effort rather than currency reform. The foreign secretary urged that Leith Ross's visit to Japan should be called off,[44] but Chamberlain was not to be moved. Though a loan might not be possible, Leith Ross must go to Tokyo to clear up misunderstandings over the mission and perhaps reach some understanding with Japan over the Chinese maritime customs. He still hoped that the final result of the mission would be an improvement of British relations with both China and Japan[45]. Chamberlain's comments and his attitude suggested that he envisaged Leith Ross undertaking work of a political nature and of course the Foreign Office protested that there were embassies in Tokyo and Peking to deal with any political problems which might arise. Furthermore, if as seemed likely, Leith Ross's mission had been an irritant to the Japanese army, his continued presence in China could even be a hindrance to an improvement in Sino-Japanese relations. The Foreign Office felt that as long as Leith Ross stayed it was unlikely that the Japanese could be persuaded that he was not pursuing a policy inimical to their interests and there appeared to be some danger that further discussion of a loan or joint financial proposals for China might inspire Japanese military extremists to more aggressive action in China or at home.

It proved impossible to convince the Treasury of this. Chamberlain blandly ignored the foreign secretary's plea that if Leith Ross should visit Tokyo on his way home it should be on the understanding that the loan and other political questions had been dropped.[46] It was not until May when Cadogan returned to London and commented that, not only would Leith Ross's departure cause no disappointment in China, but that there was already a tendency to ask what he was doing in Shanghai,[47] that Chamberlain could finally be persuaded. Eden wrote the chancellor a strong letter urging Leith Ross's recall. In a stiff reference to Chamberlain's apparent wish that Leith Ross might make some political judgments while he was in Japan, he noted, 'I cannot, you will appreciate, attach to his political opinion in fields which are so unfamiliar to him, quite the same importance that I attach to that of our resident advisers.'[48] Treasury concern for far eastern policy had resulted in fact, in the appearance of having two ambassadors in China, each controlled by a different department. This situation caused departmental machinery to grind so slowly that it scarcely worked and led to acrimonious exchanges between the permanent heads of the Foreign Office and the Treasury.

At the end of May 1936 Leith Ross finally went to Tokyo. There had been no official invitation to him from Japan. A statement was made in parliament explaining that the object of the visit was to discuss financial and economic questions of common interest to the United Kingdom and Japan in China and elsewhere.[49] One of the aims of this statement was to avoid giving the impression in China or anywhere else that the primary purpose of the visit was to obtain Japanese acquiescence in a loan to China.

When Leith Ross arrived in Japan in the first week of June 1936 he found the atmosphere much more cordial both towards Britain and to his mission in China than it had been when he had visited the country in September 1935. He put this down to Japan's desire to avoid the risk of a combination between Britain, the United States and Russia in support of China.[50] He saw Arita Hachirō, the new minister for foreign affairs, and Horinouchi Kēnsuke, the vice minister for foreign affairs, both of whom appeared to make every effort to assure him that Japan wanted friendly relations with Britain and that she had no desire to oust British influence in China. Leith Ross and Clive gained the impression that the minister for foreign affairs was embarrassed over the situation in East Hopei and was anxious to find a solution, but that it was necessary for him to proceed with caution to avoid the opposition of the military.[51] The future of the Chinese maritime customs was discussed by Leith Ross with Horinouchi who, while unwilling to commit Japan too far ahead, was agreeable to the suggestion that a British subject should succeed Sir Frederick Maze provided that a Japanese subject held the post of deputy inspector general and that the number of Japanese in the customs service was increased.[52] Such decisions were, of course, technically a matter for the Chinese government. The question of market sharing and textile competition was also raised but Leith Ross found that neither Arita nor Horinouchi was well informed on this and they appeared to be unaware of the Anglo-Japanese talks which had taken place in 1934.[53] There could, therefore, be no serious discussion on this subject. The minister of finance, Baba Eiichi, who was regarded as a nominee of the military, spoke of his interest in China's railway development and his willingness to provide credit for railway projects, subject to a better political understanding with China, but it was left to Japanese bankers and industrialists to assure Leith Ross that they welcomed currency reform in China.[54] In spite of the friendly reception, it was clear that the Japanese government officials were ready to discuss neither finance nor trade issues. In short these talks were amicable but unfruitful. Leith Ross had, of course, expected nothing more. The Japanese obviously did not care to raise the subject of joint financial proposals for China and Leith Ross, though not debarred from discussing China's financial reforms as a whole or from exchanging views with Japan on the desirability at some future date of foreign assistance to China,[55] did not initiate such discussions with the civilians he met. Leith Ross's Japanese friends in the financial world expressed regret at the ignorant criticisms levelled at his mission by the military elements in Japan but, as Leith Ross recognised, bankers and industrialists had little or no influence on policy and it was his impression that the government was unable or unwilling to modify the policy of the military authorities in China.

In fact, of course, the political situation in Japan had deteriorated since the 26 February Incident and it was increasingly difficult for British, or any western observers, to form an appreciation of the nature of government in Japan and to judge the methods with which it might be dealt. While not unfamiliar outward forms of a democratic government had been observed the British had felt that, although Japanese political attitudes and behaviour within this structure were foreign to them, Japan's government was at least stable and within it there existed a moderate civilian element which might be encouraged and to which appeal might be made. After 26 February 1936 the guide lines were less clear. Hirota was regarded as an expert politician who could be relied upon to avoid a serious clash with the military, but this also seemed to indicate that there would be increased military influence in Japan's government, and in particular in Japan's China policy.

This recognition of military influence was perhaps the reason why when Leith Ross met General Isogai, head of the military affairs bureau at the Tokyo war office, it was to him, rather than the minister for foreign affairs, that he gave a memorandum outlining his personal views on Japan's China policy. In this memorandum Leith Ross expressed his regret that political tension between China and Japan had over-shadowed economic considerations and had prevented friendly cooperation between Britain and Japan to improve the financial situation in China. He added the hope that cooperation between Britain and Japan in support of the Nanking government's financial reforms might be possible in the future. Pointing out that currency reform should have advantages for Japan as for the other powers trading in China, Leith Ross deprecated the ignorant and prejudiced criticism of the scheme and Japanese efforts to undermine it. He also criticised the 'silk-worm' tactics by which Japanese military authorities had established and maintained a corrupt and inefficient regime in north China against the wishes of the overwhelming majority of the local population as well as of the foreign interests established in the area. Leith Ross suggested that if Japanese policy could be modified, the Nanking government would go far to consider any reasonable proposals for an honourable settlement of outstanding difficulties.[56] This was strong language and an authoritative tone to adopt in what was theoretically a communication between a senior civil servant who had been engaged on a technical mission and a senior military officer in another country. Leith Ross wrote in the manner of a man accustomed to having attention paid to his opinions. The memorandum concluded with a series of questions apparently designed to point out what, from a British view, might be regarded as inconsistencies in Japanese policy. Did the Japanese not agree that the stabilisation of Chinese currency was desirable and if so, why would they not cooperate and what advantage could they see in a breakdown of the currency? Did the Japanese not agree that China needed capital for development and if so, why did Japan not welcome the assistance of the United Kingdom which had capital available for investment? Why, if the Japanese government opposed communism, did they not support rather than oppose the Nanking government, which had shown itself the main bulwark against communists in China? If the Japanese policy was still to promote the unification of China, the preservation of her territorial integrity and the restoration of order, why did Japanese authorities work for the virtual separation of the northern provinces and why did they countenance the imposition of a separate tariff by the East Hopei regime having always claimed that they would oppose the creation of a separate customs tariff by any local authority in China? There is a certain naivety in this catalogue of familiar complaints about Japan's policy. Presumably the intention was to force Japan to make out her case or to admit, at least by implication, her own selfish designs in China.

Had the Japanese been interested in taking up the question of joint action in China, the memorandum might have provided a basis for discussion of some of the points at issue between Britain and Japan. As it was, Isogai's reply, which Leith Ross believed had been drafted by him and revised by the ministry of foreign affairs, reached Leith Ross just before he left Tokyo. It made no concessions to Leith Ross's criticisms and did nothing to clear up the inconsistencies Leith Ross felt he detected in Japanese policy. On the other hand, the Japanese case set out in the document did have a logic of its own if viewed in the light of the opening proposition. This stated that, due to the complexities of the political situation in China, economic and financial questions were so intimately and inseparably interwoven with political questions that the Japanese attitude toward the question of extending economic and financial assistance to China must be determined according to the general trend of politics in China as well as the policy of the Chinese government towards Japan. It could not, therefore, be explained by discussing merely the economic aspects.[57] This was not a statement with which the Foreign Office would have disagreed. The difference between the British and Japanese view in the matter was related in part to the degree of their respective economic interest in China and to the nature of that interest. A stable China offered prospects for British capital investment but British trade with China was limited and likely to remain so. The Japanese were concerned with the expansion of a vital economic interest. The ideology of the open door to which Britain subscribed was increasingly unsatisfactory to Japan when other powers retained exclusive rights in their colonies and operated a closed door in them. Faced with the fact that Manchukuo was a disappointing exercise from the economic point of view Japan, unlike Britain, was preoccupied with China and Chinese political and economic development.

In his answers to Leith Ross's questions, Isogai stressed the oft repeated Japanese argument that China must learn self help before economic aid could be effective. He denied that the Japanese government was antagonistic towards the Nanking government as such, but declared himself sceptical of its real attitude to the Communist Party and regarding the suppression of communism. He claimed there was a misunderstanding of the Japanese position in north China. It was, he suggested, the monetary policy of the Nanking government which had given an impetus to the autonomous movement in the north. He disclaimed Japanese involvement but pointed out that, as the local administrations in north China were inclined to cooperate actively with the Japanese and, while the Nanking government's attitude with regard to the special relations between Japan, Manchukuo and north China, to the control of anti-Japanese activities and to the suppression of communism remained unsatisfactory, the Japanese government could scarcely remain indifferent. The uncompromising tone of this document made it clear that if Leith Ross had ever hoped to play the part of an honest broker between China and Japan, he could not now succeed.

Leith Ross arrived back in Shanghai on 16 June, bade farewell to Chiang Kai-shek, made a statement to the press in which he disclaimed responsibility for the 'bold step' of currency reform, congratulated the Chinese government on the progress its policy had achieved, and sailed for home on 23 June.[58]

The Leith Ross report for the Treasury and the Foreign Office was available in July. It contained sections on Japanese policy, the Chinese internal situation, the banking and currency reforms, British trade in China, defaults and railway financing, and the Chinese maritime customs.[59] Some mild criticisms of Leith Ross's political assessments of the situation in China were forthcoming from the Foreign Office but his conclusion that the Nanking government with all its faults was the only one on which Britain could build hopes for the reconstruction of China was one which was accepted there. There was general agreement too with Leith Ross's criticisms of the British banking and business community in China which he found 'defeatist' and reluctant to cooperate with the Chinese.[60] Detailed discussion of the technical matters to do with defaults, railway financing and export credits took place at an inter-departmental meeting at the Treasury at the end of July.[61]

In September, Leith Ross prepared a simplified statement and a list of largely innocuous recommendations for the cabinet.[62] The Foreign Office felt that little good was to be served by putting many of its more elementary ideas such as better publicity of Britain's interest in China and her intention to stay there, before the cabinet. There were, however, more important recommendations to do with policy towards Japan, railway financing, export credits and a customs union between Hong Kong and China. The list of recommendations, thirteen in all, was referred by the cabinet to the committee for political and economic relations with Japan.[63] The Foreign Office[64] and the Colonial Office[65] prepared their observations on Leith Ross's paper and their answers to his criticisms. Notes were prepared for the use of the foreign secretary when the cabinet committee met, but after nine months, no meeting having been called, the papers were put by.

Nothing came of the Leith Ross report because it was over-taken by events both in the far east, where the Sian Incident in 1936 and the Marco Polo bridge incident and subsequent Sino-Japanese hostilities in 1937[66] made irrelevant its recommendations for railway reform and export credit, and in Europe where the continuing Abyssinian crisis drove matters so far from Britain into the background. Leith Ross himself believed that his mission had succeeded in its object, which he described as being the solution of the acute currency crisis.[67] Sir John Pratt, however, who was at the heart of the Foreign Office discussion at the time, contended that the mission failed in its main object, that of encouraging Japanese collaboration with western powers.[68] It seems probable that these two assessments represent the views of the departments concerned with the operation of the mission and that they reflect the different expectations which each department had for it. The failure of the Treasury and the Foreign Office to establish clearly and jointly the precise aims of the mission was a weakness from the outset.

Estimates of the value of the mission vary. Leith Ross believed that the reforms for which, in his autobiography, he took responsibility, 'altered China's economic situation radically'.[69] Pratt too felt that the mission was in many ways a success.[70] Allan Everest, an American historian, whose chief interest is in the silver problem, estimated that after all the British effort, the United States won more credit in the currency stabilisation because the agreement to purchase large quantities of silver was a crucial factor.[71] Arthur Young, an American and a financial adviser to Chiang Kai-shek's government, presumably gives the Chinese point of view. He describes Leith Ross as bringing the 'needed ingredient' of British financial prestige and moral support[72] but describes the financial reforms themselves as an 'impressive example of Chinese self help'.[73] It may be there is a grain of truth in all these assessments, but what is certainly true is that today the Leith Ross mission is as interesting as a case history in dual diplomacy as it is as an aid operation to China.

THE CONTINUING PROBLEM

When the Leith Ross report appeared in 1936, the problem of Japan's position in China remained for the British the problem of the far east. In spite of Britain's acute consciousness of the problem and in spite of the various 'solutions' to the problem which had been proffered, the period from 1933 had seen both an expansion of Japan's influence in China and the recognition of the Amau statement as the cornerstone of her policy there. Observers of the far eastern scene no longer stressed Japan's fear of isolation but drew attention to Japan's increasing confidence, to her consciousness that Japan could work out her own destiny unhindered. It was noted that Japan worked without regard to the requirements or interests of the western powers in the east, not so much deliberately challenging them as simply not taking them into account.[74] Japan's defection from the naval conference was a manifestation of the new spirit and, after 26 February 1936, the Japanese government seemed less than ever likely to be amenable to standards which the British believed to be rational. These factors taken with Japan's tendency to isolate far eastern questions from global considerations increased the detachment of the far east from world affairs generally at a time when European problems were becoming increasingly difficult for those countries affected by them.

This was all rather ominous for the British who were still vainly trying to reconcile the fundamental contradictions between British interests and those of Japan in the far east. Unlike Japan, Britain had to take account of the European situation and of changes occurring in political relationships as well as naval strengths. Leith Ross had concluded that it would not be possible to persuade the Japanese to cooperate with Britain in the rehabilitation of China without Japan first obtaining satisfaction of her political demands. He thought it possible that if the British government was prepared to make some wider political and economic arrangement, the Japanese government might modify its policy towards China. In view of the difficulties in the way of such a general arrangement, Leith Ross recommended that the government should formulate its own policy and not defer to unreasonable Japanese objections. He wrote,

The Japanese are experts in the art of bluffing and the view was frequently expressed to me by British residents in Japan that H.M. [*sic*] government should not take their criticisms too seriously. The Japanese themselves pursue their objectives by presenting the world with 'faits accomplis' and we should not hesitate to do the same if necessary.[75]

On the face of it, this appeared to be sound advice, but the Foreign Office felt that unless caution was observed, such a policy could amount to a direct challenge to Japan and might lead to disaster.[76] If a violent Japanese reaction was provoked, the British were powerless to protect the Chinese against its consequences. The British public was unlikely to countenance a war to defend British interests in China and in any case the Foreign Office did not believe that these interests were, in themselves, worth one.

11 JAPANESE APPROACHES, AUSTRALIAN PROPOSALS

The Leith Ross report was shelved in 1936 but hopes for Anglo-Japanese cooperation in China by no means faded. The new Japanese ambassador, Yoshida Shigeru, arrived in London in June and, from the time of his first call at the Foreign Office, his behaviour was such as to keep alive dreams of an Anglo-Japanese *rapprochement*.[1] Assuring Anthony Eden, the foreign secretary, of his belief that, with the coming of autumn, there would be a steady increase in the authority of those who supported moderate counsels in Japan, Yoshida put forward an obscure proposal for Anglo-Japanese cooperation in China with Japan in charge of law and order and Britain in charge of irrigation and flood control.[2] While this idea was not taken seriously in Whitehall, officials were aware of a Japanese press campaign suggesting that Britain was seeking Japanese friendship[3] and the Foreign Office read the signs as indicating Japanese fear of isolation. It was felt that, rather than 'running after' Japan, it would be wiser to leave her to make the first advance.[4] A concrete approach through official channels was expected.

By September such an approach appeared to be imminent. Yoshida called on Vansittart, claiming that he had received instructions which encouraged him to pursue his plans for better Anglo-Japanese relations and cooperation in China. He suggested that the time was ripe to try the ways of diplomacy and persuasion which would strengthen the civilian and moderate elements in Japan; that Japanese psychology was changing; and that there might be a trend away from increased military expenditure. The ambassador explained that Japan found Russia stronger than expected and appeared to be sounding Vansittart about Britain's attitude to that country. Yoshida's interpretation of the Japanese political situation was of considerable interest to Vansittart but, since the ambassador had no concrete ideas on the basis for an Anglo-Japanese pact, he suggested that their conversation might be continued when Yoshida found himself in a position to be more specific.[5]

JAPAN'S CHINA POLICY 1936

After the 26 February Incident it was understandably difficult for the British to assess who was in control in Japan but it was reasonable to expect that, after such a political upheaval in Tokyo, the vital matter of Japan's policy in China should be under review. This was indeed the case although the trend of that policy was not precisely that at which Yoshida was hinting.

It was recognised in Japan that the prospect of a Sino-Japanese friendship treaty based on Hirota's 'three principles'[6] was unattainable and, in the early months of 1936, a reassessment of Japan's north China policy took place. The outcome was 'The Fundamental Principles of National Policy', a document sanctioned by the Hirota cabinet in August.[7] The policy put forward was designed to enable Japan to reorganise the east Asian sphere in a 'spirit of co-prosperity and co-existence based on the Imperial Way'. Strategic and diplomatic priorities were not stated with the result that each ministry concerned could interpret the 'Fundamental Principles' of policy as best suited its interest. The navy prepared a five year building programme on the assumption that Japan's national defence could not be stabilised without Japanese command of the western Pacific and advance towards the south seas. The army authorities decided to double the size of the Kwantung army and to build up the 'Manchurian nation' on the paternalistic principles described as the 'Imperial Way'.[8]

The officials of the Japanese Ministry of Foreign Affairs had as their primary objective the organisation of a 'special anti-communist, pro-Japanese zone in north China'.[9] This was all the more important to the Japanese since the Chinese communists were now established in the north-west province of Shensi and had, since August 1935, been advocating a 'united front' with the Kuomintang against Japanese imperialism. Such a front would leave Japan dangerously exposed to the hostility of both

China and Russia. An anti-communist zone was to be desired, therefore, to increase the security of Manchukuo and as a step towards a pact of mutual assistance between Japan, Manchukuo and China. It was visualised that steady diplomatic pressure and the negotiation of a series of special pacts and agreements would bring the Nanking government to recognise that the stability and peace of east Asia could only be secured by a policy of cooperation with Japan. If the method had changed a little since the Ho–Umetsu and Ching–Doihara agreements had established a buffer for Japan in north China in 1935,[10] the aim of Japanese political hegemony over China remained.

Japanese ideas about China in 1936 were based on the assumed weakness of the Nationalist army and of Chiang Kai-shek's determination to avoid a direct confrontation with Japan. As part of the programme of putting pressure on Nanking, the Hirota cabinet authorised the promotion of a 'Mongolia for the Mongolians' campaign and the resumption of negotiations with the Nanking government on tariff revision and a joint programme of economic development in north China. These Sino-Japanese talks began in October 1936.[11] The idea of an anti-communist pact with Germany was also approved as a check to Soviet penetration in Outer Mongolia and Comintern activities in China.

YOSHIDA'S MEMORANDUM

The facts of the situation in east Asia, even as far as they were known and understood in London in October 1936, were in direct contrast to the hopes for Anglo-Japanese cooperation expressed by the Japanese ambassador in London. As a result of Japanese pressure, a greater degree of autonomy had been introduced into the governments of Hopei and Chahar and talks between the Chinese foreign minister, Chang Chun and Kawagoe Shigeru, Japanese ambassador in China, in September 1936 suggested that Japan had not given up her plan for the reorganisation of the five northern provinces of China.[12] A north China buffer state with a separate customs administration was a matter of positive anxiety to British holders of Chinese bonds secured on the Chinese customs. Moreover the Japanese seemed to be indifferent to

British sensibilities in their refusal to grant any sort of redress for an incident at Keelung in Formosa involving the wrongful arrest of British sailors. British protests and the cancellation of a good-will visit of the British fleet to Japan left the Japanese apparently unmoved.[13]

In spite of the unfavourable impression created by these events in the east, the Foreign Office did not allow Yoshida's hints at the possibility of Anglo-Japanese cooperation to drop. Sir Alexander Cadogan, the deputy under-secretary, saw him in October and tried to find out whether Yoshida could make a definite offer. Cadogan explained that the British would welcome cooperation with Japan with a view to assisting the regeneration and development of China. Faced with this direct approach, Yoshida asked Cadogan in what way he thought their two govern-ments could cooperate. He said that, once he knew the intentions and desires of the British government, he would consult his own people. The interview ended with Cadogan reminding Yoshida that it was he who had raised the matter of Anglo-Japanese cooperation and it was from him that proposals for cooperation were expected to come.[14]

Although the Foreign Office found Yoshida's next move exceedingly annoying, it was from Yoshida's point of view quite shrewd. Making use of a 'very irregular channel' he turned to the chancellor of the exchequer, Neville Chamberlain, and placed before him a draft memorandum containing suggestions which he thought might be the basis of a definite understanding between Britain and Japan. He undertook to convey British comments on this memorandum to his government.[15]

Yoshida's basic premise was that the situation in China was the main source of mutual misunderstanding and the most vital issue to Japan. Of his ten proposals the first three were, in any case, treaty obligations already assumed by Britain and Japan: respect for the sovereignty of China south of the Great Wall;[16] support for the principle of the open door and the integrity of the Chinese customs; respect for foreign rights and interests in China. The following five proposals seemed to represent Japanese desiderata. These were: frank bi-lateral discussion on financial and political aid to China with the Leith Ross recommendations as a basis;[17] discussion with the Chinese government on the question of assisting in checking the spread of communism with, perhaps, the provision by Japan of arms, ammunition and military advisers to this end; discussion on markets and tariffs by Britain and Japan; the extension of any agreement on markets and tariffs to the British Dominions; close financial relations and the exchange of Treasury policies between Britain and Japan. The final suggestions were that, if the preceding points could be agreed, the naval conference might be revived and Japan might seek to be readmitted to the League of Nations.

There was little chance of China finding these proposals acceptable, nor did they offer any real bait to the British. In return for receiving what were essentially economic benefits, the Japanese appeared to be offering, apart from the vague reference to the naval conference, the fulfilment of existing political obligations. Furthermore, Yoshida's claim to have 'used his own initiative' and his apparent reluctance to use the 'proper' diplomatic channels gave Whitehall understandable doubts about the sincerity of this approach. Cadogan thought it might be a gambit to get Britain to lend a hand with the 'big stick' in China.[18] The Foreign Office case against the proposals was that which it had maintained since 1934: that the British government could not afford to flout the moral sense of the British or American people or world opinion by appearing as an abbetor in the spoilation of China by Japan; that Japan could not be relied on to respect British interests once she had accomplished her aims; that in the long run China would be 'too big a nut for Japan to crack' so that it was not worthwhile to antagonise the Chinese people with whom Britain wanted to trade; that cooperation with Japan might antagonise Russia, weaken Russian power to act as a check on Germany and, correspondingly, strengthen Germany.[19]

These opinions were shared by Clive, the ambassador in Tokyo, and by Sansom, the commercial counsellor there. Sansom thought the 'sad truth' was that the desire for British friendship was insufficiently widespread or deep-rooted to be counted on. He believed that there were many people in Japan who would like friendship with Britain but that each country wanted what the other could not give because British and

Japanese interests were fundamentally opposed at every point.[20]

The British response to Yoshida depended, however, on the extent to which he might have been inspired from Tokyo. Clive consulted Matsudaira Tsuneo, former Japanese ambassador in London, and now minister to the imperial household. Matsudaira told Clive that Yoshida had general instructions to see what could be done to improve Anglo-Japanese relations but indicated that Yoshida was 'rather bold' and capable of putting forward his own ideas. He was able to confirm later that Yoshida's proposals were indeed his own, though in line with the ideas of the Japanese government.[21]

A similar assessment of Yoshida came from Sugimura Yotaro, the Japanese ambassador in Rome. He said that, while Yoshida had some power as the son-in-law of Count Makino, the former lord privy seal,[22] and was therefore connected with the immediate advisers of the emperor, he was not popular with the army which had refused to accept him as a cabinet minister. Sugimura said that Yoshida had only consented to go to London provided he was given a free hand and, Sugimura thought, perhaps over-estimated the limits within which such a 'free hand' could be exercised. He did not think Yoshida could effect any far-reaching political arrangement and implied that the Japanese government was in the same position unless the military party approved.[23]

Wisely, Clive advised keeping Yoshida in play, awaiting further developments, and not committing Britain to anything. The foreign secretary saw Yoshida therefore, in spite of the general scepticism about his proposals, and went through the memorandum with him. Eden took the line that the British government could not accept obligations contrary to the covenant of the League of Nations and would not ignore the interests and views of China and the United States in considering far eastern questions. He promised to inform Yoshida of the results of inter-departmental discussion on the memorandum. Yoshida assured him that 'all the senior statesmen' he knew were agreed in their desire to restore the former good relations between Britain and Japan.[24]

There was no evidence in mid-November that such 'senior statesmen' were in control of Japan's policy. The Keelung affair continued to disturb Anglo–Japanese relations and rumours of a German–Japanese pact gathered substance. The anti-Comintern pact between Germany and Japan was duly announced on 25 November. Its publication was ill-received in Japan and it seemed to Anthony Eden that, in negotiating it, the Japanese government had 'done a bad day's work' for itself.[25]

Meantime in London it proved impossible to penetrate the smokescreen of unexceptionable platitudes and find out whether Yoshida really had anything to offer. To the annoyance of Cadogan and the far east department he had seen Sir Robert Craigie, the head of the American department, and had asked him to 'do what he could in his sphere' to assist in the promotion of friendship between Britain and Japan.[26] He later explained to Eden that he hoped to return to Japan before the Diet opened on 20 January 1937 in order to 'obtain the ear of cabinet ministers', and was anxious for some indication of the British government's desire to improve Anglo–Japanese relations. He said he wished to counter the view of many ministers in Tokyo who felt that, because of Anglo–Japanese commercial rivalry, it was impossible to improve Anglo–Japanese relations.[27] But Yoshida could not suggest what form an 'indication' of the British government's intentions should take. Further, his criticisms of the 'wrong tactics' of the Japanese government in China raised the question of whether it was wise to deal with a man who might not faithfully reflect the policy of his government.[28] Finally the Foreign Office decided that 'on balance' it might be a good idea to produce an interim reply to Yoshida's memorandum. This might help the 'moderates' in Tokyo and might engender goodwill at a time when the British were anxious to obtain Japanese adherence to the agreement to adopt 14-inch guns as a maximum for capital ships accepted by all other naval powers.[29]

Yoshida was enthusiastic at the prospect of receiving a written reply to his memorandum and spoke of taking it to Japan at once. He claimed that the Japanese cabinet had been shaken by criticism of the anti-Comintern agreement with Germany, the direction of Japan's future policy hung in the balance, and that much could be done to strengthen moderate elements if there was a favourable response from Britain.[30]

THE SIAN INCIDENT

Events in China, which were to cause a radical change in Chinese domestic politics and to have important repercussions for Japan's China policy, now startled the far east.

The reform of the currency had strengthened Chiang Kai-shek's position but the political situation in China showed no sign of becoming more stable in 1936. In June an insurrection in the south-west, where military leaders wished to mount a campaign against the Japanese, was averted but the national movement of opposition to Nanking's policies continued to grow everywhere. In October a Japanese-trained 'independent Mongolian army' attempted to establish itself in Inner Mongolia. This invasion was part of Japan's 'Mongolia for the Mongolians' campaign and the rout of the 'independent' army by Nationalist forces after a week-long battle at Pailingmiao was a surprise to and a set-back for the Japanese. In addition, the victory was a further stimulus to Chinese nationalism and increased the outcry in China for resistance to Japan. In November Chiang Kai-shek broke off talks with the Japanese ambassador in China but he had apparently no desire for an open confrontation with Japanese military power in north China.[31]

The crushing of the communist movement remained Chiang Kai-shek's first concern. On 7 December 1936 he flew to Sian in Shensi province to launch a final annihilation campaign. There Chang Hsueh-liang, the former warlord of Manchuria, was in charge of operations. Chang arrested Chiang Kai-shek on 12 December and demanded that the campaign against the communists be abandoned in favour of a united front between the Kuomintang and the Chinese Communist Party against the Japanese. Subsequent events were somewhat confused. Chiang Kai-shek was released on 25 December and, although he denied that any agreement had been reached, the outcome of the Sian incident was a truce between the Kuomintang and the Chinese Communist party. Chiang Kai-shek was forced to adopt a more anti-Japanese stance.[32]

Both in Peking and Whitehall British reaction to these events was concern lest the Chinese 'got above themselves' and, as a result of the truce, adopted a forward policy against Japan.[33] It was also feared that the dropping of the campaign against the communists might give Tokyo a 'more colourable' excuse for seeking to impose an anti-communist policy on China.[34] The Japanese were reported to be watching the situation with anxiety but at the end of December, when Amau was removed from his post as Foreign Ministry spokesman, this was thought to be a sign that the Japanese government had decided to modify their policy and in the meantime ride out the incident with soft words.

Whether or not this was so, the Sian incident added to Britain's problems in China. It greatly increased the possibility of a Sino-Japanese clash and this was not in Britain's interests any more than it was in the interests of Japan. Aggressive Chinese nationalism was, however, as much beyond British control as was Japanese militarism. Although the aims of Britain and Japan in China were so different, they had a common interest in 1937 in seeing that a confrontation did not take place there. The situation gave more meaning to the attempts to negotiate with Yoshida.

THE REPLY TO YOSHIDA'S MEMORANDUM

The Foreign Office draft reply to Yoshida's memorandum was extensively amended by the chancellor of the exchequer, Neville Chamberlain, and by Leith Ross. In spite of Foreign Office protests, most of these amendments were accepted by the foreign secretary. A document which was generally more favourable to Japan than the Foreign Office original was the result.[35]

The British *aide-mémoire* dealt point by point with the proposals in Yoshida's memorandum. It was a carefully worded document which, while it reflected a positive interest in the ambassador's approach, made clear British reservations and the caveats which might have to be entered before agreement could be reached on the main issues of China and trade. Nevertheless it left scope for negotiation and the formulation of definite proposals by Japan. Yoshida received it with every expression of delight.[36]

After this enthusiasm had lasted three days, Yoshida was back at the Foreign Office 'rather more unintelligible than usual' and declaring that he found the British *aide-mémoire* 'embarrassing'. It was hard to discover quite why this was so, but the Foreign Office impression was that either Yoshida had gone ahead of his government and now did not dare produce the British reply or he had led the Japanese government to believe the reply would be more favourable than it was. It was not clear whether he had reported any of the contents of his own *aide-mémoire* to his government. Yoshida explained that he really wanted a document expressing Britain's desire to negotiate a general agreement with Japan. He suggested that he give the Foreign Office another memorandum. The British might then reply in the way he had indicated.[37]

In the Foreign Office, Yoshida was described as 'extremely tiresome' and 'very crooked'. But in spite of his total lack of appreciation of the effort and trouble to which he had already put Whitehall's draughtsmen it was felt that the Japanese ambassador must be kept in play.[38] When the new Japanese memorandum arrived, it proved to be a list of points which the ambassador suggested 'might form the groundwork for mutual agreement' Since it was impossible to reply in general terms, Cadogan re-drafted the whole so that the British reply could be in the form which Yoshida wanted.[39] Understandably, Cadogan found the process by which he drafted both Japanese and British documents, 'laborious, embarrassing and unfruitful'.[40] Furthermore, from Tokyo, the British ambassador dismissed as 'nonsense' Yoshida's claim that the document he sought from the British would strengthen the chances of a more liberal government there.[41] Nevertheless the charade continued in London and a reply expressing Britain's sincere desire to reach an understanding with Japan was duly returned to Yoshida's redrafted memorandum. The ambassador found this document 'very better'.[42]

POLITICAL UPHEAVALS IN JAPAN

After all the British haste to prepare a paper which Yoshida could take to Tokyo, the ambassador found that he could not return to Japan. The political situation there had deteriorated steadily in January 1937 and army opposition finally brought about the resignation of the Hirota cabinet. The army was also able to prevent the next nominee, General Ugaki Issei, from forming a cabinet. General Hayashi Senjūrō, who had faithfully followed the line of the so-called Control faction in the army and whose policies as war minister in 1934 and 1935 had found favour, then became prime minister.

While these events demonstrated the control of the Japanese army in politics and observers did not expect Hayashi's government to last, the new prime minister found favour with the British. He was regarded by ambassador Clive in Tokyo as 'the best type of army leader' and his advocacy of a moderate type of China policy won British approval.[43] In his opening speech to the Diet of 15 February Hayashi declared he had 'no faith in a pugnacious foreign policy' and spoke of 'fostering mutual appreciation and cultivating cordial feelings between China and Japan'.[44] The appointment of Satō Naotake, former Japanese ambassador in Paris, as minister for foreign affairs was particularly pleasing to the British. A professional diplomat who had been 'more or less in exile from Japan for thirty years', Satō was regarded as friendly towards Britain and America. Satō had told the British ambassador in Paris that he felt Japanese policy was 'slipping away on the wrong lines' and that Japan was isolating herself from every friend.[45] He startled the House of Peers by criticising Japanese policy in Asia and by expressing the opinion that negotiations with the Chinese should be conducted on the basis of equality and in a conciliatory spirit and that Japan should respect the open door in China.[46] Japan appeared to be engaged in a 'friendship drive' in China which could perhaps be explained as being a reaction to the Sian incident. If agreement could be reached in the life-time of the Hayashi cabinet, progress towards Anglo-Japanese cooperation in China no longer seemed completely unattainable.

In May Yoshida announced that he had received a reply from Tokyo with which he did not agree on certain points and that there would, therefore, be further delay while he communicated with his government.[47]

AUSTRALIAN PROPOSALS FOR A PACIFIC PACT

Meanwhile an imperial conference opened on 14 May in London

where Dominion prime ministers had gathered for the coronation. In his opening speech, the Australian prime minister, J. A. Lyons, 'dropped a little bomb', a suggestion for a pact of regional understanding and a pact of non-aggression in the Pacific.[48] The proposal, which was clearly partly on election gambit designed to appeal to Lyons's supporters in Australia, aroused a great deal of interest at the conference. The Australian delegation had no definite ideas about the form a pact might take but suggested that the conversations with Yoshida might cover the possibility of reaching a wider understanding with all the countries in the Pacific.[49]

From Tokyo the response was cautious. Clive said that both the Japanese minister for foreign affairs and the American ambassador with whom he had discussed the question agreed that an understanding in the Pacific, especially between Britain, Japan, and the United States, was an object to be worked for but thought that a conference on the subject would be premature and an improvement in Sino-Japanese relations the first essential.[50]

At the imperial conference Eden was similarly cautious. He pointed out that, while the moment seemed ripe for a *détente* in the far east, it was no use ignoring the difficulties. Neville Chamberlain, now prime minister, was far more optimistic.[51] He thought an understanding with Japan would be an 'enormous burden' off Britain's shoulders. The danger that trouble in Europe might be Japan's opportunity to take some step to Britain's disadvantage in the far east had to be admitted. Chamberlain declared that since China was 'one of the great potential markets of the world' Britain, more than any other country, could provide her with the kind of help she needed. Increased trade with China would also be valuable to Britain in providing greater employment opportunities at home. Chamberlain claimed that, since the Leith Ross mission, which had been hailed as the beginning of a 'new attitude' on Britain's part, both China and Japan had felt more confidence in Britain. A Pacific pact would be a further step in the right direction. It was agreed by the conference that the Australian proposal should be examined by the experts of the delegations concerned.[52]

The Foreign Office foresaw difficulties but felt the idea of a non-aggression pact in the Pacific was to be encouraged. The activities of Yoshida suggested that Japan might be ready to sign such a treaty and China was known to favour one. It was clear, however, that it would be premature to approach any government before Japan and the United States had been consulted.

FURTHER HINTS FROM TOKYO

Negotiations with Yoshida were once again in a state of suspension because of changes in the Japanese political situation. The Hayashi cabinet fell at the end of May. Hayashi had failed to win popular support in Japan and lost the support of the army which disapproved of Satō's conciliatory policy towards China.[53] Until the new ministry, led by Prince Konoe Fumimaro, was established, no official reply to the British paper which had been given to Yoshida in February could be expected. Yoshida told Sir Robert Craigie privately that, if the new Japanese government did not accept the policy which he had already outlined in a draft memorandum to Tokyo which had been prepared in accordance with Satō's views, he would resign. He gave Craigie what he described as a simplified version of this draft with extensive explanatory remarks appended. These documents, however, did not make any clearer to the Foreign Office what the Japanese hoped to write into an agreement.[54]

The hiatus was annoying but the outlook was not altogether bleak. Little was known of Konoe but Hirota Koki was once again foreign minister. It was suggested in the Foreign Office that it was probably not Hirota's fault that the army had dominated Japan's China policy during Hirota's earlier time as prime minister, and the Foreign Office was encouraged by Hirota's statement that an agreement with the United Kingdom was the most important work the new government had to perform. He said that such an agreement had been his ambition since he was foreign minister in 1935 and that he hoped it would be possible to achieve one in the next two or three months. Such an understanding, he said, was essential to the peace of the world or at all events the far east. He did not know why the Anglo-Japanese alliance had been abrogated, 'but look at the result ever since'.[55]

The imperial conference to which Eden reported this conversation was delighted with this good omen and with the news that Yoshida's proposals for the betterment of Anglo-Japanese relations were apparently being considered in Tokyo. Eden told the conference that the new Japanese government appeared to be more stable and more capable of conducting important negotiations than its predecessor. Chamberlain thought the Japanese government was in a more 'reasonable' mood than for some time past.[56]

THE FATE OF THE PACIFIC PACT

The optimism with which the political situation in Japan was regarded helped to compensate for the rather pessimistic results of the detailed investigation of the Lyons proposal. Many obstacles to a Pacific pact were foreseen. It was recommended as a first step that the American and Japanese governments should be sounded and, in view of the conversations already in progress between the British and Japanese, that the United Kingdom government might be invited to undertake the soundings and be given discretion as to the time and manner of so doing.[57] The conference decided, at Chamberlain's suggestion, that first China, then Japan and the United States should be approached.[58]

The background and details of the Pacific pact proposal were not discussed with the Chinese ambassador. He gave his opinion that his government would not be interested in a pact merely relating to insular possessions and would certainly want included some provision for consultation.[59] The counsellor at the American embassy, with whom the proposal was discussed in detail, was for his part doubtful about the wisdom and flexibility of the idea of a pact. He thought the Japanese were feeling their isolation rather acutely and it would be a mistake, when they were showing signs of a chastened mood, to go running after them with a pact. He wanted evidence of a real change of heart in Japan.[60]

Yoshida was not approached on the question of a Pacific pact. Whitehall did not want to complicate manoeuvres already underway and hoped that, if the long-promised discussions went well, the opportunity for sounding the Japanese on a Pacific pact could be found.[61] In any case, the British embassy in Tokyo was convinced that no Japanese government would be prepared to bind itself to the *status quo* in the Pacific and that it would be a mistake to try and force the pace on Japan. The chargé d'affaires in Tokyo could find no evidence that the Japanese army or navy had substantially modified its semi-mystical belief in Japan's destiny to dominate east Asia and the western Pacific.[62]

On 25 June, Eden told the Commons that there were encouraging signs of an improvement in international relations in the far east. He expressed the hope that the examination of concrete proposals for a better understanding between Britain and Japan would begin soon and renewed his assurances that an Anglo–Japanese understanding would not be at China's expense. He made a cautious reference to the Pacific pact, indicating that it was hoped to consult other governments about this in the near future.[63]

THE MARCO POLO BRIDGE INCIDENT

These overtures were upset when a local unplanned clash between Chinese and Japanese troops took place near Lukouchiao, known to foreigners as Marco Polo bridge, outside Peking. In spite of Tokyo's wish to do so, the Nanking government refused to accept the agreement reached locally and within a week the Foreign Office in London realised that a grave situation had developed in north China. Eden saw Yoshida and, in an effort to encourage Japanese restraint, commented that an Anglo–Japanese understanding would hardly be possible while there was fighting in north China.[64] The fear that Japan might take some action which would precipitate widespread fighting was uppermost in the minds of Foreign Office officials in spite of the accumulating evidence of China's belligerency. It had become clear that Chiang Kai-shek was determined to preserve what remained of his authority in north China and that Japan would not accept his hostile stance. Unable to persuade the United States to join Britain in urging both China and Japan to suspend troop movements and in putting forward proposals which might lead to a settlement, Eden again sought to restrain Japan by announcing in the Commons that, as long as the existing situation in China prevailed, it did not 'seem opportune' to open the Anglo–Japanese conversations to which the government had been looking forward.[65] The Japanese were unimpressed. Hirota told the House of Representatives that it was regrettable that conversations with the British government had been suspended because of the north China incident but that plans for helping China would, in any case, have had to be suspended during the present crisis.[66]

From the beginning of August 1937, the situation in China deteriorated and hopes for an improvement in Anglo–Japanese relations faded. As hostilities extended to Shanghai, the centre of British interests in China, London's attitude hardened. From 26 August when the British ambassador in China, Sir Hughe Knatchbull-Hugessen, was seriously wounded by fire from Japanese aeroplanes as he travelled by car between Nanking and Shanghai, suspicions of Japan increased. The need to 'keep Japan in play', which had been characteristic of British diplomacy since 1934, was no longer felt. Yoshida's well-intentioned approaches now could be seen to have been misleading and increased cynicism about the 'sincerity' of Japanese diplomacy. Eden and Cadogan who had been most involved in the British response to Yoshida's proposals and with keeping the way open to the possibility of an Anglo–Japanese understanding now came to feel strongly that Japan must be restrained.[67]

A recent writer suggests that one factor underlying Britain's reluctance to appease the Japanese after 1937 was her belief that, in the end, China must win and this would bring advantages for British trade.[68] This argument had, in fact, been part of British calculations since 1933. It can also be suggested that, just as the Japanese, in a situation of intolerable tension in their relations with China in 1937, found it easier to cut the Gordian knot with what might be a short sharp campaign against Chiang Kai-shek, so too the British, faced with a deteriorating situation in Europe, found it easier to take a hard line with Japan. By abandoning the desire for appeasement which had been a consistent characteristic of British far eastern policy since the Manchurian crisis, Britain left the east Asian protagonists to a confrontation which might resolve Britain's far eastern problem, the problem of Japan's position in China.

12 THE FAILURE OF BRITAIN'S DUAL DIPLOMACY

The incident at Marco Polo Bridge in July 1937 brought to an end the manoeuvres for an Anglo–Japanese understanding and killed the Australian idea of a Pacific pact. It also eventually brought to a halt Treasury-inspired attempts to assist China with a currency loan which had, for some time, been causing consternation in the Foreign Office. H. H. Kung, Chinese minister of finance, arrived in London in May at the head of the Chinese delegation to the coronation of George VI. The political developments in Japan in the spring had raised hopes of a better attitude on Japan's part to Chinese reconstruction and it was known before the delegation arrived that Kung hoped to raise a large loan in London.[1]

The British commercial counsellor in Shanghai warned that the loan proposal, when looked at in conjunction with the supplies of railway and other equipment which it was expected that Kung would obtain from Germany, was designed to secure Chiang Kai-shek's strategic aims.[2] But this possibility does not seem to have been taken seriously at the Treasury. Leith Ross, who had been so deeply involved in the reform of China's currency in 1935, was anxious to promote the stability of that currency and thought the time to do this was when the sky was clear and there were 'no storms in sight'.[3] He was keen, therefore, to explore the possibility of a currency loan. The Treasury saw Kung's mission as an opportunity to carry out some of the reforms to China's financial structure which Leith Ross had failed to put through in 1935. Cyril Rogers of the Bank of England, the central banking expert who had accompanied Leith Ross and stayed behind in China to assist in the organisation of a Central Reserve Bank, had made little headway with the project by 1937,[4] nor had the question of a successor to the British-born inspector-general of Chinese customs, Sir Frederick Maze, been settled.

The Chinese consortium remained as a stumbling block to a

British loan to China but, even before Kung's visit was mooted, the British had taken the initiative to try to dismantle this. In January 1937 the Chinese had forced the issue by offering British banking interests a loan for the construction of the Canton–Meihsien railway but flatly refusing to treat with the consortium or admit Japanese cooperation.[5] Since it was regarded as desirable that British banks should make this loan and British firms construct the line, action to break the consortium deadlock followed. The American government was sounded about its attitude to the dissolution of the consortium[6] and, when its favourable reply had been received, the French and Japanese governments were consulted.[7] Their replies were still awaited in May but the Treasury had high hopes that, by the autumn, the consortium would no longer exist to prevent an individual loan to China.

In London Kung held separate meetings with the chancellor of the exchequer, Leith Ross, Treasury and Foreign Office officials as well as the governor of the Bank of England and the leading executives of the Hong Kong and Shanghai bank. By the beginning of June when he left England, the idea of a currency loan had been agreed in principle and the Chinese had agreed to the conditions which the Treasury imposed. These included the setting up of a Central Reserve Bank, the employment of a special financial adviser, the appointment of a British successor to Sir Frederick Maze and the resumption of foreign recruitment into the customs service. There were also certain purely financial arrangements for the security and disposal of the loan designed to try to ensure that the money did reinforce China's financial stability and was not used simply to buy arms. The loan could not, of course, be issued while the consortium was in existence. The Treasury was still confident this difficulty would be overcome but Konoe's government had just taken office in June 1937 and, until the political situation was more settled, there was no point in pressing Japan for her attitude to the proposed dissolution or her agreement to a currency loan.[8]

During the pause which these political changes in the far east brought to negotiations, opposition developed to Treasury policy. From Shanghai, Sir Louis Beale, the commercial counsellor, reported that Christopher Chancellor of Reuters and Keswick of

Jardine Matheson, representing 'responsible British interests' were disturbed about rumours of a loan. They maintained that it would be construed by China and Japan as a political loan to the Kung–Chiang Kai-shek faction; that, in view of the anti-Japanese attitude of the Kung faction, the loan would prejudice the chances of improving relations with Japan; and that, regardless of safe-guards, the loan would be used for the purchase of arms and would not directly assist British trade. They maintained that, if a currency loan was necessary, it should be the joint responsibility of interested countries, and they described unilateral support of China by the United Kingdom as 'simply quixotic'.[9]

Although the Foreign Office did not have much respect for the political flair of the British taipans on the Chinese coast, the British commercial community in Shanghai was clearly implying that Leith Ross's 'antics' were leading Britain into deep waters and political factors were being ignored.[10] Leith Ross himself dis-missed the assessment from Shanghai as underestimating the importance to China and to British trade and prestige in China of getting central bank reform. He did not despair of getting Japanese goodwill for a loan, especially if Yoshida's general talks got underway in June or July.[11] Things had reached the stage in the currency loan negotiations when the question of Kung's face, to say nothing of Leith Ross's face, could not be ignored.

The importance of keeping Japan informed of the progress of the talks with Kung was recognised. The Japanese financial com-missioner in London was told of the negotiations and of British hopes for expediting the formation of a central bank and for the future organisation of the Chinese customs. It was stressed that the government was not trying to obtain exclusive advantages for Britain but was anxious for the issue of a loan entirely from the point of view of helping China.[12] Such expressions of altruism seem likely to have fallen on stony ground. Hall-Patch, the financial adviser to the British embassies in China and Japan, warned from Tokyo that, unless the ground was carefully pre-pared, a proposal for a currency loan would cause considerable resentment.[13] He was authorised to explain the British terms, should a loan be granted, to Japan's vice-minister of finance and to Tsushima Juichi, vice-governor of the Bank of Japan, who had been Japanese financial commissioner in London and was known to Leith Ross.[14] In London the French, Japanese and American ambassadors were given a memorandum describing Kung's requirements and the British terms for meeting these.[15]

The Japanese had obvious misgivings. They wanted to know whether a British adviser to the Central Reserve Bank would be a condition of the loan. They were told that it was hoped that an adviser would be appointed on grounds of technical qualifications and not on political grounds. This was a specious argument and one which made the Foreign Office nervous. It was hoped, and confidently expected in Britain and China, that Cyril Rogers of the Bank of England would be the man appointed.[16]

The Foreign Office did not wonder at Japan's doubts about the loan and, especially after the Sino-Japanese clash on 7 July, recognised that any attempt to push the negotiations was bound to cause keen resentment in Japan. The loan was not necessary to secure the success of currency reform but would serve as a lever for various desiderata which smacked unpleasantly of British tutelage and was apparently being pursued by the Treasury because in its opinion Chiang Kai-shek and the Nanking government would be strengthened by British support. The Foreign Office was inclined to think that, far from assisting Chiang Kai-shek, the loan might become a propaganda weapon against him, used by his enemies at home and abroad.

The danger was that so much would be agreed between Treasury and Chinese negotiators that, if Sino-Japanese tension relaxed sufficiently for a loan actually to be granted, it would be impossible for the Foreign Office to put forward political considerations. Cadogan therefore wrote to Leith Ross, expressing some tentative doubts about the importance of the loan from the point of view of Chinese finance but stressing particularly its likely political effects. He thought that Britain would have to admit that a loan would not be conducive to improved Sino-Japanese relations and that, though bureaucrats and financiers in Tokyo might not be unfavourably disposed towards it, there was always the risk that the Japanese military would see in it an element of provocation no matter how tightly the funds might be tied up. A loan, he argued, might give those who opposed Chiang

Kai-shek a stick with which to beat him, rather than strengthening him against them. It would be used by Chiang Kai-shek's detractors to represent him as a puppet of Britain. The Treasury was committed to the principle of a loan but Cadogan asked that no special effort should be made to push it through at that time and that, while the loan should be tied up as tightly as possible, it should avoid such a semblance of control over the Reserve Bank as might compass Chiang Kai-shek's downfall.[17]

Leith Ross dismissed Cadogan's letter as a 'long grouse' which did not 'amount to much.'[18] The Treasury went ahead and an agreement was reached for the Canton–Meihsien railway loan, when market conditions permitted and this, with an exchange of letters recording points accepted as a preliminary to a currency loan, was ready for Kung's signature.[19] The Foreign Office objected. It was anxious that it should be made clear to Kung that, owing to the existing situation in China, the British government could give no assurance, even when market conditions permitted, that a loan would not be withheld on political grounds.[20] Leith Ross could not accept this reservation. He did not think the government should step in and raise political arguments if the market was prepared to issue a Chinese loan and reiterated the view he had expressed in 1935 that Britain could not afford to give Japan a veto on loans to China. Such timidity would, he thought, gain Britain neither advantages nor respect.[21]

Taking up the cudgels for the Foreign Office, Orde, the head of the far east department, pointed out that, however the fighting in China went and however soon it stopped, the effect of a loan to China on Chinese internal politics, Sino-Japanese relations and Anglo-Japanese relations was liable to be entirely different from what it had been before the fighting began. Again he urged that Kung should be warned.[22] Orde's personality and his tenacity had been a persistent irritant to the Treasury since 1934. Thanking God that this gentleman was shortly to be transferred to Riga,[23] Leith Ross told the Foreign Office that, since China had met all the conditions for a loan, it was impossible to turn round and say that the government might have further political objections to raise even if market requirements were satisfied. This was not, he said, the way to do business.[24] The Foreign Office repeated that, because Britain had agreed to a currency loan in 1937, it should not be assumed that she would automatically agree to one the next year. Orde now suggested that the British ambassador might be asked to indicate to Chiang Kai-shek that approval might eventually have to be withheld on political grounds.[25] The Treasury remained adamant. Leith Ross felt that there was no point in worrying about the 'very hypothetical contingency' that, when peace was restored in the far east, the then existing Chinese government might be such as to make a loan undesirable on political grounds. He thought a message of the kind the Foreign Office was contemplating could not fail to be interpreted as meaning that the sympathies of the British government in the conflict were against China and that the British were taking the opportunity of China's difficulties to inflict on her a deliberate rebuff. He unbent sufficiently, however, to suggest that the Foreign Office might be content with an understanding as between the Treasury and the Foreign Office that, if and when the question of a currency loan arose as a practical issue, the Treasury would consult the Foreign Office before giving its blessing.[26]

Leith Ross wrote as if the Foreign Office was incompetent to choose a suitable moment to make a tactful and diplomatic approach to Chiang Kai-shek, but the undertaking to consult when the question of a currency loan arose was a concession and it was felt better to let the matter rest rather than putting this difference of opinion between Treasury and Foreign Office on record to the cabinet.[27] As the situation in China continued to deteriorate in September 1937, it seemed highly unlikely that borrowing would be possible in the very near future and the Foreign Office retired from the battle over a loan allowing time and events in the far east to solve its problems with the Treasury.

THE FOREIGN OFFICE VERSUS THE TREASURY IN THE
FAR EAST

In the period between the end of the Manchurian crisis and the outbreak of the Sino-Japanese war the British sought to sustain Japanese goodwill while cultivating Chinese friendship. As the Leith Ross mission and, to some extent, the currency loan negotiations of 1937 demonstrated, unless the greatest care was exercised, the effect of this policy could be to transform the policy of the Nanking government from one of drift into one of action inimical to Japan's interests. The British supplied the 'needed ingredient' of their moral support and prestige to carry out reforms which promoted China's capitalism and the driving power behind Chiang Kai-shek's movement for the unification of China. On the admission of Chiang's American financial adviser, the vital central banking reforms were carried out at Leith Ross's insistence.[28] The hardening of the Nanking government's attitude to Japan in 1937 was not simply the result of the united front but also of the greater financial security of the Nanking regime.

The Leith Ross report and Leith Ross's memorandum to General Isogai[29] had both pointed to the prospects for long-term investment in China, which, from a Japanese point of view, was undesirable if it meant the persistence of western capital in China. In 1937 when war broke out it was clear that the Nanking government was embarking on a new phase of borrowing that involved both private interests and governmental agencies in Britain, Europe and the United States. The trend was highly unfavourable to Japan. China's capacity to borrow successfully in 1937 was based to a large extent on the success of the currency reform in which Britain had been so deeply involved. Given political developments in China after the Sian incident and Chiang's refusal to meet Japan's advances in 1937, there was some reason for Japan to feel injured by events in China and to regard Britain as having a hand in China's ability to be a threat.[30] Once war had broken out, anti-Japanese feeling developed in Britain and anti-British feeling increased in Japan. There the recent currency loan negotiations were cited to support the claim that British financial assistance was behind Chiang Kai-shek.[31]

The British would have denied that their policy after the Manchurian crisis was in any way anti-Japanese. But the cultivation of Chinese friendship, the purpose of which was to protect British interests and prospects in China, had the effect also of chanelling Chinese anti-imperialism against the Japanese. This aspect of British policy was intensified by the dual diplomacy of Whitehall which was the result of Treasury influence in the making of policy in the far east.

It is, of course, nothing new to suggest that forces outside the Foreign Office or outside the government were having an effect on Britain's policy-making in the 1930s. Dawson of *The Times*, the Cliveden set, the Bank of England, have been variously blamed for appeasement of Germany, though scholarly studies have recently played down these outside influences.[32] It is less common to be able to document policy-making being shared between two departments of government, yet it is clearly a common factor in the far eastern area. It came about because of the strong position of Neville Chamberlain; because coordination between Treasury civil servants and the chancellor of the exchequer was better than between Foreign Office civil servants and the foreign secretary; because the quality and rank of Treasury officials was higher so they carried more weight in practical decision-making; and because of the special character and experience of Leith Ross who was able to over-ride Wellesley and Orde who had no direct far eastern experience.

Dual diplomacy has been thought of as a characteristic of Japanese policy in the 1930s and the unwillingness or inability of successive Japanese governments to resist the military or make any fundamental changes in the status quo has been criticised by historians.[33] At the time this dual diplomacy made it difficult for western observers to discover the origins, and predict the course, of Japanese policy and frequently created the impression that Japanese politicians and diplomats were deliberately 'insincere'.

The effect of British dual diplomacy can have been no less confusing to the Japanese. It was the Treasury's confidence in the practicability and the necessity of cooperating with Japan which forced the Foreign Office into attempts to discover a basis for a *rapprochement*. The Foreign Office assessment of the pros and cons of a pact with Japan and of the possibilities open to Britain in the far east, remained remarkably consistent from 1933 until the outbreak of the Sino-Japanese war. The interference of the Treasury in far eastern policy, which was the result of the special economic circumstances of the post-depression period, the problems associated with the decision to rearm, and the powerful personalities of Chamberlain, Fisher and Leith Ross, put the Foreign Office view under constant pressure and ultimately distorted the policy which it sought to carry out. The Treasury attempts to find 'solutions' to British problems in the far east, to find a basis for the appeasement of Japan, to find the means for international cooperation in China's finance, to reinforce China's new-found currency stability with a loan, had the effect of making British far eastern policy appear far more positive and ultimately far more pro-Chinese than the Foreign Office intended or had hitherto been the case. Because the Sino-Japanese war genuinely increased pro-Chinese sentiment in the Foreign Office and in Britain, the very real effort which had characterised the years after 1933 to 'keep Japan in play' even though an understanding was regarded as improbable, was obscured.[34]

The 'new attitude' which the Leith Ross mission symbolised, was the result of pressure which orthodox policy-makers had been unable to resist. The mission itself illustrated the risks which may be attached to the employment of 'special envoys' whose very success with an immediate problem is likely to undermine the standing and policy of the representatives of the regular foreign service who must be preoccupied with political problems and the niceties of maintaining the delicate balance between long-term political aims and immediate interests.

SOME REFLECTIONS

The British had neither the willingness nor the capacity to police the kind of balance of power which would have best suited their interests in the far east in the period between 1933 and 1937. In these circumstances a confrontation with Japan had to be avoided. Though aware of a 'genuine but disconcertingly abstract Japanese desire for good relations with the United Kingdom', the Foreign Office did not find cooperation with Japan a feasible alternative in its dilemma. Japan did not respond to Britain's tentative feelers for a *rapprochement* in 1934 and rejected cooperation in promoting Chiang Kai-shek's government on the basis the Leith Ross mission offered. Japan's domestic political difficulties after February 1936 increased the difficulty of negotiation. The British feared that a wider political and economic agreement with concessions to Japan in China would amount to an agreement to permit Japan to swallow up British interests. The loss of these interests would not have been economically shattering to Britain but it would have broadcast British impotence to the world. Once Japan had made it clear that she would not be a party to any naval limitation agreement, there was no *quid pro quo* which could be obtained from her which could compensate for a revelation that Britain could not police her interests or carry out her imperial role in the far eastern and Pacific areas. The Foreign Office was not prepared, therefore, to recommend that a step involving such risks to Britain's image as an imperial power should be taken.

Britain and Japan had interests in common in the future of China and the question of naval policy in the Pacific. For Britain, the China question was one aspect of the wider problem of imperial defence and Britain's world-wide economic interests. But Japan's China policy was an issue of central importance to every Japanese government in the 1930s and the future of China was of vital interest to Japan in economic and cultural terms. It was as hard for the British to appreciate the significance of China for Japan as it was for the Japanese to understand that, for Britain, the east Asian situation was assessed in the light of European, Mediterranean and imperial problems, not simply in terms of competition or cooperation with Japan in the exploitation of an area in which Japan felt she had special claims.[35]

It has been suggested that, in diplomacy, an element of make-believe is essential if any result is to be produced at all.[36] The persisting British attempts to encourage the 'moderates' in Japan illustrates this point. A belief in the long-term possibility of the emergence of a moderate government justified attempts at appeasement of Japan from which little benefit was expected in the short-term. For this reason the Foreign Office was prepared to explore suggestions for a better understanding with Japan despite the inhospitable climate. In reality, whether it appeared in the guise of an east Asian Monroe Doctrine, the Amau statement, 'positive diplomacy' or the east Asian co-prosperity sphere, the direction of Japanese diplomacy in China between 1933 and 1937 was consistent.[37] Except perhaps for the brief and precarious period of Hayashi–Satō diplomacy in 1937, when the British ambassador in Tokyo thought Japan had been offered by destiny a last chance for cooperation in China,[38] this national policy left no room for economic or political power-sharing in China. Hindsight also suggests that, while there were men in Japan who were well disposed towards Britain and moderate in their political outlook, they were never capable of, or interested in, challenging the general trend of Japan's national policy. If the existence of an effective moderate group was assumed, however, it was worthwhile responding to diplomatic gestures by Hirota Koki, even if they might prove to be superficial, and to the nebulous suggestions of Yoshida Shigeru.

In both Britain and Japan, the problems of the far east were seen as the concern primarily of Britain, Japan and China. The Japanese army and Japanese political observers appear to have discounted the possibility of American intervention in the mid-1930s[39] and the British regarded the possibility of cooperation with the United States as a 'broken reed'.[40] The British studiously avoided any action which might smack of a 'common front' between Britain and the United States in naval and other matters affecting the far east and their experience was that the United States could not be persuaded into joint action of any kind. The 'excessive timidity' displayed by the Roosevelt administration when the British sought American cooperation to keep Japan from interfering with Anglo-American shipping in September 1937 was therefore no surprise to the Foreign Office.[41] All the same, the British were reluctant to antagonise the United States over the far east, and the dream of a tripartite political arrangement between Britain, Japan and the United States offered the means of keeping Japan in check and cooperating with her without offending the Americans. The reaction of the American president at the time of the naval conference in 1936 to the idea of a tripartite agreement made it clear that this suggestion was probably less attractive to the Americans than it was to the Japanese and was impracticable. Suggestions that the United States might be interested in the neutrality of the Pacific were made in 1936 and 1937 but, although Norman Davis 'havered' about a 'great peace area in the Pacific' which would be an example to the world, he would not commit himself to the possibility of an

American signature to a pact of any kind.[42] Nor did the American president respond to the idea of a Pacific pact in 1937.

The British felt that they were left with no alternative but to sustain the bluff and play for time. The Foreign Office complained that this was a policy of perpetually making bricks without straw[43] but the alternative of cooperating with Japan or abandoning British interests altogether was seen to be both politically and psychologically unacceptable.

BRITAIN, JAPAN AND CHINA

British observers tended to believe that Japanese professed fears of the expansion of Chinese communism were an exaggeration by the Japanese in their own interests.[44] Furthermore a state of tension with no blows between Japan and the Soviet government suited British interests by acting as a check on the expansionist proclivities of both these countries.[45] From the Japanese point of view, however, not only was Soviet activity in the far east a menace, but it could be argued that, without British encouragement and assistance, Chiang Kai-shek would be compelled to yield to the communists or to cooperate with Japan for help in his economic programme and his political and military struggle against the Chinese communists. On the basis of this argument, the stumbling block to Japanese interests in China came not from Chinese nationalism, but from Britain.[46] An Anglo-Japanese political agreement would have weakened the link between Britain and the Nationalist government and, as such, was a possible solution to Japan's problems in China. This was, no doubt, one reason for the persistent, if tentative, feelers from Japan for such an agreement in the years between 1933 and the outbreak of the Sino-Japanese war in 1937. If this was the basis of the Japanese desire for cooperation with the British, those observers who claimed that cooperation with Japan in China could only mean the end of British interests there, were probably correct in their deduction. Another alternative for the Japanese was to attempt to sever the link between Britain and the Nationalists. The increasing tendency of the Japanese to isolate far eastern questions from world affairs made it difficult for them to assess accurately the consequences of this alternative.

Altogether this situation best suited Chiang Kai-shek who found room to manoeuvre between the dilemmas of Britain and Japan in China. Between 1933 and 1937 he was able to avoid a confrontation or a compromise with the Japanese and he increased his military strength so that by mid-1937 he not only refused to respond to the conciliatory gestures of the Hayashi government but took a stronger line in the disputes which arose. The British regarded this recalcitrant Chinese attitude without much sympathy.[47] Chiang Kai-shek had made use of British expertise and promises of financial help to increase the stability of his government and had evaded conditions which might have secured British long-term interests.

The British believed that there could be room for both Britain and Japan in a China undergoing reconstruction. They placed their hopes on the Nanking government. Their attitude suited a power without the means to support its interests or its imperial image. The open door and the growth of a Nationalist government sufficiently strong to be anti-Japanese were obstacles to Japan's hopes for a tripartite relationship between Japan, China and Manchukuo in economic, political and cultural fields.[48] British and Japanese policies were, therefore, fundamentally opposed. Neither Britain nor Japan was without goodwill toward the other in the period from 1933 to 1937 but Britain's formula for survival in the far east was at odds with Japan's increasing sense of mission in Asia. The difficulties became more acute after 1935 when British policy appeared to make a 'forward' move in China while at the same time the role of the Japanese army in politics became increasingly obvious. In these circumstances the basis for an improvement in Anglo-Japanese relations was impossible to discover and, with the outbreak of the Sino-Japanese war, the search for such a basis was abandoned. Britain's role in the far east and her far eastern problem, the problem of Japan's position in China, seemed likely to be conditioned by the outcome of the struggle between China and Japan. It was a struggle which the British believed China must win.[49] In this certainty lay the key to British policy in the next two years and the case for ending attempts to conciliate the Japanese.

NOTES

NOTES TO PREFACE

1. Christopher Thorne, *The Limits of Foreign Policy, The West, the League and the Far Eastern Crisis of 1931-1933* (London, 1972); Bradford A. Lee, *Britain and the Sino-Japanese War 1937-1939, A Study in the Dilemmas of British Decline* (Stanford, Cal., 1972).

NOTES TO CHAPTER I

1. Jordan to Balfour, 23 December 1918, FO 371/3693 [3057].
2. I. H. Nish, *Alliance in Decline. A Study in Anglo-Japanese Relations 1908-1923* (London, 1972), pp. 387-97.
3. F. S. Northedge, *The Troubled Giant. Britain among the Great Powers 1916-1939* (London, 1966), p. 629.
4. Nish, p. 389.
5. S. W. Roskill, *Hankey, Man of Secrets*, Volume II *1919-1931* (London, 1972), pp. 4-9, Hankey to Beatty, 10 July 1925.
6. Nish, p. 394.
7. K. Middlemas, *The Diplomacy of Illusion* (London, 1972), pp. 2-8.
8. Christopher Thorne, 'The Quest for Arms Embargoes: Failure in 1933', *Journal of Contemporary History*, v, No. 4 (1970), p. 149.
9. Orde, 9 May 1933, Foreign Office minute, FO 371/17167 [F3128].
10. Cabinet 50, 11 October 1932, conclusion 9.
11. Middlemas and Barnes, *Baldwin* (London, 1969), pp. 730-6, 745-7. The best-known example is the East Fulham bye-election of October 1933. The Labour candidate made disarmament the major issue of his campaign and the Conservative majority of 15,000 was transformed into a Labour one of nearly 5,000. The result, in June 1935, of the Peace Ballot which had been conducted over eight months in 1934-5 indicated the continuing political importance of pacifist sentiment.
12. Note by the Treasury on the Annual Review for 1932 by the chiefs of staff sub-committee, 11 March 1932, CID paper 1087-B, CAB 4/21.
13. See Chamberlain's statement at the 11th meeting of the Imperial Conference 1937, 2 June 1937, CAB 32/128. See also Chapter 11.
14. K. Feiling, *The Life of Neville Chamberlain* (London, 1946), Diary, 12 May 1934, p. 258.
15. Neville Chamberlain to Ida Chamberlain, 19 September 1931, Neville Chamberlain papers. Quoted by Thorne, p. 94.

16. Thorne, p. 188, pp. 210–11, 217–18, 247–66.

17. Austen Chamberlain to Ida Chamberlain, 3 February 1934, Austen Chamberlain papers.

18. Austen Chamberlain to Ida Chamberlain, 9 February 1935, Austen Chamberlain papers. Austen Chamberlain was quoting a comment of William Ormsby-Gore who was first clerk of works, an office not in the cabinet at that time.

19. See for example Simon's change of line between August and September 1934, Chapter 6, pp. 100–1.

20. Middlemas and Barnes, p. 833; The Right Honourable the Earl of Avon, *Facing the Dictators* (London, 1962), pp. 192–214, 220–30, 236–311. Italian and Ethiopian troops had clashed at Wal Wal in December 1934. On 3 January 1935 Emperor Haile Selassie appealed to the League Council. Diplomatic manoeuvres had been going on since then.

21. Hoare, 23 June 1935, minute, FO 371/19287 [F4296].

22. See chapter 9 which illustrates Eden's reluctance to clash with Chamberlain over the Leith Ross mission.

23. F. T. Ashton Gwatkin, *The British Foreign Service* (Syracuse, N.Y., 1950), pp. 20, 24. The author of the schemes was the deputy under-secretary, Sir Victor Wellesley. His desire to see the integration of trade, finance and diplomacy, and his wish to establish a politico-economic intelligence department at the Foreign Office were interpreted by the Treasury and the Board of Trade as an attempt to seize their spheres of interest for the Foreign Office. The immediate result of the inter-departmental quarrel was that the Department of Overseas Trade was put under the joint control of the Board of Trade and the Foreign Office.

24. Robert Craigie, head of the American department, was an important figure because he was the Foreign Office negotiator on naval matters as well as head of this department. In 1933 Ralph Wigram became head of the central department (Belgium, France, Germany, Poland, Danzig) and A. W. A. Leeper became head of the League of Nations and western department (League of Nations, Disarmament, Holland, Luxembourg, Switzerland, Spain, Portugal). Both these men were personal friends of Vansittart. See I. Colvin, *Vansittart in Office* (London, 1965), p. 93; R. G. Vansittart, *Mist Procession* (London, 1958), p. 399.

25. As a member of the consular service Pratt was, in theory, junior to all Foreign Office members of the department.

26. Orde seems to have been specially irritating to Sir Warren Fisher, see below p. 128. Orde was appointed minister in Riga in 1937 and ambassador in Santiago in 1940. He retired in 1946.

27. See W. R. Louis, *British Strategy in the Far East 1919–1939* (London, 1971), pp. 4, 27–8, 39, 95, 144, 153, for evidence of Wellesley's interest in the far east in the 1920s. See Thorne, pp. 150–2, 188, 234ff, 294–5, for his attitude during the Manchurian crisis.

28. The chief interest of Sir Robert Vansittart, the permanent under-secretary, was in Europe and in the growing power of Germany. Vansittart was publicly involved with the formulation of the Hoare–Laval pact in 1935. This pact would have conceded many of Italy's demands in Abyssinia. Public outcry against the pact brought Hoare's resignation on 18 December 1935 and in 1936 Cadogan was offered the post of joint deputy under-secretary and obvious heir to Vansittart. Until his retirement in 1938, Vansittart tended to be less involved in the making of important decisions. See Colvin, p. 92; and D. Dilks, *The Diaries of Sir Alexander Cadogan* (London, 1972), p. 12.

29. Austen Chamberlain to Hilda Chamberlain, 31 March 1935, Austen Chamberlain papers.

30. See note p. 10 n. 28 above.

31. Vansittart, 3 January 1935, minute, FO 371/18116 [F7054].

32. Fisher, 21 January 1935, memorandum for the chancellor of the exchequer, chancellor of the exchequer's papers, T172/1831.

33. Fisher, 23 February 1937, minute, Leith Ross papers, T188/162.

34. Admiral Sir Ernle Chatfield, chief of naval staff, described the Treasury as 'frightened to death of having to fight a war on two fronts'. Chatfield to Admiral W. W. Fisher (Commander-in-chief, Mediterranean fleet) 2 August 1934, Chatfield papers.

35. Nish, p. 387.

36. It was suggested at the time that Chamberlain was pro-Japanese and that he led a pro-Japanese lobby. See Foreign Relations of the United States (hereafter cited as FRUS) Volume I, 1934, pp. 351–3. The first charge was an over-simplification and there is no evidence of a pro-Japanese lobby in cabinet.

37. Simon to MacDonald, 29 January 1932, Simon papers.

38. Pratt. 1 December 1933, memorandum on British policy in the Far East, FO 371/17148 [F7818].

39. Similar sentiments were expressed by Sir John Tilley, under-secretary at the Foreign Office, in 1919. See Documents on British Foreign Policy (hereafter cited as DBFP), I (vi), No. 617 and Nish, p. 277.

40. Nish, p. 369.

41. B. B. Schofield, *British Sea Power* (London, 1967), p. 110.

42. Dorothy Borg, *American policy and the Chinese Revolution 1925–1928* (New York, 1947), pp. 51–4. (Hereafter cited as Borg, *American Policy, 1925–1928*.)

43. Borg, *American Policy, 1925–1928*, pp. 20–46, gives a detailed account of the 30 May Incident and the spread of the anti-foreign movement.

44. Borg, *American Policy 1925–1928*, pp. 95–121; China (ministry of foreign affairs) *Special conference on the Chinese Customs Tariff 1925–26*, (Peking, 1928) gives a detailed account of proceedings.

45. A. Iriye, *After Imperialism* (Cambridge, Mass., 1965), p. 56.

46. Royal Institute of International Affairs, *Survey of International Affairs 1926* (London, 1928), p. 488–94.

47. For details of this group and the split in the Japanese navy see chapter 4.

48. *Taiheiyō sensō e no michi* (Road to the Pacific war), 8 volumes (Tokyo, 1963), Vol. I, p. 156 (hereafter cited as TSM). For assistance with Japanese sources I am grateful to Miss T. Tani, Fellow, Centre of International Studies, London School of Economics.

49. Royal Institute of International Affairs, *Survey of International Affairs, 1932* (London, 1933), pp. 27–34.

50. Pratt, 25 October 1934, minute, FO 371/18101 [F6337].

51. Sir George MacDonough and others, 3 April 1935, note presented to the chancellor of the exchequer, FO 371/19287 [F2600].

52. Chi-ming Hou, *Foreign Investment and Economic Development in China 1840–1937* (Cambridge, Mass., 1965), pp. 97–8. In 1938 the *per capita* foreign capital investment in China was $US 5.7. The figure for India was $US 9.7 and for Argentina $US 228.1.

53. Hou, p. 117.

54. C. F. Remer, *Foreign Investments in China* (New York, 1933), p. 403.

55. Hou, pp. 17–18.

56. Hou, pp. 119–20.

57. F. J. Rippy, *British Investment in Latin America* (Minneapolis, Minn., 1959), p. 159. Rippy estimates British investment as £357.7 million in 1934.

58. Hou, p. 103. Hou estimates that 60 per cent of the profits were re-invested in China; pp. 113–15 show that these profits were not high.

59. Pratt, 23 January 1934, memorandum respecting foreign investments in China, FO 371/18078 [F414].

60. Lindley, 20 May 1933, The policy of Japan, CP 143(33), CAB 24/241.

61. Foreign Office memorandum, 23 November 1937, FO 371/20989 [F100017].

62. Snow to Simon, 13 May 1933, FO 371/17154 [F3757].

63. Far Eastern Department, 25 July 1935. The protection of British interests in China against Japan, FO 371/19287 [F4811].

64. Chihiro Hosoya, 'Retrogression in Japan's Foreign Policy Decision-Making Process', chapter in *Dilemmas of Growth in Prewar Japan*, J. W. Morley (ed.), (Princeton, N.J., 1971), p. 88.

65. This thinking prevailed when the Foreign Office agreed to the Treasury plan to send a financial mission to China in 1935. See chapter 8.

66. Vansittart, 28 July 1935, minute, [F4811] above.

NOTES TO CHAPTER 2

1. Ashton Gwatkin, 5 December 1933, Memorandum respecting the economic position in Japan, FO 371/17166 [F7764]. This shows Japanese cotton exports to China were 120 million yen less in 1932 than in 1930 and that over half this loss, or 63 million yen, was made up by gains in the Indian market.

3. Major (Consul-general, Mukden) to Simon, 3 February 1933, FO 371/17111 [F1202].

3. Snow to Simon, 27 July 1933, FO 371/17166 [F5730].

4. Wellesley, 2 August 1933, minute FO 371/17319 [W8965]. Wellesley seems to have been particularly sensitive on this issue.

5. Pratt, 1 December 1933, British policy in the Far East, FO 371/17148 [F7818].

6. Hou, Chapter 6 and pp. 220–1.

7. G. E. Hubbard, *Eastern Industrialisation and its Effect upon the West* (London, 1938), pp. 227–31.

8. Pratt, 1 December 1933, memorandum above, FO 371/17148 [F7818].

9. Remer, p. 92.

10. Minutes of a meeting of the British Chamber of Commerce and the China Association, 2 November 1933, China Association, London.

11. Pratt, 6 August 1936, minute, FO 371/20218 [F4498].

12. Chairman's report, 28 May 1935, China Association, London.

13. Clive to Vansittart, 5 December 1935, FO 371/20241 [F156].

14. The Manchester Chamber of Commerce papers contain evidence of the activity of local members of parliament on the question of Japanese competition. See, for example, letter from Lancashire, Cheshire and Westmorland M.P.s to the Chamber of Commerce, 10 May 1933, Manchester Chamber of Commerce papers, Vol. 18.

15. Manchester Chamber of Commerce, memorandum for submission to the secretary of state for India and the president of the Board of Trade, 31 January 1933, Manchester Chamber of Commerce papers, Vol. 18.

16. Board of Trade, 11 December 1933, memorandum, Japanese competition, FO 371/17157 [F7706].

17. Snow to Wellesley, 13 May 1933, FO 371/17152 [F5080].

18. Overton (Board of Trade) to Mallet, 23 February 1933, FO 371/17153 [F1256]. Article 27 of the Anglo-Japanese commercial treaty allowed British Dominions, colonies, possession and protectorates which were parties to the treaty to terminate separately by giving twelve months notice.

19. *Manchester Guardian*, 14 January 1933.

20. Runciman to Simon, 31 March 1933, FO 371/17153 [F2334].

21. Turner (India Office) to Simon, 3 March 1933, FO 371/17160 [F1493].

22. Cabinet 15, 8 March 1933, conclusion 1; cabinet 22, 29 March 1933, conclusion 4.

23. *Aide-mémoire* handed to the Japanese ambassador, 25 April 1933, FO 371/17153 [F2755].

24. *Japan Chronicle*, 13 June 1933.

25. Snow to Simon, 20 April 1933, FO 371/17160 [F2600].

26. Snow to Wellesley, 13 May 1933, FO 371/17152 [F5080].

27. Vansittart, 6 August 1933, minute, [F5080] above.

28. Orde to Twentyman (Treasury), 14 September 1933, FO 371/17156 [F5999].

29. The preferences granted to British textiles under the Ottawa agreement were insufficient because the Japanese article was so much cheaper in the first place. The real competition in India came, however, from the Indian manufacturer rather than Japan. The Lancashire delegation hoped to have talks with the Japanese delegation in India but these did not prove feasible. See Manchester Chamber of Commerce, meeting to hear a special report of Mr A. D. Campbell, 24 November 1933, Manchester Chamber of Commerce papers, Vol. 18.

30. *The Times*, 8 November 1933; Secretary of State for India, 27 November 1933 Negotiations between India and Japan, CP 282(33), CAB 27/245.

31. Cabinet 65, 28 November 1933, conclusion 12; India committee, third meeting, 1 December 1933, CAB 27/556.

32. Feiling, extract from diary, January 1934, p. 235.

33. The Indo-Japanese treaty was initialled in January 1934.

34. Lindley to Simon, 11 January 1934, FO 371/18166 [F731].

35. Committee on Japanese trade competition, meeting 11 April 1934, CAB 27/568; Committee on Japanese trade competition, 12 April 1934, CP 106(34), CAB 24/248.

36. *Hansard's Parliamentary Debates*, fifth series, House of Commons, Vol. 289, 7 May 1934, columns 713–18.

37. *The Times*, 8 May 1934.

38. Hereafter referred to as Manchukuo.

39. Lampson to Simon, 13 December 1933, FO 371/17191 (F7733); Sansom to Crowe, 30 March 1934, FO 371/18178 (F2753).

NOTES TO CHAPTER 3

1. Ashton Gwatkin, 3 August 1933, The Far East – Changing Situation, FO 371/17148 [F5189] and minutes on this memorandum.

2. Lampson to Simon, 18 June 1933, FO 371/17081 [F5709]; Snow to Simon, 14 August 1933, FO 371/17081 [F5950]; Ingram to Lampson,

23 June 1933, FO 371/17081 [F6008]. These communications were all received in London between mid-August and mid-September 1933.

3. DBFP, second series, Vol. XI, 1932–3, pp. 558–98. This is a long review of events in China between 1926 and 1933 and contains a good account of the major events during Lampson's time as ambassador.

4. DBFP, second series, Vol. XI, 1932–3, p. 597.

5. Avon, p. 27. This connection was to be valuable to Cadogan when Eden became foreign secretary in December 1935. Eden offered Cadogan the post of deputy under-secretary. See Dilks p. 12. For the background to Cadogan's promotion see Chapter 1, p. 10 n. 28.

6. Joseph Grew diary, 22, 28 June, 13 July 1932, quoted by Thorne p. 99.

7. Lindley to Wigram, 26 October 1932 and 7 July 1933, Royal Archives Windsor, quoted by Thorne, p. 99.

8. K. Sansom, *Sir George Sansom and Japan* (Talahassee, Fla, 1972), pp. 78, 95.

9. Sansom had published an *Historical Grammar of the Japanese Language* in 1928 and *A Short Cultural History of Japan* in 1931 and had also written various papers on Japanese language, literature and history.

10. Simon, 11 January 1935, note introducing CP 8(35), CAB 24/253. In the original draft, Simon used the phrase 'one of the very best authorities'. Vansittart altered this to the wording quoted and added, 'This is no exaggeration of Mr Sansom's credentials. His reputation is immense, even in the United States, particularly in American universities.' This comment is to be found on the copy of this memorandum in the Foreign Office library, Cornwall House. A number of memoranda on Anglo-Japanese relations are to be transferred from Cornwall House to the Public Record Office where they will be added to Class FO 899. These memoranda will be referred to hereafter as FO Cornwall House.

11. Fergusson to the chancellor of the exchequer, 15 January 1935 T172/1831.

12. Lampson to Simon, 18 June 1933 [F5709] above. Snow (chargé d'affaires in Tokyo) was more pessimistic. His views had been set out in detail in an earlier letter, Snow to Orde, 25 May 1933, FO 371/17158 [F4284].

13. Imperial Defence Policy, Annual Review (1933) by the chiefs of staff sub-committee, 12 October 1933, CID paper 113-B, CAB 4/22. The Committee of Imperial Defence advised the prime minister on matters affecting the security of the British empire. The only permanent member was the prime minister but its membership was usually made up of cabinet ministers, military leaders and key civil servants. The chiefs of staff sub-committee was a permanent sub-committee set up in 1923 to report on defence policy. See F. A. Johnson, *Defence by Committee* (London, 1960), pp. 1–2.

14. See for example cabinet 8, 13 February 1933, conclusion 3.

15. Extract from draft minutes of 261st meeting of CID held on 9 November 1933, enclosure in CP 264(33) CAB 24/244.

16. Cabinet 57, 26 October 1933, conclusion 2.

17. Foreign Office memoranda on the situation in the far east 1933-4, 15 March 1934, CP 77(34) CAB 24/248. This is the collection of the memoranda which were written between November 1933 and January 1934.

18. In the Foreign Office naval matters were dealt with by one very experienced negotiator, Robert Craigie, who was head of the American department in 1933. Craigie became ambassador to Japan in 1937.

19. Pratt, 1 December 1933, His Majesty's government's policy in the far east, CP 77(34) above.

20. Harcourt Smith, 2 January 1934, British and Japanese interests in China; Pratt, 23 January 1934, Foreign investments in China; Orde, 14 December 1934, His Majesty's government's relations with Japan, CP 77(34) above.

21. Allen, 25 November 1933, The advent of a militarist government in Japan, CP 77(34) above.

22. Orde, 14 December 1933, memorandum above, CP 77(34).

23. Vansittart to Admiralty, War Office, etc., 12 March 1934, FO 371/18160 [F295].

24. Cabinet 62, 15 November 1933, conclusion 5b. The committee consisted of the three defence chiefs, Vansittart, permanent under-secretary at the Foreign Office, Fisher, permanent under secretary at the Treasury and Sir Maurice Hankey, secretary to the cabinet. Hankey became chairman.

25. Ultra nationalist political group led by Toyama Mitsuru.

26. Lindley to Simon, 27 December 1933, FO 371/18184 [F677].

27. Lindley to Simon, 23 January 1934, FO 371/18180 [F411].

28. Lindley to Simon, 6 February 1934, FO 371/18181 [F138].

29. Snow to Orde, 22 December 1933, FO 371/18184 [F591].

30. See chapter 2.

31. Report of the Defence Requirements Committee, 28 February 1934, CP 64(34), CAP 24/247.

32. CP 64(34) above, CAB 24/247.

33. Cabinet 9, 14 March 1933, conclusion 13.

34. Feiling, p. 252.

35. CP 64(34) above, CAB 24/247.

36. Note by the prime minister, March 1934, CP 70(34), CAB 24/248.

37. Cabinet 9, 14 March 1934, conclusion 13.

38. Simon, 16 March 1934, memorandum CP 80(34), CAB 24/248.

39. Thorne, p. 380; N. Thompson, *The Anti-Appeasers* (Oxford, 1971), p. 37.

40. TSM, Vol. I, p. 156.

41. President of Board of Trade, 20 March 1934, Japanese Trade Competition, CP 81(34) CAB 24/248.

42. Cabinet 10, 19 March 1934, conclusion 2.

43. Orde, 31 October 1934, minute, FO 371/18184 [F2109].

44. Orde and Randall, 13 April 1934, Anglo-Japanese Relations, [F2109] FO Cornwall House.

45. Barnes (Admiralty) to Orde, 28 June 1934, FO 371/18184 [F3960]. Chatfield explained to Warren Fisher that he did not want friendship with Japan to be looked on as a reason for reducing Britain's naval world power. Chatfield to Fisher, 4 June 1934, Chatfield papers.

NOTES TO CHAPTER 4

1. See chapter 1, pp. 12–13.

2. Schofield, pp. 101–8.

3. The rule had been operating since 1919. S. W. Roskill, *Naval Policy between the Wars* (London, 1968), pp. 214–15.

4. Schofield, pp. 110–12.

5. M. M. Postan, *British War Production: History of the Second World War*, civil series (London, 1952), p. 3.

6. Postan, p. 23.

7. Chief of naval staff, memorandum in preparation for the 1935 naval conference, 23 March 1934, NCM(35) 1, CAB 29/148. Papers relating to the 1935 naval conference have been given the description NCM(35) and are numbered in order of presentation to the ministerial committee on the naval conference.

8. Shigemitsu Mamoru, *Japan and her Destiny* (London, 1958), pp. 89–90.

9. Shigemitsu, p. 90.

10. I. Morris, *Nationalism and the Right Wing in Japan* (London, 1960), introduction by Maruyama, p. xxv.

11. Saionji–Harada Memoirs, Pt. v, ch. 104 (1 November 1933). Saionji in November once remarked, 'I would like to remove his highness [Fushimi] from his responsible position by some means or other.' Quoted by R. Storry, *The Double Patriots* (London, 1957), p. 150n.

12. Saionji–Harada Memoirs, Pt. vi, ch. 107 (18 November 1933). Admiral Okada (to Harada) 'We are annoyed by the young officers who are trying to entice the navy . . .' Quoted by Storry, p. 151n.

13. TSM Vol. 1, p. 156.

14. J. D. Potter, *Admiral of the Pacific* (London, 1965), p. 25.

15. Craigie, Japanese official or semi-official statements on the ratio, 27 January 1934 to 25 April 1934, FO 371/17597, [A3955].

16. Snow to Simon, 21 June 1933, FO 371/17158 [F4126].

17. Craigie, 9 January 1934, Foreign Office memorandum, FO 371/17596 [A1977].

18. Craigie, 9 January 1934, memorandum [A1977] above.

19. Report of a meeting between Vansittart, Stanhope, Orde and Craigie, 6 February 1934, and Simon, 10 February 1934, minute on this report, FO 371/17597 [A2060].

20. Craigie, 9 March 1934, minute, FO 371/17596 [A1938]; FRUS I 1934, p. 222.

21. FRUS I 1934, pp. 15–16, 221.

22. On other occasions the line taken was discussed. This appears not to have been the case at this meeting.

23. FRUS I 1934, pp. 224–7.

24. Notes of a meeting held in the prime minister's room, 26 February 1934, CAB 29/149.

25. FRUS I 1934, p. 222.

26. Record of a meeting between the prime minister and Mr Norman Davis, 5 March 1934, CAB 29/149.

27. Vice-Admiral Little and Mr Craigie, 12 April 1934, reports of a meeting with Mr Norman Davis and Mr Bingham, NCM (35) 2, CAB 29/148.

28. Craigie to Lindsay, 17 April 1934, FO 371/17597 [A2966].

29. Craigie to Lindsay, 17 April 1934, FO 371/17597 above.

30. Chief of naval staff, 23 March 1934, memorandum in preparation for the 1935 naval conference, NCM(35) 1, CAB 29/148.

31. Note of a meeting held at the Admiralty on 20 March 1934, FO 371/17596 [A2416].

32. Stanhope, 19 March 1934, minute, FO 371/17596 [A2176].

33. Meeting of cabinet committee on the naval conference 1935 (hereafter cited as NCM(35)), 16 April 1934, CAB 29/147.

34. NCM(35), first meeting 16 April 1934, above.

35. Orde and Randall, 13 April 1934, Anglo-Japanese Relations, FO Cornwall House, [F2109].

36. NCM(35) third meeting, 23 April 1934, CAB 29/147.

37. NCM(35) third meeting above, CAB 29/147.

38. See p. 53 above.

39. NCM(35) second meeting, 19 April 1934 and third meeting above, CAB 29/147.

40. Fisher, 19 April 1934, memorandum, Naval Conference 1935, NCM(35) 3, CAB 29/148.

41. Chief of naval staff, 29 May 1934, memorandum, NCM(35) 10, CAB 29/148; Chatfield to Warren Fisher, 4 June 1934, Chatfield papers.

42. Chancellor of the exchequer, 23 April 1934, NCM(35) 3 above, CAB 29/148.

43. Vansittart to Fisher (undated, but accompanying minute by Craigie dated 18 May 1934) FO 371/17597 [A4114].

44. Vansittart to Fisher, FO 371/17597 above.

45. Ministerial committee on disarmament (hereafter cited as DC(M)32) paper 100, 17 April 1934, CAB 27/510.

46. Prime minister, 25 April 1934, memorandum, Naval Conference 1935, NCM(35) 4, CAB 29/148.

47. *The Times*, 18 April 1934.

48. For details see chapter 5.

49. *The Times*, 25 April 1934.

50. Vansittart, 26 April 1934, minute, FO 371/17597 [A3955].

51. DC(M)32, 40th meeting, 1 May 1934, CAB 27/506.

52. Simon, 16 May 1934, minute, FO 371/17597 [A3955].

53. NCM(35) fourth meeting, 17 May 1934, CAB 29/147.

54. NCM(35) fourth meeting, 17 May 1934, CAB 29/147.

55. Foreign Office telegram to Dodd, 18 May 1934, NCM(35) 9 above.

56. Prime minister, 25 April 1935, memorandum, above NCM(35) 4, CAB 29/148.

57. Foreign Office, 23 May 1934, memorandum respecting Anglo-Japanese relations and the question of naval parity, NCM(35) 8, CAB 29/148.

NOTES TO CHAPTER 5

1. Pratt, 11 July 1933, League 'Cooperation' with China, FO 371/17128 [F4808]; C. Y. W. Meng, 'China goes to Geneva for Technical Assistance in Reconstruction Programme', *China Weekly Review*, 29 July 1933.

2. Annual Report of the National Economic Council 1935–36 (Nanking, March 1936), p. 4.

3. Appeal by the Chinese government: *Report of the commission of enquiry.* ([Lytton Report] Geneva, 1933) pp. 17–24.)

4. The boycotts had been instituted when the Manchurian crisis began in 1931. They continued with decreased intensity after the Tangku truce until the end of 1933.

5. F. V. Field, *American Participation in the China Consortium* (American Council Institute of Pacific Relations, 1931), pp. 165-6, 189.

6. Beale (Commercial counsellor, Shanghai) to Lampson, 24 April 1933, FO 371/17135 [F3997].

7. Lampson to Simon, 4 June 1933, FO 371/17124 [F3730].

8. Addis to Orde, 9 June 1933, FO 371/17108 [F3908].

9. Dorothy Borg, pp. 62–3. *The United States and the Far Eastern Crisis 1933–1938* (Cambridge Mass., 1964) (Hereafter cited as Borg, *Far Eastern Crisis 1933–1938*).

10. Harrison, 22 June 1933, minute, FO 371/17108 [F4129].

11. Simon to Lampson, 18 August 1933, FO 371/17108 [F4487].

12. Addis to Orde, 19 June 1933, FO 371/17108 [F4116].

13. Holman (Peking) to Simon, 19 June 1933, [F4129] above.

14. Orde, 23 June 1933, minute, [F4129] above.

15. Holman (Peking) to Simon, 19 June 1933, [F4129] above.

16. Pratt, 4 July 1933, The China Consortium, FO 371/17135 [F4411].

17. Pratt, 4 July 1933, memorandum, [F4411] above.

18. Orde, 10 July 1933, minute, [F4411] above.

19. Simon to Lampson, 4 July 1933, FO 371/17136 [F4548].

20. Pratt, 27 July 1933, minute, FO 371/17136 [F4779].

21. Simon to Lampson, 19 June 1933, FO 371/17136 [F4432].

22. Pratt, 14 July 1933, Foreign Office minute, FO 371/17136 [F4753].

23. Simon to Lampson, 4 July 1933, FO 371/17136 [F4548].

24. The Export Credits Guarantee Department provided credits for a maximum of three years to United Kingdom merchants only.

25. Pratt, 14 July 1933, minute [F4753] above.

26. Pratt, 14 July 1933, minute [F4753] above.

27. FRUS III 1933, p. 505–6.

28. Simon to Lampson, 11 August 1933, FO 371/17136 [F5350].

29. *Annual Report Economic Council 1935–36*, p. 4.

30. FRUS III 1933, p. 502.

31. Pratt, memorandum, League 'Cooperation' in China, 11 July 1933, FO 371/17128 [F4808].

32. Pratt, 6 June 1933, memorandum, FO 371/17127 [F3872].

33. Pratt, 6 June 1933, memorandum, [F4808] above.

34. Borg, *Far Eastern Crisis 1933–1938*, pp. 65–6; FRUS III 1933, pp. 503–4, 508–10.

35. Iriye, p. 87.

36. Ingram to Simon, 1 January 1934, FO 371/18142 [F1261].

37. Ingram to Simon, 1 January 1934, FO 371/18142 above.

38. Cadogan to Simon, 1 January 1935, FO 371/19325, [F1482].

39. *The Times*, 29 March 1934.

40. FRUS III 1934, p. 372.

41. Pratt, 8 May 1934, memorandum, FO 371/18090 [F2683].

42. Ingram to Simon, 1 March 1934, FO 371/18078 [F1933].
43. Cadogan to Simon, 30 April 1934, FO 371/18078 [F3858].
44. Cadogan to Simon, 6 March 1934, FO 371/18096 [F1339].
45. Wellesley, 12 March 1934, minute, [F1339] above.
46. *The Times*, 18 April 1934.
47. Reuters message, 19 April 1934, FO 371/18097 [F2204].
48. *Nichi Nichi*, 18 April 1934.
49. *The Times*, 19 April 1934.
50. *The Times*, 20 April 1934.
51. Lindley to Simon, 20 April 1934, FO 371/18097 [F2211].
52. Allen, 20 April 1934, minute, [F2211] above.
53. Orde, 20 April 1934, minute, [F2211] above.
54. Allen, 20 April 1934, minute, FO 371/18096 [F2193].
55. *The Times*, 20 April 1934.
56. *The Times*, 20 April 1934.
57. Orde, 20 April 1934, minute, [F2211] above.
58. Vansittart to secretary of state, 20 April 1934, [F2211] above.
59. Simon to Lindley, 23 April 1934, [F2211] above.
60. D. C. Watt, *Personalities and Policies* (London, 1965), p. 89, suggests that the British reaction was a 'strong' one. This does not seem to have been the impression the government intended to convey.
61. Borg, *Far Eastern Crisis 1933–1938*, pp. 78–9 gives an account of these events based on the American documents.
62. FRUS III 1934, pp. 122–3.
63. FRUS III 1934, pp. 126–7.
64. Randall, 20 April 1934, minute, FO 371/18097 [F2313].
65. Orde, 21 April 1934, minute, [F2313] above.
66. *Hansard's Parliamentary Debates*, fifth series, Vol. 288, 23 April 1934, columns 1363–5.
67. *The Times*, 23 April 1934.
68. Simon to Cadogan, 23 April 1934, FO 371/18097 [F2306].
69. Seymour (private secretary) 24 April 1934, note, FO 371/18097 [F2430].
70. FRUS III 1934, pp. 132–3.
71. Wellesley, 24 April 1934, minute, FO 371/18097 [F2430].
72. Simon, 25 April 1934, minute [F2430] above.
73. Vansittart, 24 April 1934, minute, [F2430] above.
74. Wellesley, 25 April 1934, [F2430] above.
75. FRUS III 1934, p. 166.

76. Borg, *Far Eastern Crisis 1933–1938*, p. 79.

77. Lindsay to Simon, 24 April 1934, FO 371/18097 [F2316].

78. Simon to Lindsay, 25 April 1934, FO 371/18097 [F2136].

79. Simon to Lindsay, 27 April 1934, FO 371/18097 [F2339].

80. Cabinet 17, 25 April 1934, conclusion 1.

81. Lindley to Simon, 25 April 1934, FO 371/18097 [F2325].

82. Lindley to Simon, 25 April 1934, FO 371/18097 [F2326].

83. Lindley to Simon, 26 April 1934, FO 371/18097 [F2350].

84. *The Times*, 26 April 1934.

85. Simon to Lindley (telegrams 81 and 82), 27 April 1934, FO 371/18097 [F2351].

86. Lindley to Simon, 26 April 1934, [F2351] above.

87. Lindley to Simon, 27 April 1934, FO 371/18097 [F2375].

88. Allen and Randall, 27 April 1934, minute, [F2375] above.

89. Lindley to Simon, 28 April 1934, FO 371/18097 [F2418].

90. Wellesley, 30 April 1934, minute, [F2418] above.

91. Lindsay to Simon, 4 May 1934, FO 371/18097 [F2579].

92. Simon to Lindley, 23 April 1934, FO 371/18097 [F2211]. See pages 72–4 for the background to this telegram.

93. *Hansard's Parliamentary Debates*, fifth series, Vol. 288, 30 April 1934, column 13.

94. Randall, 1 and 3 May 1934, minutes, FO 371/18097 [F2481].

95. FRUS III 1934, p. 168.

96. *Hansard*, 30 April 1934, column 13 above.

97. CAB 27/506, DC(M) 32, 40th meeting, 1 May 1934.

98. FRUS III 1934, p. 163; Borg, *Far Eastern Crisis 1933–1938*, p. 80.

99. J. C. Grew, *Ten Years in Japan* (London, 1944), Diary entry, 29 April 1934, p. 123.

100. *The Times*, 2 May 1934.

101. Stanhope, 9 May 1934, minute, FO 371/18097 [F2560].

102. Allen, 4 May 1934, minute, [F2560] above.

103. *The Times*, 2 May 1934.

104. Dodd to Simon, 2 May 1934, FO 371/18097 [F2500].

105. *The Times*, 2 May 1934.

106. Simon to Dodd, 4 May 1934, [F2500] above.

107. Dodd to Simon, 7 May 1934, FO 371/18097 [F2606].

108. *Hansard's Parliamentary Debates*, fifth series, Vol. 289, 7 May 1934, columns 710–12.

109. Speech by Lord Ponsonby of Shulbrede, *Hansard's Parliamentary Debates*, fifth series, House of Lords, Vol. 92, columns 21–34.

110. *Hansard's Parliamentary Debates*, fifth series, Vol. 289, 18 May 1934, columns 2061–2.

111. Charles (Moscow) to Simon, 8 May 1934, FO 371/18098 [F2791].

112. Allen and Randall, 20 April 1934, minutes, FO 371/18096 [F2193]; Randall, 20 April 1934, FO 371/18097 [F2211]; Pratt, 24 April 1934, FO 371/18097 [F2339]; Lindley to Simon, 23 April 1934, FO 371/18097 [F2255]; Cabinet 17, 25 April 1934, conclusion 1.

113. Harcourt Smith, 19 April 1934, minute, FO 371/18096 [F2193].

114. Lindley to Simon, 26 April 1934, FO 371/18097 [F2351].

115. Wellesley, 8 May 1934, minute, FO 371/18097 [F2606].

116. Lindley to Simon, 27 April 1934, FO 371/18098 [F3010].

117. Iriye, Japanese Imperialism and Aggression, essay in *The Origins of the Second World War*, E. M. Robertson (ed.), (London, 1971), p. 251.

118. FRUS III 1934, p. 161.

119. Cadogan to Simon, 26 April 1934, FO 371/18097 [F2378].

120. Chinese minister, 7 May 1934, *Aide-mémoire*, FO 371/1809 [F3029].

121. Randall, 11 May 1934, minute, FO 371/18098 [F2849].

122. Cadogan to Simon, 19 May 1934, FO 371/18101 [F2983].

123. Phillips (Canton) to Simon, 26 July 1934, FO 371/18082.

124. Blunt (Nanking) to Simon, 17 October 1934, FO 371/18084 [F6978].

125. *The Times*, 19 April 1934.

126. Pratt, 26 April 1934, memorandum, FO 371/18098 [F2353].

127. Report of discussion held at the Board of Trade, 7 May 1934, FO 371/18100 [F2806].

128. NCM(35), 4th meeting 17 May 1934, CAB 29/147. See chapter 4 pp. 57–9 for a fuller treatment of this episode.

129. Conversation between head of far east department and Atherton and Millard of United States embassy, 20 April 1934, FO 371/18100 [F2294].

130. Dodd to Simon, 9 May 1934, FO 371/18099 [F3508].

131. Dodd to Simon, 9 May 1934, [F3508] above.

NOTES TO CHAPTER 6

1. French reply to a *Note Verbale* communicated to the French government by Lord Tyrrell on 28 March 1934, DC(M) 32, 100, 17 April 1934, CAB 27/510.

2. Vansittart, 6 April, The Future of Germany, CP 104(34), CAB 24/248; Secretaries of State for war, and air and first lord of the Admiralty, 20 April

1934, Imperial Defence Policy, CP 113(34), CAB 24/249; Vansittart, 23 April 1934, memorandum, CP 116(34), CAB 24/249.

3. See chapter 3, above, pp. 36, 40–1.

4. Cabinet 19, 2 May 1934, conclusion 2.

5. Ministerial Committee on Disarmament (hereafter referred to as DC(M)32), 41st meeting, 3 May 1934, CAB 16/110.

6. Sir Maurice Hankey had been secretary to the C.I.D. since 1912, and became secretary to the cabinet in 1919. He was knighted in 1916.

7. DC(M)32, 41st meeting above, CAB 16/110.

8. Cabinet 9, 14 March 1934, conclusion 13.

9. DC(M)32, 41st meeting above, CAB 16/110.

10. S. Roskill, *Hankey, Man of Secrets* Vol. II, p. 409, Hankey to Beatty, 10 July, 1925.

11. Note by the chancellor of the exchequer on the report of the defence requirements committee, 20 June 1934, DCM(32), 120, CAB 27/511.

12. Hankey to prime minister, 3 August 1934, CAB 21/398.

13. Hankey to Monsell, 22 June 1934, Hankey papers CAB 63/49.

14. Hankey to prime minister, 22 June 1934, Hankey papers CAB 63/49.

15. Hankey, 22 June 1934, Secret memorandum for the prime minister, Hankey papers, CAB 63/49.

16. Hankey to prime minister, 3 August 1934, Hankey papers, CAB 63/49.

17. DC(M)32, 50th meeting 25 June 1934, CAB 16/110.

18. DC(M)32, 50th meeting above, CAB 16/110.

19. With the exception of Hoare all those whom Hankey had lobbied opposed Chamberlain and used his actual arguments. See, for example, Baldwin's contribution at the 50th meeting above.

20. DC(M)32, 51st meeting, 26 June 1934, CAB 16/110.

21. Cabinet 31, 31 July 1934, conclusion 1.

22. Naval Conference, Conversations with representative of USA, hereafter cited as NC USA; see 4th meeting, 27 June 1934, CAB 29/149.

23. FRUS I 1934, pp. 272–4; see also Borg, *Far Eastern Crisis 1933–1938*, p. 104 for discussion of American reaction.

24. FRUS I 1934, p. 272.

25. FRUS I 1934, p. 284.

26. MacDonald to Roosevelt, 28 June 1934. Baldwin papers Vol. 131.

27. Craigie, 28 June 1934, minute, FO 371/17598 [A5834].

28. Craigie, 28 June 1934, minute, FO 371/17598 [A5428].

29. Hankey, 2 July 1934, Naval Conference 1935, note, NCM(35) 14, CAB 29/148.

30. Fisher to Chatfield, 11 July 1934, Baldwin papers, Vol. 131.

31. Chatfield to Fisher, 16 July 1934, Baldwin papers, Vol. 131.

32. Cabinet 31, 31 July 1934, conclusion 1.

33. Bruce to Hankey, 14 December 1933, Hankey papers, CAB 63/70.

34. Hankey to Bruce, 6 February 1934, Hankey papers, CAB 63/70.

35. Parr to Hankey, 18 July 1934, Hankey papers, CAB 63/70.

36. Diary, Outline of speech to be delivered in South Africa, Hankey papers, CAB 63/68.

37. Hankey to lord president, 30 July 1934, Hankey papers, CAB 63/66; Hankey to prime minister, 3 August 1934, CAB 21/398.

38. Hankey, *aide-mémoire* enclosed in a letter to lord president, 30 July 1934, Hankey papers, CAB 63/66.

39. Hankey to lord president, 30 July 1934, Hankey papers, CAB 63/66.

40. Hankey to prime minister, 3 August 1934, CAB 21/398.

41. Hankey to Baldwin, 23 August 1934, Baldwin papers, Vol. 1. In this Hankey said of Fisher, 'I don't think he is a fit man or that his judgment is at its best.' The official letter written at the same time is in Hankey papers, Hankey to lord president, 23 August, 1934, CAB 63/66.

42. TSM, Vol. 1, p. 137.

43. TSM, Vol. 1, p. 137.

44. Clive to Simon, 5 July 1934, FO 371/18181 [F4798].

45. Craigie, 5 July 1934, minute, FO 371/17852 [A5306]. This minute appeared on the telegram dated 3 July in which the conversation was first described.

46. Osborne to Simon, 27 June 1934, FO 371/18169 [F4270].

47. Craigie, 23 August 1934, minute, FO 371/17599 [A7695].

48. Simon to Vansittart, 20 August 1934, [A7695] above.

49. TSM, Vol. 1, p. 157. The policy was decided on 7 September 1934.

50. Craigie, 23 August 1934, minute, [A7695] above.

51. Saionji–Harada memoirs (7 September 1934). In reply to a question about Japan's conditions for the termination of the treaties, Hirota said, 'We must terminate them, no matter how much the powers agree to our proposals.' Quoted by J. B. Crowley, *Japan's Quest for Autonomy* (Princeton, N.J., 1966), p. 199.

52. Orde, 28 August 1934, minute, [A7695] above.

53. Vansittart to secretary of state, 29 August 1934, [A7695] above.

54. Chamberlain to Simon, 1 September 1934, Simon papers.

55. See above p. 97.

56. *The Times*, 30 August 1934.

57. Chamberlain to Simon, 1 September 1934, above.

58. Chamberlain was referring to the undertaking that no increase in Japan's ratio would be agreed by either side without first consulting the other.

59. Comments on Mr Neville Chamberlain's proposals, memorandum, Orde, 4 September 1934, [F6189], FO Cornwall House.

60. The Amau statement of 17 April 1934. See above, Chapter 5 pp. 71–2.

61. Simon to Chamberlain, 7 September 1934, Simon papers.

62. Cabinet 32, 25 September 1934, conclusion 4.

63. Cabinet 32, 25 September 1934, above.

64. Hankey to lord president, 23 August 1934, Hankey papers, CAB 63/66. See above p. 96.

65. Cabinet 32, 25 September 1934, above.

66. Clive to Simon, 29 September 1934, FO 371/18184 [F5846].

67. Sainoji–Harada Memoirs, 7 September 1934, quoted by Crowley, p. 199.

68. Far East department, 1 October 1934, memorandum, [F6190], FO Cornwall House.

69. Pratt, 3 October 1934, China Policy and the proposed Anglo-Japanese pact, [F6191], FO Cornwall House.

70. Craigie, 3 October 1934, Proposed Non-Aggression Pact with Japan, [F6191], FO Cornwall House.

71. Craigie, 5 October 1934, Non-aggression Pact with Japan, [F6192], FO Cornwall House; Craigie, 5 October 1934, minute, FO 371/18184, [F6192].

72. Simon to Clive, 8 October 1934, NCM(35) 24, CAB 29/148.

73. Matsudaira's father, Marquis Katamori Matsudaira, had been lord of Aizu. His daughter was married to Prince Chichibu, younger brother of emperor Hirohito.

74. Clive to Simon, 5 October 1934, FO 371/18184 [F5996].

75. Clive to Simon, 12 October 1934, FO 371/18195 [F6101].

76. The chancellor of the exchequer and the secretary of state for foreign affairs, 16 October 1934, The Future of Anglo-Japanese Relations, CP 223(34), CAB 24/250.

77. Cabinet 35, 17 October 1934, Conclusion 7.

78. Simon to Clive, 30 October 1934, FO 371/18184 [F6740].

79. Simon to Clive, 19 November 1934, NCM(35) 31, CAB 29/148.

80. In 1933, the Four Power treaty of 1922 had become terminable at a year's notice by any one of the parties to the treaty.

81. *The Times*, 17 November 1934, announcing the arrival of Yoshida, described him as 'Japanese ambassador at large' making a personal visit to the Japanese ambassador in London. Yoshida does not appear to have been officially entertained and was not among the guests at the functions associated with the naval talks.

82. Cabinet 41, 21 November 1934, conclusion 5.

83. Simon to Clive, 21 November 1934, NCM(35) 32, CAB 29/148.

84. Borg, *Far Eastern Crisis 1933–1938*, p. 108; Watt, p. 95.

85. Wigram to Latham, 3 January 1935, Latham papers, MS 1009, Series A, general correspondence.

86. Vansittart, 9 February 1935, minute, FO 371/18160 [F7373].

87. Watt, p. 98.

88. Hankey to prime minister, 23 November 1934, Baldwin papers, Vol. I.; Hankey to Baldwin, 17 November 1934, Baldwin papers, Vol. I.

89. Latham to Pearce, 19 December 1934, Latham papers, MS 1009, Series A, general correspondence.

90. Pearce to Latham, 21 December 1934, Latham papers above.

91. Hankey to prime minister, 23 November 1934, Baldwin papers, above; M. P. Lissington, *New Zealand and Japan 1900–1941* (Wellington, New Zealand, 1972), pp. 125–35.

92. NCM(35), 6th meeting, 16 October 1934, CAB 29/147.

93. Naval conference, Japan [hereafter cited as NC(J)], 1st meeting, 23 October 1934, CAB 29/149.

94. NC(J), 2nd and 3rd meetings, 26 October 1934, CAB 29/149.

95. Simon to Clive, 30 October 1934, FO 371/18184 [F6470].

96. NC(J), 4th and 5th meetings, 7 November 1934, CAB 29/149.

97. Craigie, 15 November 1934, minute, FO 371/17601 [A9224].

98. Wigram to Latham, 3 January 1935, Latham papers, MS 1009, Series A, general correspondence.

99. NC(USA), 7th meeting,. 14 November 1934, CAB 29/149; Craigie, 17 November 1934, FO 371/17601 [A9264]. At Craigie's insistence, Simon had, on 13 November, told Davis of the approach to Matsudaira. Subsequently Davis appears to have suggested that Simon indicated that Craigie should have informed Davis of the conversation. Simon indignantly repudiated the suggestion that he might criticise a Foreign Office official in front of a foreigner. Simon had not, however, made a record of the original conversation. Davis's official and quite uncritical account of it is in FRUS I 1934, p. 328.

100. Simon to Clive, 19 November 1934, NCM(35) 31, CAB 29/148.

101. Simon to Clive, 21 November 1934, NCM(35) 32, CAB 29/148.

102. Points for discussion at the 9th meeting of the ministerial committee, circulated by direction of the secretary of state for foreign affairs, 26 November 1934, NCM(35) 33, CAB 29/148.

103. NCM(35), 9th meeting, 27 November 1934, CAB 29/148.

104. Craigie, 28 November 1934, Foreign Office minute, FO 371/17602 [A9682].

105. Record of a conversation between Secretary of state for foreign affairs and Japanese ambassador, 6 December 1934, NCM(35) 38, CAB 29/148.

106. FRUS I 1934, p. 399.

107. *The Times*, 20 December 1934.

108. TSM Vol. I, p. 158.

109. Simon, Diary, 19 December 1934, Simon papers.

110. Clive to Simon, 8 December 1934, FO 371/17602 [A9824].

111. Conversation between Matsudaira and Craigie, 29 December 1934, NCM(35) 43, CAB 29/148.

112. Survey of the present position of naval conversations and recommendations as to future procedure, 17 January 1935, NCM(35) 46, CAB 29/148.

113. Cabinet 12, 27 February 1935, conclusion 3.

114. Craigie, 4 March 1934, Foreign Office minute, FO 371/18732 [A2968].

115. Clive to Eden, 28 March 1935, FO 371/18732 [A2932].

NOTES TO CHAPTER 7

1. Federation of British Industries, *Report of Mission to the Far East, August–November 1934* (London, 1934).

2. In March 1932, the Manchukuo minister of foreign affairs had declared that the 'open door' would be maintained.

3. Sir Edward Crowe to Randall, 31 August 1933, FO 371/17112 [F5850].

4. Relton (Department of Overseas Trade) to Randall, 9 May 1934, FO 371/18109 [F2689]. The Manchukuo government held one-fifth of the shares, two-fifths were in the hands of the South Manchurian Railway company, a Japanese government agency, and the remainder were held by the Mitsui and Mitsubishi interests and the Nippon and Ogura Oil Companies.

5. Snow to Simon, 20 November 1933, FO 371/17113 [F7846]. Japan's share of the trade increased from 40 to 56 per cent in the same period. China's share dropped from 25 to 13 per cent. Britain's share had risen from a mere 2 per cent to 3 per cent.

6. Butler (consul-general Mukden) to Department of Overseas Trade, 30 April 1934, FO 371/18114 [F3483].

7. Simon to Cadogan, 12 June 1934, FO 371/18100 [F3542].

8. Snow to Orde, 27 July 1933, FO 371/17141 [F5756].

9. Randall to Sir Edward Crowe, 7 September 1933, FO 371/17112 [F5805].

10. Sir Edward Crowe to Orde, 21 June 1934, FO 371/18114 [F3841].

11. After the dismissal of Aglen, inspector general of the Chinese maritime customs, in 1925, Edwardes was, for a time, the acting inspector general. He appears to have been unsatisfactory and displeased the Chinese government

by continuing policies which had caused Aglen's dismissal. He resigned in 1929, complaining of intrigues against him. Though he forfeited his pension, he received considerable compensation from the Chinese government, which was understandably displeased when he found employment with the Manchukuo government.

12. Snow to Simon, 18 July 1933, FO 371/17140 [F5534].

13. Randall, 26 June 1934, minute, FO 371/18114 [F3841].

14. Crowe to Orde, 21 June 1934, [F3841] above. This letter gives the background to the choices finally made. MacGowan was only prepared to lead an official government mission. Crowe suggested unkindly that this was because he wanted a peerage. Piggot, whose name was Julian Ito Piggott, had been born in Japan in 1888. His father, an English barrister, was an adviser to Count Ito Hirobumi while Japan's constitution was being drafted. The Piggott family left Japan in 1891, but kept in touch with Japanese friends. F. S. G. Piggott, brother of Julian Piggott, became British military attaché in Tokyo in 1936. See F. S. G. Piggott, *Broken Thread* (Aldershot, 1950).

15. *The Times*, 10 August 1934.

16. Wellesley to Lord Cecil, 31 July 1934, FO 371/18114 [F4691].

17. Clive to Simon, 8 August 1934, FO 371/18114 [F4835]; Crowe to Orde, 9 August 1934, FO 371/18114 [F4939].

18. Quo Tai-chi to Crowe, 14 August 1934, FO 371/18115 [F5032].

19. Quo Tai-chi to Orde, 1 September 1934, FO 371/18115 [F5360].

20. Clive to Simon, 16 August 1934, FO 371/18115 [F5594].

21. Collier (head of northern department), 28 December 1934, minute, FO 371/18306 [N7104].

22. Clive to Simon, 19 September 1934, FO 371/18115 [F5652].

23. Simon to Clive, 19 September 1934, [F5652] above.

24. Cadogan to Simon, 17 September 1934, FO 371/18115 [F6230].

25. Clive to Simon, 9 October 1934, FO 371/18115 [F6523].

26. Butler to Simon, 19 October 1934, FO 371/18116 [F6595].

27. Clive to Simon, 9 October 1934, FO 371/18115 [F6524].

28. Sansom to Crowe, 12 October 1934, FO 371/18184 [F6577].

29. Orde, minute, 5 November 1934, [F6577] above. The oil issue with Manchukuo and Japan persisted and at this time the Foreign Office favoured economic retaliation against Japan and Manchukuo by the British and American oil companies withholding supplies. The Board of Trade feared this would ruin Anglo-Japanese relations. See Harcourt Smith, 18 September 1934, FO 371/18190 [F5694], cabinet 41, 21 November 1934, conclusion 4. In any event, the United States government refused to cooperate in the Foreign Office plan and the oil monopoly was established in 1935.

30. Chamberlain, 19 November 1934, minute, chancellor of exchequer's papers, T172/1831.

31. Fisher, 17 November 1934, minute and notes on [6577] above. Edwardes to Fisher, 26 November 1934, chancellor of exchequer's papers, T172/1831. It seems highly irregular that a private letter to a head of department should have been passed by the head of another department to a complete outsider for analysis.

32. Clive to Simon, 9 October 1934, FO 371/18115 [F6521]; Clive to Simon, 9 October 1934, FO 371/18115 [F5624].

33. Federation of British Industries Report of Mission to the Far East, above.

34. Crowe to Orde, 9 November 1934, FO 371/18116 [F6746].

35. Harcourt Smith, 4 January 1935, minute, FO 371/18116 [F7561].

36. Sansom to Crowe, 25 October 1934, FO 371/18116 [F7402]; Butler to Cadogan, 19 October 1934, FO 371/19277 [F62].

37. Locock to Wilson, 24 November 1934, FO 371/18116, [F7054].

38. Locock to Wilson, 24 November 1934, [F7054] above.

39. Wellesley, 11 December 1934, minute, [F7054] above.

40. Orde, 14 December 1934, Foreign Office minute, FO 371/18116, [F7461].

41. Seligman is reported as saying that as between standing in with USA and Japan, he would prefer the latter. Fisher suggested that Canadian opinion had changed since the time of the abrogation of the Anglo-Japanese alliance. [F7461] above.

42. Orde, 14 December 1934, Foreign Office minute, [F7461] above.

43. Clive to Simon, 22 December 1934, FO 371/18116 [F7590].

44. Allen, 3 January 1935, minute, FO 371/18116 [F7561].

45. Note by Mr Sansom respecting the economic conditions in Japan at the end of 1934, 21 January 1935, FO 371/19361 [F1116].

46. Orde, 2 January 1935, minute, FO 371/18116 [F7054].

47. Vansittart, 3 January 1934, minute [F7054] above.

48. Boothby to Eden, 6 November 1934, FO 371/18305 [N6328]; N. Thompson, *The Anti-Appeasers* (Oxford, 1971), p. 62.

49. Simon to Charles, 9 November 1934, FO 371/18305 [N6462].

50. Soviet ambassador conversation, 13 December 1934, FO 371/18305 [N6953]; Soviet ambassador conversation, 19 December 1934, FO 371/18035 [N7104].

51. Soviet ambassador conversation, 13 December 1934 [N6953] above.

52. Collier, 28 December 1934, minute, FO 371/18305 [N7104].

53. Soviet ambassador conversation, 27 December 1934, FO 371/18036 [N7155].

54. Orde, 8 January 1935, minute, FO 371/19277 [F132].

55. The papers became CP 8(35), 11 January 1935, and CP 9(35), 4 January 1935, CAB 24/253. They were considered in cabinet on 16 January 1935. Cabinet 4, conclusion 5.

56. President of the Board of Trade, 4 January 1935, memorandum introducing CP 9(35), CAB 24/253.

57. Locock to Wilson, 10 December 1934, CP 9(35) above CAB 24/253.

58. Secretary of state for foreign affairs, 11 January 1935, note introducing CP 8(35), CAB 24/253.

59. Sansom, 29 October 1934, memorandum by Mr Sansom respecting Anglo-Japanese relations, enclosure in CP 8(35), CAB 24/253.

60. Sansom, memorandum in CP 8(35) above, CAB 24/253.

61. Orde, 7 January 1935. The political Aspects of Trade Rivalry or Co-operation with Japan in China, CP 8(35), CAB 24/253.

62. Fisher, 21 January 1935, memorandum for the chancellor of the exchequer, chancellor of exchequer's papers, T172/1831.

63. Cabinet 35, 17 October 1934, conclusion 7.

64. Fergusson, 15 January 1935, note for the chancellor of the exchequer, chancellor of the exchequer's papers, T172/1831.

65. Edwardes, 14 January 1934, note, chancellor of exchequer's papers, T172/1831.

66. Fergusson, 15 January 1935, T172/1831 above.

67. China was sixteenth when listed with nations in order of their value as customers of Britain.

68. Cabinet 4, 16 January 1935, conclusion 5.

69. Cabinet 5, 23 January 1935, conclusion 2.

70. Orde to Cadogan and to Clive, 22 February 1935, FO 371/19356 [F1026].

NOTES TO CHAPTER 8

1. From 1921–31, the world price of silver was low, China's exports were competitive, China was relatively prosperous and large stocks of silver were built up. When in 1931, the pound sterling, yen and rupee left gold, the price of silver rose in terms of sterling, China's exports lost their price advantage and contracted, credit in China was restricted and silver was exported to make up the unfavourable balance. The American silver policy aggravated an already difficult situation.

2. Allan Seymour Everest, *Morgenthau, The New Deal and Silver* (New York, 1940), pp. 101–7, explains the effect of the American silver policy on China. Also Borg, *Far Eastern Crisis 1933–1938*, pp. 121–2.

3. FRUS III 1934, pp. 424, 428, 438, 440, 442; *The Times*, 16 October 1934; Cadogan to Simon, 12 December 1934, FO 371/18137 [F7390].

4. Maze to the Chinese minister of finance, 14 September 1934, Maze papers, Vol. 10. This comment is written at a later date on the copy of this letter.

5. Hopkins to governor of the Bank of England, 15 October 1934, T160, Box 544, F13963.

6. *Hansard's Parliamentary Debates*, fifth series, Vol. 292, 19 July 1934, column 1260.

7. Conversation between Sir John Pratt and Sir Frederick Maze, 2 November 1934, FO 371/18079 [F6531].

8. Simon to Cadogan, 14 November 1934, FO 371/18137 [F6760]; Cadogan to Simon, 30 November 1934, FO 371/18137 [F7148]; Cadogan to Simon, 12 December 1934, FO 371/18137 [F7390].

9. Pratt, 19 December 1934, FO 371/18138 [F7483].

10. Fergusson to Seymour, 12 December 1934, FO 371/18138 [F7523]. The committee eventually was made up of representatives from the Treasury, India Office, Colonial Office, Department of Overseas Trade, Foreign Office and Bank of England.

11. Borg, *Far Eastern Crisis 1933–1938*, pp. 122–4.

12. Cadogan to Simon, 27 December 1934, FO 371/18138 [F7681].

13. Cadogan to Simon, 31 December 1934, FO 371/19238 [F6].

14. China committee report, 17 January 1935, FO 371/19238 [F479]. Sassoon's made their request to the Bank of England on 28 December 1934. The committee met on 2 January 1935.

15. Ashton Gwatkin, 1 January 1935, Foreign Office minute, FO 371/19238 [F50].

16. Pratt, 2 January 1935, minute, FO 371/19238 [F9]; China committee report, 17 January 1935, above.

17. See p. 133–4.

18. Pratt, 11 January 1935, minute, FO 371/19283 [F233]; Simon to Cadogan, 19 January 1935, FO 371/19238 [F458].

19. President of the Board of Trade, 4 January 1935, Anglo-Japanese Relations, CP 9(35), CAB 24/253.

20. Fergusson, 15 January 1935, Note for the chancellor of the exchequer, chancellor of exchequer's papers, T172/1831.

21. Secretary of state for foreign affairs, 11 January 1935, introductory note for CP 8(35), CAB 24/253.

22 Ashton Gwatkin and Collier, 7 January 1935, Foreign Office memorandum, FO 371/19283 [F192].

23. Cabinet 4, 16 January 1935, conclusion 5.

24. Cabinet 5, 23 January 1935, conclusion 2.

25. Cabinet 9, 13 February 1935, conclusion 3. The committee for political

and economic relations with Japan (PEJ) was made up of the prime minister, chancellor, foreign secretary, president of Board of Trade, and secretary of state for war.

26. Simon, 21 January 1935, Anglo-Japanese Relations, Simon papers, FO 800/290.

27. Fisher, 21 January 1935, memorandum for the chancellor of the exchequer, chancellor of the exchequer's papers, T172/1831.

28. The conversation took place at a farewell luncheon for Admiral Yamamoto, the purpose of which, according to Fisher, was to make sure that Yamamoto was 'fully seized' of Britain's needs and difficulties.

29. Fisher, 21 January 1935, memorandum above, T172/1831.

30. Chancellor of the exchequer, 8 February 1935, Note on the financial and economic position of China, CP 35(35), CAB 24/253.

31. Fisher, 8 February 1935, memorandum forming part of CP 35(35), CAB 253.

32. Orde, 9 February 1935, minute, FO 371/19239 [F975].

33. Simon to Cadogan, 22 February 1935, FO 371/19239 [F1017].

34. Clive to Simon, 7 February 1935, FO 371/19283 [F853].

35. Pratt, 14 February 1935, memorandum, FO 371/19239 [F1017].

36. Foreign Office telegrams for Washington, Peking and Tokyo, 22 February 1935, [F1017] above.

37. Wellesley to Lindsay, 12 March 1935, FO 371/19287 [F1659].

38. Clive to Simon, 26 February 1935, FO 371/19239 [F1291].

39. FRUS III 1935, p. 533.

40. Borg, *Far Eastern Crisis 1933–1938*, pp. 125–8.

41. FRUS III 1935, p. 550.

42. Lindsay to Simon, 1 March 1935, and minutes on this telegram, FO 371/19239 [F1443].

43. Simon to Cadogan, 4 March 1935, FO 371/19239 [F1364].

44. Cadogan to Simon, 18 March 1935, FO 371/19239 [F1823].

45. Cadogan to Simon, 20 March 1935, FO 371/19240 [F1888].

46. Arthur N. Young, *China's Nation Building Effort, 1927–1937* (Stanford, 1971), p. 230. Young, an American, was a financial adviser to Chiang Kai-shek's government at this time. He says that cooperation with Japan in this matter was deemed 'unadvisable' by the government.

47. Pratt, 22 March 1935, minute, FO 371/19240 [F1888].

48. Chaplin, 19 September 1935, minute, FO 371/19244 [F5932].

49. Fisher to chancellor of the exchequer, 28 March 1935, communicated by Treasury to Foreign Office, April 1935, FO 371/19240 [F2384].

50. Cadogan to Orde, 25 July 1935, FO 371/19244 [F5932].

51. Simon to Cadogan, 5 April 1935, FO 371/19240 [F2280].

52. Cadogan to Simon, 31 May 1935, FO 371/19241 [F3562].

53. Wellesley, 18 April 1935, minute, FO 371/19240 [F2504].

54. Pratt, 15 May 1935, minute, FO 371/19241 [F2998].

55. Board of Trade to far east department, 7 May 1934, Notes on an informal discussion relating to trade in China, FO 371/18100 [F2806].

56. Sir Harry MacGowan (chairman), 18 July 1934, Report to the president of the Board of Trade; China, FO 371/18101 [F4469]. The other members of the committee were Sir Arthur Balfour, O. J. Barnes, D. G. M. Bernard, Sir Hugo Cunliffe-Owen, Sir Richard Holt, Andrew Agnew, J. Hanbury Williams, L. B. Lee, Colin C. Scott.

57. Crowe to Orde, 7 September 1934, FO 371/18101 [F5438].

58. Pratt, undated minute October 1934, Notes on Mr Beale's draft memorandum, FO 371/18102 [F6337].

59. Simon to Orde, 18 April 1935, FO 371/19287 [F2870].

60. Orde to Crowe, 25 October 1934, FO 371/18101 [F6337].

61. Orde to Cadogan, 21 August 1935, FO 371/19287 [F4447].

62. W. J. Keswick to Runciman, 7 September 1934, FO 371/18102 [F7403].

63. Cadogan to Vansittart, 21 February 1935, FO 371/19287 [F1623].

64. Pratt, 14 March 1935, minute, [F1623] above.

65. Orde, undated minute March 1935, [F1623] above.

66. Sir Archibald Rose, Sir George Macdonough, W. J. Keswick, G. W. Swire, 3 April 1935, Note presented to the chancellor of the exchequer, FO 371/19287 [F2600].

67. Crowe to Orde, 30 April 1935, FO 371/19287 [F2799].

68. Randall, 14 May 1935, minute of conversation with Mr Archibald Rose, FO 371/19287 [F3444].

69. President of the Board of Trade, 13 May 1935, circulating a memorandum, British Interests in the Far East in Relation to the Crisis in China, PEJ(35)3, CAB 27/596; Louis, pp. 227–9. Louis lists the signatories of this memorandum.

70. Mounsey, 15 May 1935, minute on [F3444] above; Cadogan to Orde, 31 May 1935, FO 371/19287 [F4447].

71. Simon to Orde, 18 April 1935, [F2870] above.

72. Chancellor of the Exchequer and President of the Board of Trade, 3 May 1935, Further note on the financial and economic position in China, PEJ(35)2, CAB 27/596.

73. Vansittart, 16 May 1935, minute [F3444] above.

74. Cadogan to Orde, 31 May 1935, [F4447] above.

75. PEJ(35) second meeting, 14 May 1935, CAB 27/596.

76. Orde to Cadogan, 21 August 1935, [F4447] above.

77. Clive to Simon, 8 May 1935, FO 371/19290 [F2920]. The American and French governments were consulted and it was decided that the status of all legations should be raised. The announcement was made on 18 May 1935.

78. Simon to Cadogan, 6 June 1935, FO 371/19241 [F3666]; Vansittart, 6 June 1935, minute, [F3666] above. The post of chief economic adviser was one of the principal posts in the civil service. In 1924 Leith Ross became adviser to the government on financial relations between Britain and foreign countries. He was the chief permanent official in the United Kingdom delegation at the two Hague conferences of 1929 and 1930, of the London conference of 1930 and the Lausanne conference of 1931. Since the economic crisis in 1931 he had been chief adviser to the government on questions of foreign exchange, currency and foreign loans. He travelled to the U.S.A. with the prime minister in 1933 and was one of the chief advisers to the government at the world economic conference in London in 1933. He represented the government in the financial negotiations with the German and Italian governments in 1934. Leith Ross took a prominent part in the work of the economic committee of the League of Nations.

NOTES TO CHAPTER 9

1. *New York Times*, 27 November 1935.

2. Both these men were to stay in China. Hall Patch became financial counsellor to the embassies in Peking and Tokyo and Rogers was asked by T. V. Soong to assist with Central Bank reform. See chapter 12.

3. Cadogan to Hoare, 11 June 1935, FO 371/19242 [F3810].

4. Deputation to meet Leith Ross, 17 July 1935, Manchester Chamber of Commerce papers, Vol. 25.

5. Orde to Cadogan, 26 July 1935, FO 371/19243 [F4699]. This deputation was led by Sir Harry MacGowan, chairman of ICI and the most energetic speaker appears to have been General Woodruffe, chairman of the Peking Syndicate which was deeply involved in mining and railways in China.

6. Turner (Reuters London) to Maze, 29 July 1935, Maze papers Vol. 11.

7. Morgenthau to Stamp, 9 July 1935, T160/Box 611, F14233/1, Borg, *Far Eastern Crisis 1933–1938*, pp. 130–1.

8. Clive to Wellesley, 6 July 1935, FO 371/19243 [F4890].

9. Clive to Hoare, 9 July 1935, FO 371/19242 [F4342].

10. Leith Ross, 31 July 1935, Secret memo for Sir R. Hopkins and chancellor of the exchequer, FO 371/19243 [F5081].

11. Chamberlain, 31 July 1935, minute, [F5081] above.

12. Hoare 10 August 1935, minute, [F5081] above.

13. Pratt, 20 August 1935, minute, FO 371/19243 [F5195].

14. Leith Ross to Waley, 19 October 1935, T160/Box 620 F14233/02/1. The

original draft of the plan, dated September 1935, and written on paper headed 'Canadian Pacific Steamship Lines' is among the Leith Ross papers, T188 (128).

15. F. Leith Ross, *Money Talks* (London, 1968), p. 198.

16. Leith Ross to Fisher, 12 September 1935, Leith Ross papers, T188 (123).

17. Leith Ross to Fisher, 12 September 1935, above.

18. Leith Ross, 31 July 1935, Secret memorandum above, FO 371/19243 [F5081]. It was hoped that the consortium banks might issue such a loan.

19. Clive to Hoare, 11 September 1935, FO 371/19244 [F5853].

20. Leith Ross to Vansittart, 29 July 1935, FO 371/19243 [F4922].

21. The king to the emperor of Japan, 7 August 1935, FO 371/19243 [F5011].

22. Hosoya, p. 88.

23. Northedge, p. 626.

24. Leith Ross to Fisher, 12 September 1935, Leith Ross papers above.

25. Cadogan to Hoare, 26 September 1935, FO 371/19244 [F6159].

26. Chinese counsellor (London), 5 October 1935, conversation, FO 371/19244 [F6386].

27. Vansittart, 6 October 1935, minute, [F6386] above.

28. Randall, 7 October 1935, minute, [F6386] above.

29. Hoare to Cadogan, 8 October 1935, [F6386] above.

30. Leith Ross to Fisher, 4 October 1935, T160/Box 620 F14233/02/1. In fact the Chinese did not begin their effort to sell their silver until 8 October, when the ambassador in Washington was instructed to offer 100 million ounces to be sold in two lots at $0.65 over six months. For various reasons the ambassador was unable to see Morgenthau until 28 October. An agreement was not reached until 13 November by which time the currency reforms had been announced. Young, pp. 234–6; FRUS III 1935, pp. 628, 641–2.

31. Leith Ross to Warren Fisher, 9 October 1935, FO 371/19245 [F6415].

32. Pratt, 25 November 1935, memorandum, FO 371/19247 [F7505].

33. Leith Ross to Treasury, 12 October 1935, FO 371/19245 [F6481].

34. Young, p. 230. Young makes it clear that the Chinese hoped that British efforts to secure international cooperation had failed by the time Leith Ross arrived.

35. Pratt, 22 February 1935, memorandum, FO 371/19243 [F1017].

36. Leith Ross to Fisher, 24 October 1935, FO 371/19245 [F6673].

37. Fisher to Leith Ross, 24 October 1935, FO 371/19245 [F6704].

38. Cadogan to Hoare, 24 October 1935, FO 371/19245 [F6711].

39. Wellesley, 28 October 1935, minute, FO 371/19245 [F6729].

40. Leith Ross to Sir Warren Fisher, 26 October 1935, FO 371/19245 [F6739].

41. Orde, 28 October 1935, minute, FO 371/19245 [F6379].

42. Clive to Hoare, 28 October 1935, FO 371/19245 [F6750].

43. Fisher, 29 October 1935, minute on [F6750] above, Hopkins papers T175/91.

44. Vansittart, 28 October 1935, minute, FO 371/19245 [F6711].

45. Vansittart, 29 October 1935, minute for the secretary of state, FO 371/19245 [F6729].

46. Sir Samuel Hoare, 31 October 1935, Foreign Office minute, FO 371/19245 [F6832].

47. Hoare to Cadogan, 30 October 1935, [F6832] above.

48. Leith Ross to Fisher, 1 November 1935, FO 371/19245 [F6885].

49. FRUS III 1935, pp. 632–3. The agreement was finalised on 13 November, FRUS III 1935, pp. 641–2.

50. Hoare to consul-general Shanghai, 2 November 1935, FO 371/19245 [F6865].

51. Leith Ross to Treasury, 13 November 1935, FO 371/19246 [F7162].

52. Leith Ross to Treasury, 13 November 1935, [F7162] above.

53. Treasury to Leith Ross, draft telegram, [F7162] above.

54. Cowan (Peking) to Hoare, 18 November 1935, FO 371/19337 [F7311].

55. Hoare to Leith Ross, 26 November 1935, FO 371/19247 [F7404].

56. Leith Ross to Warren Fisher, 8 November 1935, FO 371/19246 [F6962].

57. Pratt, 12 November 1935, [F6962] above.

58. Clive to Hoare, 10 November 1935, FO 371/19246 [F7045].

59. Pratt, 14 November 1935, memorandum, FO 371/19246 [F7160].

60. Royal Institute of International Affairs, *Survey of International Affairs, 1933* (London, 1934), pp. 181–2.

61. Clive to Simon, 30 May 1935, FO 371/19310 [F3513].

62. Harcourt Smith, 12 June 1935, memorandum, FO 371/19311 [F3760].

63. Clive to Simon, 6 June 1935, FO 371/19311 [F4330].

64. Cadogan to Eden, 28 February 1936, FO 371/20249 [F1177]. General Ho was chairman of the Peking military council, General Umetsu was chief of staff of the Japanese army in north China, General Ching was the Nationalist army commander in Chahar and General Doihara was in charge of the intelligence division of the Japanese general staff. See J. B. Crowley, *Japan's Quest for Autonomy* (Princeton, N.J., 1966), pp. 214–17.

65. I. S. Friedman, *British Relations with China 1931–1939* (New York, 1940), pp. 71–9.

66. Ingram to Simon, 18 January 1934, FO 371/18184 [F1148].

67. Clive to Hoare, 28 September 1935, FO 371/19314 [F6516].

68. Cadogan to Hoare, 24 November 1935, FO 371/20227 [F34].

69. Cowan (Peking) to Hoare, 13 November 1935, FO 371/19337 [F7144].

70. Cadogan to Hoare, 10 December 1935, FO 371/19248 [F7775]. This despatch reflects Leith Ross's anxiety about the threat to British interests in the Yangtse valley. Smuggling increased sharply in the latter half of 1935 after Leith Ross's arrival in China. See Friedman, p. 71.

71. Wellesley, 20 November 1935, minute, FO 371/19247 [F7254].

72. Cadogan to Hoare, 24 November 1935, FO 371/20227 [F34].

73. Cadogan to Hoare, 25 November 1935, FO 371/19337 [F7424].

74. *The Times*, 26 November 1935. In his autobiography, *Money Talks* (London, 1968) p. 212, Leith Ross notes that he cabled to the public relations officer at the Treasury and he calmed down the Foreign Office spokesman whose apprehensions about this incident Leith Ross felt were exaggerated.

75. Wiggin (Tokyo) to Hoare, 28 November 1935, FO 371/19337 [F7530].

76. Cadogan to Hoare, 18 November 1935, FO 371/19337 [F7308].

77. Pratt, 21 November 1935, minute, FO 371/19337 [F7319].

78. Secretary of state for foreign affairs, 18 November 1935, FO 371/19247 [F7430].

79. Hoare to Cadogan, 25 November 1935, [F7430] above.

80. Cadogan to Hoare, 6 December 1935, FO 371/19248 [F7715].

81. Wellesley, 10 December 1935, minute, [F7715] above.

82. See above chapter 1, p. 10, n. 28.

83. Eden to Cadogan, 21 December 1935, FO 371/19248 [F 8010].

84. Cadogan to Eden, 15 January 1936, FO 173/20249 [F1177].

85. Leith Ross to Treasury, 7 January 1936, FO 371/20215 [F137].

86. The question of railway loan defaults was crucial to Leith Ross because there was bound to be an outcry from the holders of Chinese railway bonds who had received no interest for years if a loan was made to China before the issue of the defaults was settled. At Leith Ross's suggestion, a bond holders committee was set up in London in November 1935. Leith Ross acted as intermediary in China and eventually new arrangements involving the cancellation of most of these arrears were accepted for the Tientsin–Pukow railway. *The Times*, 25 February 1936. Arrangements for the Hukuang railway were underway when Leith Ross left China.

87. Cadogan to Eden, 16 January 1936, FO 371/20215 [F320]. Cadogan supported him.

88. Leith Ross to Fisher, 2 January 1936, Leith Ross papers, T188 (122).

89. Pratt, 22 January 1936, minute, FO 371/20215 [F320].

90. Wellesley, 22 January 1936, minute, [F320] above.

NOTES TO CHAPTER 10

1. Wellesley to Lindsay, 12 March 1935, FO 371/19287 [F2659].

2. Cabinet 33, 19 June 1935, conclusion 2.

3. Report by the British representatives, 5 June 1935, Anglo-German naval conversations, NCM (35) 50, CAB 29/148. Japan's total strength by tonnage was about 64 per cent of Britain's. If this strength remained the same when Germany's reached 35 per cent, Britain's margin of safety would just be adequate.

4. CID sub-committee on defence policy and requirements, 1 July 1935, Revision of Defence Requirements, DPR 6, CAB 16/112.

5. Mounsey, 20 September 1935, minute, FO 371/19035 [F6059].

6. Hankey to Vansittart, 20 November 1935, Hankey papers, CAB 63/50.

7. Wellesley, 25 July 1935, minute, FO 371/19287 [F4811].

8. Far Eastern Department Memorandum, 25 July 1935, FO 371/19287 [F4811].

9. Hoare to Clive, 8 October 1935, FO 371/18739 [A8587].

10. Clive to Hoare, 31 July 1935, FO 371/18737 [A6788].

11. Holman, 28 December 1935, summary of meeting of the naval conference, December 9–December 20, FO 371/19803 [A164].

12. Record of a meeting with the Japanese delegation, London Naval Conference/United Kingdom delegation (hereafter cited as LNC(35)UK), 13 December 1935, paper LNC(35)UK 1, FO 371/18744 [A10612].

13. Craigie, 29 December 1935, minute, [A164] above.

14. Meeting with the United States delegation, 17 December 1935, LNC(35)UK 3, [A10612] above.

15. Clive to Hoare, 17 December 1935, FO 371/18744 [A10617].

16. Clive to Eden, 6 January 1936, FO 371/19803 [A126].

17. Craigie, 1 January 1936, minute, FO 371/18744 [A10985].

18. Fisher, 21 January 1935, memorandum, T172/1831 above.

19. Chancellor, 27 June 1935, Text of lecture at Chatham House, FO371/19395 [F4633] and Orde minute 30 June 1935 on this paper.

20. Sansom to Crowe, 12 October 1934, FO 371/18115 [F7042].

21. Wellesley, 4 January 1936, minute [A10985] above. Cf. this attitude with that of Japan at the Washington Conference, 1921, where she accepted the naval ratio in return for the non-fortification agreement.

22. Eden to Clive, 4 January 1936, [A10985] above.

23. Nagai Matsuo, Japanese ambassador to Berlin 1933–4, had been a member of the Japanese delegation to the naval conference in 1930. He was, therefore, already known to Craigie and his English was better than that of Admiral Nagano, leader of the Japanese delegation. M. D. Kennedy, *The Estrangement of Britain and Japan* (Manchester, 1969), pp. 333–4, describes Nagai incorrectly as the chief delegate. Nagai apparently felt he had been treated with indifference by the foreign secretary. The political drama associated with Hoare's resignation on 22 December should not be forgotten. Eden had been foreign secretary for less than a month at the time of the conversation Kennedy reports.

24. Craigie, 6 January 1936, Foreign Office memorandum, FO 371/19804 [A277].

25. Craigie, 6 January 1936, Foreign Office memorandum, FO 371/19804 [A278].

26. Clive to Eden, 6 January 1936, FO 371/19803 [A126]; Clive to Vansittart, 21 December 1935, FO 371/19804 (A401). The letter to Vansittart was received at the Foreign Office after the telegram.

27. Eden to Lindsay, 13 January 1936, [A126] above.

28. Clive to Eden, 9 January 1936, FO 371/19804 [A279].

29. Lindsay to Eden, 13 January 1936, FO 371/19804 [A415].

30. Eden, 13 January, minute, [A279] above.

31. Cabinet 3, 29 January 1936, conclusion 6.

32. Cabinet conclusion, 29 January 1936, FO 371/20279 [F607]. This copy of the report of the cabinet meeting has been annotated by Orde, head of the far east department. He wrote 'by the chancellor?' against the comment on the Leith Ross mission and put a number of question marks against the claim that Leith Ross was liked by the Japanese.

33. Clive to Eden, 7 February 1936, FO 371/20215 [F720].

34. Clive to Eden, 7 February 1936, FO 371/20215 [F727].

35. Chancellor (Reuter's) to Amau, 20 January 1936, JMFA archives, S 120025.25ff.

36. Amau to Chancellor, 30 January 1936, JMFA archives above. I am grateful to Dr I. H. Nish who searched the Japanese archives on this point.

37. Clive to Eden, 14 February 1936, FO 371/20215 [F847].

38. Leith Ross to Eden, 12 February 1936, FO 371/20215 [F289].

39. Orde, 8 February 1936, minute, FO 371/20215 [F720].

40. Clive to Eden, 19 February 1936, FO 371/20215 [F987].

41. Crowley, pp. 244–79; Storry, pp. 180–91.

42. Eden to Cadogan, 29 February 1936, FO 371/20216 [F1213].

43. Leith Ross to Eden, 9 March 1936, FO 371/20216 [F1355].

44. Eden to Chamberlain, 23 March 1936, [F1355] above.

45. Chamberlain to Eden, 27 March 1936, FO 371/20216 [F1702].

46. Eden to Chamberlain, 7 April 1936, [F1702] above; Chamberlain to Eden, 28 April 1936, FO 371/20216 [F2359]. Vansittart felt that Sir Warren Fisher attached most importance to Leith Ross staying in China and either drafted or inspired Chamberlain's letters to the foreign secretary. See minute of 3 May on the above document.

47. Cadogan, 8 May 1936, minute, [F2359] above.

48. Eden to Chamberlain, 8 May 1936, [F2359] above.

49. *Hansard's Parliamentary Debates*, fifth series, vol. 312, 29 May 1936, col. 2382.

50. Leith Ross, July 1936, Notes by Sir F. Leith Ross on his mission to China, T160/Box 620, F14233/03.

51. Clive to Eden, 13 June 1936, FO 371/20277 [3417].

52. Horinouchi, 11 June 1936, memorandum of conversation with Sir F. Leith Ross, Section VII, Annex I and II in notes by Leith Ross above.
53. Clive to Eden, 10 June 1936, FO 371/20290 [F3348].

54. Leith Ross, July 1936, notes above, section II.

55. Eden to Howe (Nanking), 21 May 1936, FO 371/20217 [F2905].

56. Leith Ross, 8 June 1936, memorandum handed to General Isogai, notes by Leith Ross above, section II, annex I. Leith Ross had met General Isogai in China where he had been military attaché at the Japanese embassy.

57. Isogai, 13 June 1936, memorandum sent to Sir F. Leith Ross, in Notes by Sir F. Leith Ross above, section II, annex II.

58. *The Times*, 23 June 1936.

59. Leith Ross, July 1936, Notes on mission to China, above.

60. Pratt, 6 August 1936, minute, FO 371/20218 [F4498].

61. Record of meeting held on 29 July 1936 to discuss questions arising out of the Leith Ross mission to China, FO 371/20218 [F4974].

62. Leith Ross, 4 September 1936, Financial mission to China, recommendations, CP 251(36), CAB 27/596.

63. Cabinet 57, 14 October 1936, conclusion 14.

64. Eden, 3 November 1936, Sir Frederick Leith Ross's Report on his Financial mission to China, PEJ(35)5, CAB 27/596.

65. Ormsby Gore, 16 November 1936, Sir Frederick Leith Ross's Report on his Financial mission to China, PEJ(35)6, CAB 27/256.

66. See chapter 11 below.

67. Leith Ross, p. 195.

68. Sir John Pratt, *War and Politics in China* (London, 1943), p. 326.

69. Leith Ross, p. 225.

70. Pratt, p. 236.

71. Everest, p. 116.

72. Young, p. 232.

73. A. N. Young, *China's Wartime Finance and Inflation 1937–1945* (Cambridge, Mass., 1965), p. 7.

74. Cadogan to Hoare, 5 December 1935, FO 371/20241 [F502].

75. Leith Ross, July 1936, Notes on mission to China above.

76. Pratt, 6 August 1936, minute, FO 371/20218 [F4498].

NOTES TO CHAPTER 11

1. Yoshida was the 'special messenger' who had visited London in 1934 at the time of the Anglo-Japanese naval talks. See above pp. 105–07.

2. Eden to Clive, 17 July 1936, FO 371/20279 [F4320]; Eden to Clive, 30 July 1936, FO 371/20277 [F4625].

3. Clive to Eden, 7 August 1936, FO 371/20279 [F4778].

4. Craigie, 10 August 1936, minute, [F4778] above.

5. Vansittart, 23 September 1936, minute, FO 371/20279 [F5842].

6. See p. 163.

7. International Military Tribunal Far East (hereafter cited as IMTFE), Exhibit 979. Imperial Way expressed the relationship between the emperor at the centre of the nation and all Japanese people. See Nobuya Bamba, *Japanese Diplomacy in a Dilemma* (Vancouver, B.C., 1973) pp. 75–6, 82–3.

8. Crowley, pp. 297–8.

9. IMTFE Document 1044.

10. See chapter 9 above p. 162.

11. Knatchbull-Hugessen to Eden, 8 April 1937, Annual Report for 1936, FO 371/21006 [F2836].

12. Knatchbull-Hugessen to Eden, 8 April 1937 [F2836] above.

13. The incident occurred on 7 October 1936. The sailors were accused of not paying a taxi fare and were arrested and beaten by the police. An officer who asked for their release was insulted. The foreign secretary reported the cancellation of the visit of the fleet at the cabinet meeting on 28 October 1936, cabinet 60, conclusion 4.

14. Cadogan, 7 October 1936, minute, FO 371/20277 [F6132].

15. Draft memorandum communicated to the chancellor of the exchequer by the Japanese ambassador (undated) FO 371/20279 [F6511]; Orde, 30 October 1936, minute on the memorandum [F6511] above. A. H. F. Edwardes who, as adviser to the Manchukuo government, had accompanied the FBI mission to Japan and Manchukuo in 1934 and whose opinions had been sought be Sir Warren Fisher (see chapter 7 above) was employed by Yoshida as adviser and as a liason officer between the Japanese embassy and the Foreign Office. (I am grateful to Captain M. D. Kennedy for this

information.) This may have been one reason for an approach through the Treasury.

16. Recognition of China's sovereignty 'south of the Wall' would have conceded to Japan's sphere of influence areas of Jehol and Chahar not under her control. This fact was not appreciated by the Treasury and the phrase became a matter of contention between the Foreign Office and the Treasury. Cadogan finally settled the matter by showing Leith Ross a map.

17. China and the United States were to be excluded from these talks in the first instance.

18. Cadogan, 29 October 1936, minute, [F6511] above.

19. Orde, 30 October 1936, minute, [F6511] above.

20. Clive to Eden, 6 November 1936, FO 371/20279 [F7400]; Sansom, 22 September 1936, minute on the military attaché's report of 17 September 1936, FO 371/20285 [F7223].

21. Clive to Eden, 3 November 1936, FO 371/20279 [F6714] and [F6724]; Clive to Eden, 6 November 1936, FO 371/20279 [F7403].

22. Count Makino Nobukai was lord privy seal to emperor Hirohito from 1926 until his resignation in December 1935. Storry, p. 169.

23. Drummond to Eden, 23 November 1936, FO 371/20287 [F7427]. The information of Clive and Sugimura was, in fact, remarkably accurate in view of the findings of Japanese scholars today. Yoshida was acting on his own and possibly not reporting fully. He had been deputy minister of foreign affairs 1927–1930 but he was not especially popular in 1936. Though he was to be prime minister in 1946, Yoshida had no political following at this time.

24. Eden to Clive, 6 November 1936, FO 371/20279 [F6826]; Japanese ambassador to secretary of state, 7 November 1936 FO 371/20279 [F6861].

25. Eden, 13 December 1936, minute on Foreign Office memorandum on the German-Japanese pact, 4 December 1936, FO 371/20286 [F7504]. Collier, the head of the northern department, was alone in seeing the pact was incompatible with British interests in Europe and the far east. Eden and Orde refused to take the matter 'tragically'.

26. Craigie, 4 December 1936, minute, FO 371/20279 [F7660]. Cadogan accused Yoshida of having an 'irresistible desire to discuss policy with everyone except those primarily and directly concerned'.

27. Eden to Clive, 8 December 1936 FO 371/20279 [F7569].

28. Cadogan, 15 December 1936, minute, FO 371/20279 [F7922].

29. Eden to Clive, 16 December 1936 and Eden, 15 December 1936, minute, [F7922] above.

30. Cadogan, 12 January 1937, minute, FO 371/21029 [F304].

31. These had begun in October.

32. For detailed accounts of the Sian incident see L. P. Van Slyke, *Enemies and Friends: The United Front in Chinese Communist History* (Stanford,

Cal., 1967), pp. 48–90; C. B. McLane, *Soviet Policy and the Chinese Communists, 1931–1946* (New York, 1958), pp. 79–97.

33. Knatchbull-Hugessen to Eden, 31 December 1936, FO 371/20969 [F1048] and Cadogan, 16 March 1937, minute on this despatch.

34. Cadogan, 1 January 1937, minute, FO 371/20969 [F35].

35. Chamberlain to Eden, 13 January 1937 and Foreign Office minutes on this, FO 371/21029 [F290]; Cadogan, 15 January 1937, minute, FO 371/21029 [F345]; *Aide-mémoire*, 18 January 1937, [F345] above.

36. Eden to Clive, 18 January 1937, FO 371/21029 [F357].

37. Cadogan, 21 January 1937, minute, FO 371/21029 [F417].

38. Cadogan, 21 January 1937 and Vansittart, 21 January 1937, minutes, [F417] above.

39. Japanese ambassador to Cadogan, 23 January 1937, FO 371/21029 [F545]; Cadogan, 25 January 1937, FO 371/21029 [F546].

40. Cadogan, 28 January 1937, minute, FO 371/21029 [F570].

41. Clive to Eden, 27 January 1937, [F570] above.

42. Eden to Clive, 5 February 1937, FO 371/21029 [F754].

43. Clive to Eden, 30 January 1937, FO 371/21038 [F64].

44. Knatchbull-Hugessen to Eden, 7 June 1937, FO 371/20970 [F4531]; Crowley, pp. 316–17.

45. Clerk (Paris) to Cadogan, 6 March 1937, FO 371/21038 [F1310].

46. Knatchbull-Hugessen to Eden, 7 June 1937, [F453] above; Crowley, pp. 317–19.

47. Yoshida to Cadogan, 3 May 1937, FO 371/21029 [F2939].

48. Statement by the prime minister of the Commonwealth of Australia, 14 May 1937, 1st meeting of principal delegates to the imperial conference 1937 (hereafter cited as E(PD)37), CAB 32/128; MacDonald, 21 May 1937, minute, FO 371/21029 [F2939].

49. Suggestion for a regional pact in the Pacific, memorandum prepared by His Majesty's government in the Commonwealth of Australia, (E(37)29), 28 May 1937, CAB 32/129.

50. Clive to Eden, 20 May 1937, FO 371/21025, [F2919].

51. Chamberlain took office on 28 May 1937.

52. E(PD)37, 11th meeting, 2 June 1937, CAB 32/128.

53. Clive to Eden, 1 January 1938, Japan annual report, FO 371/22190 [F2286]. Hayashi threw the support of his government behind a pro-militarist party, the Showa-Kai. In an election in April 1937 this party was totally defeated.

54. Yoshida, 2 June 1937, draft memorandum handed to Sir Robert Craigie, FO 371/21029 [F3416]; Craigie, 2 June 1937, minute on [F3416] above.

55. Dodds to Eden, 7 June 1937, FO 371/21029 [F3308]; Orde, 3 June 1937, minute, FO 371/21029 [F3232].

56. E(PD)37, 15th meeting, 8 June 1937, CAB 32/128.

57. Report of the Technical Committee of the Pacific Pact, E(37)33, June 1937, CAB 32/129. In a note written to Eden on 7 June 1937, Cadogan described the Canadian delegates as being 'distinctly sticky' and the New Zealanders as 'none too accommodating either'. He thought this might be due to the fact that they were nettled at the way Australia had sprung the idea on the conference. See FO 371/21025 [F3385].

58. E(PD)37, 15th meeting, 8 June 1937 above.

59. Cadogan, 11 June 1937, minute, FO 371/21025 [F3437].

60. Cadogan, 17 June 1937, minute, FO 371/21025 [F3516].

61. Orde, 17 June 1937, Cadogan, 17 June 1937, FO 371/21025 [F3486].

62. Dodds to Eden, 17 June 1937, FO 371/21025 [F4002].

63. *Hansard's Parliamentary Debates*, fifth series, Vol. 325, 25 June 1937, column 1602.

64. Eden to Dodds, 12 July 1937, FO 371/21029 [F4227].

65. Bradford A. Lee, *Britain and the Sino-Japanese War 1937–1939* (Stanford, Cal., 1973), pp. 28–9; *Hansard's Parliamentary Debates*, fifth series, Vol. 326, 21 July 1937 column 2182.

66. Dodds to Eden, 11 August 1937, FO 371/21029 [F6087].

67. Lee, p. 32.

68. Lee, p. 48.

NOTES TO CHAPTER 12

1. Young, *China's Nation Building Effort, 1927–1937* (Stanford, 1971) p. 373; Knatchbull-Hugessen to Eden, 17 April 1937, FO 371/20945 [F2252].

2. Beale to Department of Overseas Trade, 2 April 1937, FO 371/20945, [F1993].

3. Leith Ross to Warren Fisher, 29 April 1937, and memorandum, 'Loans to China', attached to this paper, Leith Ross papers, T188 (187).

4. Hall-Patch to Eden, 21 January 1937, FO 371/20945 [F406]; Rogers to Leith Ross, 1 April 1937, Leith Ross papers, T188 (187).

5. Addis to Cadogan, 5 January 1937, FO 371/20972 [F101]; Hall-Patch to Eden, 19 January 1937, FO 371/20972 [F407].

6. Cadogan, 10 February 1937 and memorandum handed to the counsellor at the United States embassy, FO 371/20994 [F881].

7. United States ambassador, memorandum, 13 March 1937, FO 371/20994 [F1640]; Cadogan, minute, 20 April 1937, FO 173/20994 [F2280].

8. Eden to Knatchbull-Hugessen, 8 June 1937 four telegrams, FO 371/20946 [F3246].

9. Beale to Eden, 25 May 1937, FO 371/20945 [F3049].

10. Chaplin, 28 May 1937, Pratt, 28 May 1937, Cadogan, 30 May 1937, minutes, FO 371/20945, [F3066].

11. Leith Ross to Cadogan, 26 May 1937 [F3066] above; Leith Ross to Hall-Patch, 27 May 1937, Leith Ross papers, T188 (188).

12. Eden to Knatchbull-Hugessen, 8 June 1937, FO 371/20946 [F3292].

13. Dodds to Eden, 14 June 1937, FO 371/20946 [F3443].

14. Eden to Dodds, 19 June 1937, FO 371/20946 [F3488]; Dodds to Eden, 23 June 1937, FO 371/20946 [F3602]; Dodds to Eden, 1 July 1937, FO 371/20946 [F3721]. Hall-Patch went to China in 1935 with Leith Ross.

15. Eden to Dodds, 19 June 1937, [F3488] above; Eden to Dodds, 19 June 1937, FO 371/20946 [F3488] above.

16. Eden to Dodds, 1 July 1937, FO 371/20946 [F3733]; Orde, 5 July 1937, minute on [F3804] above.

17. Cadogan to Leith Ross, 20 July 1937, FO 371/20946 [F3894].

18. Leith Ross to Waley, 23 July 1937, Leith Ross papers, T188 (188).

19. Leith Ross to Warren Fisher, 29 July 1937, Leith Ross papers, T188 (188). The Canton–Meihsien railway loan agreement was actually signed on 30 July 1937. See British China Corporation to Under secretary of State, 6 August 1937, FO 371/20993 [F14965]. The loan was never made.

20. Heppel to Leith Ross, 28 July 1937, FO 371/20946 [F4600].

21. Leith Ross to Heppel, 29 July 1937, FO 371/20946 [F4677].

22. Orde to Leith Ross, 29 July 1937, [F4677] above.

23. Leith Ross to Warren Fisher, 29 July 1937, Leith Ross papers, T188(188). Orde took up his post as minister at Riga in April 1938.

24. Leith Ross to Orde, 29 July 1937, FO 371/20946 [F4768].

25. Orde to Waley, 5 August 1937, [F4768] above.

26. Leith Ross to Orde, 30 August 1937, FO 371/20946 [F6038]. This was the final letter in the correspondence. Orde had also been in correspondence with Sir Frederick Phillipps, deputy to Warren Fisher, when Leith Ross was on leave in August.

27. Orde, 6 September 1937, minute, [F6083] above.

28. Young, *China's Nation Building Effort 1927–1937*, p. 233. The charter of the Central Bank was finally passed by the Executive Yuan on 24 June 1937. This was the direct result of British pressure during the currency loan negotiations.

29. See pp. 182–83.

30. Usui Katsumi *Nitchu Sensō [Sino-Japanese War]* (Tokyo, 1967), p. 18.

31. Howe to Eden, 12 December 1937, FO 371/20948 [F10959]; Craigie to Eden, 17 December 1937, FO 371/20948 [F11203]; Howe to Eden, 22 December 1937, FO 371/20948 [F11461].

32. See for example, Donald McLachlan, *In the Chair: Barrington-Ward of The Times* (London, 1971); F. R. Gannon, *The British Press and Germany 1936–1939* (Oxford, 1971).

33. Bamba, pp. 359–60; A. Iriye, *Across the Pacific* (New York, 1967), pp. 175–8.

34. Lee, pp. 47–9; Pratt, 6 September 1937, minute, FO 371/20946 [F6038]. Pratt's book, *War and Politics in China* (London, 1943), illustrates this point. Pratt himself tended to be 'pro-Chinese' but his minutes in the period between 1933 and 1937 do not indicate that he was quite as partisan as the book suggests.

35. Usui, p. 18, quotes various Japanese reactions to China's currency reform which show that this was regarded as the climax of a battle between Britain and Japan for the control of China's economy.

36. D. Dilks, 'Appeasement Revisited', *University of Leeds Bulletin 1972*, p. 49.

37. Crowley, pp. 188–9, 195–7, 289–300; Borg, *United States and the Far Eastern Crisis 1933–1938*, pp. 55–92, p. 177.

38. Craigie to Eden, 1 January 1938, FO 371/22190 [F2286].

39. A. Iriye, 'The Failure of Military Expansionism', in *Dilemmas of Growth in Pre-war Japan*, J. W. Morley (ed.), (Princeton, N.J., 1971), pp. 116–20

40. Far Eastern Department memorandum, 25 July 1935, FO 371/19278 [F4811].

41. Lee, p. 42. Roosevelt's attitude to events in Europe and the far east is discussed by D. C. Watt in 'Roosevelt and Neville Chamberlain: two appeasers', *International Journal*, Vol. xxvii, No. 2, Spring 1973, pp. 184–203.

42. Cadogan, 3 May 1937, minute, FO 371/21024 [F2586]. Borg, *United States and the Far Eastern Crisis 1933–1938*, pp. 244–8. The British believed the Americans were trying to solve their problems in the Philippines.

43. Vansittart, 25 May 1936, minute, FO 371/20279 [F2872].

44. Cadogan to Hoare, 24 November 1935, FO 371/20227 [F34].

45. Vansittart, 22 February 1934, minute, FO 371/18176 [F823].

46. J. B. Crowley, 'Intellectuals as Visionaries of the New Asian Order', in Morley above, pp. 340–1. Crowley gives an account of the argument of Ozaki Hotsumi, one of the 'bright young men' of the Showa Kenkyukai who, in his paper 'British influence on China' set out to prove that Britain was Nanking's prop.

47. Clerk Kerr to Halifax, 29 April 1938, FO 371/22160 [F6312]; Knatchbull-Hugessen to Eden, 7 June 1937, FO 371/20970 [F4531].

48. Hosoya, 'Retrogression in Foreign Policy', in Morley above, pp. 90–1.

49. Lee, pp. 48–9.

BIBLIOGRAPHICAL NOTE

The Foreign Office archives for the period covered by this study have been open only since 1 January 1968 and, up to the present time, lack of sources has restricted writing about British far eastern policy in the 1930s and has limited its scope. In 1972 two detailed studies based on Foreign Office archives for east Asia in the 1930s appeared: Christopher Thorne's *The Limits of Foreign Policy: The West, the League and the Far Eastern Crisis of 1931–1933* (London, 1972) and Bradford A. Lee's *Britain and the Sino-Japanese War 1937–1939, A Study of the Dilemmas of British Decline* (Stanford, Cal., 1972). These studies hint at the problems of British policy-makers between 1933 and 1937 but there has been no detailed study of this period and in fact there is a remarkable paucity of published material about these years.

One of the problems for writers who have not had access to the Foreign Office archives has been that critics of British policy and individuals with a particular view of what that policy should be frequently made their voices heard in newspapers like *The Times*, and in journals like *Round Table* and *International Affairs*. Without the Foreign Office documents to balance the account, the available evidence might suggest that there were more clear-cut divisions within the government, that effective lobbies existed, and that backstage influences had more weight in deciding far eastern policy than was actually the case.

I. S. Friedman's book, *British Relations with China 1931–1939* (New York, 1940), is one of the few studies of British policy in the 1930s. Considering the time at which it was written and the fact that it is a pioneer work written without the benefit either of official documents or of a previous compilation of sources, this book gives a good, if not very detailed, account of the events and issues with which the British were involved in China at this time. Interpretation of Britain's policy is not always reliable for the reasons given above. This remains, however, a basic work from which to begin a study of Britain's China policy in the mid-1930s.

Sir John Pratt's book, *War and Politics in China* (London, 1943), is written with more vigour than detachment. Pratt never believed that a *rapprochement* with Japan was possible and the fact that he wrote when the Pacific war was under way reinforced his view. The book, however, suggests some of the problems the Foreign Office faced in policy-making in the far east and is of interest as an expression of the view of a Foreign Office official who knew a great deal of the inside story of Britain's difficulties in China.

The American archives for the 1930s were opened soon after the second world war. This encouraged detailed writing about American policy in the far east in the 1930s. The fullest and best account of American policy after

1933 is that of Dorothy Borg in *The United States and the Far Eastern Crisis 1933–1938* (Cambridge, Mass., 1964). While this book reveals a good deal about British policy and the problems the British faced as far as trying to interest the United States in involvement of the far east were concerned, the absence of the British documents made it impossible to check the motives attributed to British politicians and the Foreign Office by American observers. This has resulted in some faulty deductions in matters of detail.

Attention was drawn to a particularly complicated period in British–Japanese–American relations in an essay, 'Britain, the United States and Japan in 1934' by D. C. Watt in his collection *Personalities and Policies* (London, 1965). The availability of the American documents, and of private papers, including those of the well known publicist, Lord Lothian, made possible a much fuller account than hitherto of the events surrounding the preliminary naval talks of the year 1934. Nevertheless, as with Friedman's much earlier work, the conclusions reached in this essay are inevitably slanted by the unrepresentative selection of material available and this interpretation of a particularly important stage in Anglo-Japanese relations is not so satisfactory in the light of the Foreign Office documents now available.

In his recent book, *British Strategy in the Far East 1919–1939* (Oxford, 1971), W. R. Louis does make use of the Foreign Office archives and has provided new and basic information about British policy in the far east. The book is concerned, however, with identifying a specific aspect of British policy and this fact, together with the reliance, inevitable in a work of this scope, on confidential print rather than the files of general correspondence, has led to simplifications about the nature of British policy and aims in the far east after 1933.

Of the books available in English, J. B. Crowley's *Japan's Quest for Autonomy* (Princeton, N.J., 1966), is essential for an understanding of the Japanese side of the case. A recent publication, *Dilemmas of Growth in Prewar Japan*, edited by J. W. Morley (Princeton, N.J., 1971), contains a great deal of valuable material and the essays in it by Iriye, Hosoya and Crowley provide important insights into the nature of Japanese policy and Japanese perception of British policy.

The chief problem for the researcher is the quantity of material available at the Public Record Office in London. The files on both China and Japan for the period 1933–7 are vast, consisting of well over one hundred volumes for each year. Matters relating to Manchukuo and to Sino-Japanese relations appear in the China files. Complicating the problem of the control of material is the fact that it is necessary in this period to use the American files which contain all the material relating to the naval conference in 1935. This means that much of the discussion of the question of the feasibility of a non-aggression pact with Japan actually appears in the American files because the question arose in connection with the preliminary naval talks in 1934.

In the course of this research, a number of important gaps in the FO 371 series for Japan in 1934 became apparent. Between April and October 1934 seven different memoranda on questions relating to the advantages and drawbacks of a political agreement with Japan were produced in the far eastern department of the Foreign Office. None of these was actually seen by the cabinet because on 16 October the foreign secretary and the chancellor of the exchequer produced a memorandum, The Future of Anglo-Japanese Relations (CP 223(34), CAB 24/250). The far eastern department papers had very little bearing on the memorandum which the foreign secretary and the chancellor produced, but these papers were, nevertheless, classified as working papers for cabinet paper CP 223(34) and as such were filed in the Foreign Office library. These memoranda properly belong in the volume FO 371/ 18184 where comment on them will be found but, as they were not placed in the files at the time of the binding of the volume, it has now been decided that they will be transferred from the Foreign Office library in Cornwall House, where they are at present stored, to the Public Record Office and that they will be added to class FO 899 (cabinet papers). In the meantime, two of these papers have appeared in *Documents on British Foreign Policy 1919–1939*, second series, Volume XIII (1973) which was published after this manuscript was prepared. Items No. 14 and No. 15, pages 24–34 are taken from the Cornwall House documents. This volume, which covers naval policy and defence requirements from July 1934 to March 1936, contains a great many other documents referred to in this study.

The Treasury files proved a rich source for this study. The Leith Ross papers which became available in 1972 form a large collection within which the section on China consists of seventy-five files of varying sizes. Much of this material consists of memoranda and records of conversations, copies of which can also be found in the Foreign Office files on China. The correspondence between Leith Ross and Warren Fisher, however, illuminates a number of Leith Ross's telegrams from China. These papers with the Foreign Office material make it clear that Leith Ross's mission was a less straightforward and successful affair than is suggested by Leith Ross in his autobiography, *Money Talks* (London, 1968). The Hopkins and Phillips papers, while less important for the purposes of this study, nevertheless included some interesting material on the silver issue and the question of loans to China.

The attitude of the Treasury to the Foreign Office far eastern policy was clarified by some interesting comments to be found in the miscellaneous papers of the chancellor of the exchequer (T172). The material was particularly illuminating about the attitude and activities of Warren Fisher in connection with the Federation of British Industries mission and the preliminary naval talks with Japan.

The Hankey papers, CAB 63, are a considerable collection which Hankey evidently intended to use in the preparation of an important work based on his experiences as secretary both to the committee of imperial defence and the cabinet. The papers include correspondence and memoranda and reports largely prepared by Hankey. CAB 63/66–82 consists of papers relating to Hankey's visit to the Dominions and his discussions with Dominion ministers on questions of defence.

The material available in Australia was restricted by the fact that a thirty year rule had not come fully into operation in 1971. The Latham and Pearce papers were, however, useful in their comment on Hankey's visit and in providing a Dominion view of British policy in general.

BIBLIOGRAPHY

I PRIMARY MATERIAL

A. UNPUBLISHED

(i) *Official Documents*

Documents held at the Public Record Office, London

Admiralty:

Admiralty records were consulted as required but little Admiralty material which was useful for the purposes of this study has survived in Admiralty records. The most useful Admiralty material is to be found in the Foreign Office records.

Board of Trade:

Papers concerning China, Japan and India (BT 11).

Cabinet Office:

Cabinet papers, especially those printed for circulation to the cabinet (CAB 24).

Cabinet minutes (CAB 23).

Files concerning the visit of Sir Maurice Hankey to the Dominions (CAB 21).

Papers and minutes of sub-committees of the Committee of Imperial Defence; chiefs of staff committee (CAB 53), Defence Requirements committee and Defence Policy and Requirements committee (CAB 16).

Papers and minutes of ministerial committees especially those of the disarmament committee, DC(M) 32(CAB 27); the naval conference committee, NCM 35 (CAB 29); the committee on political and economic relations with Japan, PEJ (CAB 27); the committee on Indian cotton, IC (CAB 27); the committee on Japanese trade and competition, JTC (CAB 27).

Foreign Office:

General correspondence relating to China and Japan in the series FO 371.

Treasury:

Chancellor of the exchequer's papers; miscellaneous papers (T172).

Files concerning finance (T160).

Documents held at the Imperial War Museum, London
International Military Tribunal for the Far East, Proceedings, Exhibits and Judgment.

Documents held at the Commonwealth Archives, Canberra, Australia
Papers relating to Australian Eastern Mission 1934 (CP/290/1–10).
External Affairs, relations with China (A981/114/1–6).

(ii) *Private papers*

Baldwin, Stanley; University library, Cambridge.
Baldwin was lord privy seal in 1933 and in June 1935 became prime minister. He was chairman of the ministerial committee on disarmament and of the committee on the naval conference. Letters from Hankey, Fisher and Chatfield were especially interesting.

Cadogan, Sir Alexander; Public Record Office, London.
Papers in the FO 800 series which includes the private correspondence of ministers and officials with representatives overseas. There are a few letters from Cadogan in China but little of interest in this collection.

Chamberlain, Sir Austen; University library, Birmingham.
Correspondence between Chamberlain, at this time a revered back-bencher, and members of his family. These letters are most interesting for their comments on the leading political figures of the day.

Chatfield papers; National Maritime Museum, Greenwich.
The material for the period 1933 to 1937 is most interesting for those letters written by various admirals to Chatfield and for a number of letters from Sir Warren Fisher to Chatfield. There are fewer letters of interest from Chatfield himself.

China Association papers; China Association, London.
Minutes of meetings of the association in London and copies of minutes of meetings in Shanghai. These papers are of interest in revealing the complaints of British businessmen in China and the workings of a pressure group in London.

Hankey, Sir Maurice; Public Record Office, London.
Papers in the series CAB 63 relating to Hankey's Dominions tour and his discussions with Dominion prime ministers on questions of defence.

Hopkins, Sir Richard; Public Record Office, London.
Hopkins was second secretary at the Treasury during the 1930s. His papers are to be found in the Treasury files (T175). All proposals with regard to foreign exchange, debts and loans had to be submitted to Hopkins. The silver question and the question of a loan to China thus came to his attention.

Hughes, W. M.; National Library, Canberra, Australia.

This is a large collection but the papers of this Australian politician appeared to contain little material of interest for the purposes of this study.

Latham, Sir John; National Library, Canberra, Australia.

This proved to be a valuable collection in terms of this study. Latham, who was deputy prime minister in 1934 and who led an Australian goodwill mission to Japan, corresponded with Foreign Office officials as well as other Australian politicians.

Maze, Sir Frederick; School of Oriental and African Studies, London.

As Inspector General of the Chinese Maritime Customs, Maze was closely concerned with matters of Chinese finance. He undertook the task of trying to raise a huge loan in 1934. Maze was very interested in the Leith Ross mission. He was not, however, consulted as frequently, or regarded as highly, as he would have wished and this correspondence proved less rewarding than might have been expected.

Pearce, Sir George; War Memorial Archives, Canberra, Australia.

These papers relate to Pearce's activities as minister of defence and external affairs and contain reports of the defence talks with Hankey in Australia and New Zealand.

Phillips, Sir Frederick; Public Record Office, London.

Phillips, who became joint second secretary at the Treasury in 1942, was an under-secretary at this time and with Leith Ross next in the hierarchy at the Treasury to Hopkins. These papers (T177) contain reference to the silver question and China.

Ross, Sir Frederick Leith; Public Record Office, London.

These papers, which form a very large collection, have the Treasury file number T188. Papers regarding the mission to China 1935–6 form one section of this collection. There is a good deal of evidence that Leith Ross came to be regarded as something of a China expert.

Manchester Chamber of Commerce; Central Library, Manchester.

Minutes of meetings and minutes of sub-committees dealing with Indian cotton and Japanese cotton are useful in revealing the problems members faced and the organisation of this effective pressure group.

Simon, Sir John; Papers held by the Right Honourable the Viscount Simon, C.M.G.

These papers, which are as yet not well indexed, contained some interesting material, notably the correspondence between Chamberlain and Simon on the question of a non-agression pact with Japan in September 1934.

Simon, Sir John; Public Record Office, London.

These papers in the FO 800 series were of limited interest.

Wigram, Clive; Public Record Office, London.
The papers of this Foreign Office official, which are in the FO 800 series, contained little of interest.

B. PUBLISHED

Documents on British Foreign Policy 1919–1939, edited by E. L. Woodward, Rohan Butler and others, especially second series Volumes x (1969), xi (1970) and xiii (1973), and third series Volume ix (1965).
Franklin D. Roosevelt and Foreign Affairs, edited by Edgar B. Nixon, Volumes i and ii, Harvard, 1969.
Foreign Relations of the United States, especially Volume iii 1933, Volumes i and iii 1934, Volumes i and iii 1935 and Volume iv 1936.
China Association Annual Reports 1933–6.
Imperial Chemical Industries *Annual Reports 1933–6.*
Japan Bibliographical Encyclopaedia and Who's Who, Tokyo, 1958.
National Economic Council Annual Report 1935–36, Peking 1936.
Hansard's Parliamentary Debates, fifth series.
Stock Exchange Year Book 1936.

II SECONDARY SOURCES

Akagi, R.H., *Japan's Foreign Relations*, Tokyo, 1936.
Allen, G.C., *A Short Economic History of Modern Japan*, London, 1946.
Japan : The Hungry Guest, London, 1938.
Amery, L.C.S., *My Political Life*, Volumes ii and iii of three volumes, London 1953–5.
Ashton Gwatkin, F.T., *The British Foreign Service*, Syracuse, N.Y., 1950.
Avon, The Right Hon. the Earl of, *Facing the Dictators*, London, 1962.
Bamba, Nobuya, *Japanese Diplomacy in a Dilemma, New Light on Japan's China Policy 1924–1929*, Vancouver, B.C., 1973.
Bassett, R., *Democracy and Foreign Policy*, London, 1952.
Beasley, W.G., *The Modern History of Japan*, London, 1963.
Beloff, M., *Imperial Sunset, Vol. I, Britain's Liberal Empire, 1897–1921*, London, 1969.
Bergamini, D., *Japan's Imperial Conspiracy*, London, 1971.
Bianco, L., *Origins of the Chinese Revolution 1915–1949*, London, 1971.
Bisson, T.A., *American Policy in the Far East 1931–1941*, New York, 1941.
Japan in China, New York, 1938.
Borg, Dorothy, *American Policy and the Chinese Revolution 1925–1928*, New York, 1947.
(compiler) *Historians and American Far Eastern Policy*, New York, 1968.
The United States and the Far Eastern Crisis 1933–1938, Cambridge, Mass., 1964.
Borg, Dorothy and Okamoto Shumpei (eds), *Pearl Harbour as History : Japanese American Relations 1931–1941*. New York 1973.

Borton, H., *Japan's Modern Century*, New York, 1955.
Japan Since 1931, New York, 1940.
Boyle, J.H., *China and Japan at War 1937–1945, The Politics of Collaboration*, Stanford, Cal., 1972.
Brown, D.M., *Nationalism in Japan*, Berkley, Mich., 1955.
Buhite, R.D., *Nelson T. Johnson and American Policy toward China 1921–1941*, East Lansing, Mich. 1968.
Butler D.E. and Freeman, J., *British Political Facts 1900–1968* (3rd edit.), London, 1969.
Butow, R.J.C., *Tojo and the Coming of the War*, Princeton, N.J., 1961.
Byas, H., *Government by Assassination*, London, 1943.
Chang Kia-ngau, *China's Struggle for Railroad Development*, New York, 1943.
Chatfield, A.E.M., *The Navy and Defence*, Volume I, London, 1942.
It Might Happen Again, London, 1947.
China (Ministry of foreign affairs), *Special Conference on the Chinese Customs Tariff, October 1925–April 1926*, Peking, 1928.
China Year Books, 1933–1936.
Churchill, W.S., *The Second World War*, Volume I, *The Gathering Storm*, London, 1948.
Clifford, N., *Retreat from China, British Policy in the Far East, 1937–1941*, Seattle, Wash., 1967.
Clubb, O.E., *Twentieth Century China*, New York, 1964.
Coghlan, F., 'Armaments, Economic Policy and Appeasement: Background to British Foreign Policy 1931–1937', *History*, Vol. 57, No. 190, June 1972.
Collier, B., *The Defence of the United Kingdom: History of the Second World War*, H.M.S.O., 1957.
Collis, M.S., *Wayfoong: The Hong Kong and Shanghai Banking Corporation*, London, 1965.
Colvin, Ian, *Vansittart in Office, The Origins of World War II*, London, 1965.
Connell, J., *The 'Office', A Study of British Foreign Policy and its Makers*, London, 1958.
Craig, A.M. and Shively, D.H., (eds.) *Personality in Japanese History*, Berkeley, Cal. 1970.
Craigie, R., *Behind the Japanese Mask*, London, 1946.
Crowley, J.B., 'Japanese Army Factionalism in the 1930s', *Journal of Asian Studies*, Vol. XXI, No. 3, May 1962.
Japan's Quest for Autonomy, Princeton, N.J., 1966.
(ed.) *Modern East Asia, Essays in Interpretation*, New Haven, Conn., 1970.
Denlinger, S. and Gary, Charles B., *War in the Pacific: a study of navies, peoples and battle problems*, New York, 1936. Reissue, New York, 1974.
Dilks, D., 'Appeasement Revisited', *University of Leeds Bulletin, 1972.*
(ed.) *Cadogan, The Diaries of Sir Alexander Cadogan, O.M., 1938–1945*, London, 1972.
Dull, Paul S. and Umera, Michael T. *The Tokyo Trials, A Functional Index*, Ann Arbor, Mich., 1957.

Evans, Trefor (ed.), *The Killearn Diaries 1934–1936*, London, 1972.
Everest, A.S., *Morgenthau, The New Deal and Silver*, New York, 1950.
Federation of British Industries, *Report of the Mission to the Far East, August–November 1934*, London, 1934.
Feiling, K., *The Life of Neville Chamberlain*, London, 1946.
Feuerwerker, A., Murphy R., and Wright, M.C., (ed.), *Approaches to Modern Chinese History*, Berkeley, Cal. 1967.
Field, F.V., *American Participation in the China Consortium*, Chicago, 1931.
Friedman I.S., *British Relations with China 1931–1939*, New York, 1940.
Gannon, F.R., *The British Press and Germany 1936–1939*, Oxford, 1971.
Gilbert M. and Gott, R., *The Appeasers*, London, 1963.
Gore-Booth, Paul, *With Great Truth and Respect*, London, 1974.
Gray, J. (ed.), *Modern China's Search for a Political Form*, London, 1969.
Grew, J.C., *Ten Years in Japan*, London, 1944.
Griswold, A.W., *The Far Eastern Policy of the United States*, New York, 1938.
Gull, E.M., *British Economic Interests in the Far East*, London, 1943.
Hancock, W.K. and Gowing, M.M., *The British War Economy: History of the Second World War*, H.M.S.O., 1949.
Hata, Ikuhiko, *Reality and Illusion, The Hidden Crisis between Japan and U.S.S.R. 1932–1934*, Occasional paper of the East Asian Institute, Columbia University, New York, 1967.
Harada Kumao (Baron), *Saionji–Harada Memoirs*, Wayne, Detroit, 1968.
Harvey, John (ed.), *The Diplomatic Diaries of Oliver Harvey 1937–1940*, London, 1970.
Herzog, James H., *Closing the open door, American–Japanese diplomatic negotiations, 1936–41*. Annapolis, 1973.
Hou Chi-ming, *Foreign Investment and Economic Development in China 1840–1937*, Cambridge, Mass., 1965.
Hubbard, G.E., *British Far Eastern Policy*, New York, 1943.
Eastern Industrialisation and its Effect on the West, London, 1938.
The Far East in 1935, London, 1936.
Hudson, G., *The Far East in World Politics*, London, 1939.
Hull, C., *The Memoirs of Cordell Hull*, 2 volumes, London, 1948.
Iriye, A., *Across the Pacific*, New York, 1967.
After Imperialism, Cambridge, Mass., 1965.
Johnson F.A., *Defence by Committee*, London, 1960.
Jones, F.C., *Japan's New Order in East Asia, Its Rise and Fall, 1937–1945*, London, 1954.
Shanghai and Tientsin, New York, 1940.
Jones, T., *Diary with Letters 1931–1940*, London, 1954.
Kemp, P.K., *The Key to Victory: The Triumph of British Sea Power in World War II*, Boston, Mass., 1958.
Kennedy, M.D., *The Estrangement of Great Britain and Japan*, Manchester, 1969.
King, F.H.H., *A Concise Economic History of Modern China*, Bombay, 1968.
Kirby, S.W., *Singapore, Chain of Disaster*, London, 1971.
The War Against Japan, Volume I, H.M.S.O., 1957.

Larkin, T., *New Zealand and Japan*, Wellington, New Zealand, 1969.

League of Nations, Appeal of the Chinese Government: *Report of the Commission of Enquiry (Lytton Report)*, Geneva, 1932.

Records of Special Session of the Assembly 1932, Special Supplements 101–102, 111–113, Geneva, 1932.

Lee, Bradford A., *Britain and the Sino-Japanese War 1937–1939, A Study in the Dilemmas of British Decline*, Stanford, Cal., 1972.

Lensen, George A. *The damned inheritance: The Soviet Union and the Manchurian crises, 1924–35*. Tallahasie, 1974.

Lissington, M.P., *New Zealand and Japan 1900–1941*, Wellington, New Zealand, 1972.

Lockwood, W.W., *The Economic Development of Japan*, Princeton, N.J., 1954.

Louis, W.R., *British Strategy in the Far East 1919–1939*, Oxford, 1971.

Luard, Evan, *Britain and China*, London, 1962.

McCarthy, J.M., 'Australia and Imperial Defence: Cooperation and Conflict 1919–1939', *Australian Journal of Politics and History*, Vol. VII, April 1971.

McLachlan, Donald, *In the Chair: Barrington-Ward of The Times*, London, 1971.

McLane, C.B., *Soviet Policy and the Chinese Communists, 1931–1946*, New York, 1958.

Macleod, Ian, *Neville Chamberlain*, London, 1960.

Marshall, B.K., *Capitalism and Nationalism in Pre-War Japan: The Ideology of the Business Elite 1868–1941*, Stanford, Cal., 1967.

Maruyama Masao, *Thought and Behaviour in Modern Japanese Politics*, London, 1965.

Maxon, Y., *Control of Japanese Foreign Policy 1930–1945*, California University Publications in Political Science, Volume 5, 1957.

May, E.R. and Thomson, J.C. (ed.), *American East-Asian Relations: A Survey*, Cambridge, Mass., 1972.

Medlicott, W.M., *British Foreign Policy Since Versailles 1919–1962*, 2nd edition, London, 1968.

Millard, T.F.F., *America, Europe and the Manchurian Question*, Geneva, 1932.

Milner, I.F.G., *New Zealand's Interests and Policies in the Far East, 1932*, New York, 1940.

Middlemas, K., *The Diplomacy of Illusion: The British Government and Germany 1937–1939*, London, 1972.

Middlemas, K. and Barnes, J. *Baldwin*, London, 1969.

Morley, J.W. (ed.), *Dilemmas of Growth in Pre-war Japan*, Princeton, N.J., 1971.

Morris, I., *Nationalism and the Right Wing in Japan*, London, 1960.

Neumann, W.L., *America Encounters Japan*, Baltimore, Md., 1963.

Nish, I.H., *Alliance in Decline. A Study in Anglo-Japanese Relations 1908–1923*, London, 1972.

Norman, E.H., *Japan's Emergence as a Modern State*, New York, 1940.

Northedge, F.S. (ed.), *The Foreign Policies of the Powers*, London, 1968. *The Troubled Giant. Britain among the Great Powers 1916–1939*, London, 1966.

Piggott, F.S.G., *The Broken Thread*, Aldershot, 1950.
Postan, M.M., *British War Production: History of the Second World War*, H.M.S.O., 1952.
Potter, J.D., *Admiral of the Pacific*, London, 1965.
Pratt, Sir John, *War and Politics in China*, London, 1943.
Pratt, L., 'The Anglo-American Naval Conversations on the Far East of January 1938', *International Affairs*, Vol. 47, No. 4, October 1971.
Raymond, J. (ed.), *The Baldwin Age*, London, 1960.
Reischauer, E.O., Fairbank, J.K., and Craig, A.M., *East Asia: The Modern Transformation*, London, 1965.
Remer, C.F., *Foreign Investments in China*, New York, 1933.
Rippy, J.F., *British Investments in Latin America 1822–1949*, Minneapolis, Minn., 1959.
Robertson, E. (ed.), *The Origins of the Second World War*, London, 1971.
Roskill, S.W., *Hankey, Man of Secrets*, Vol. II *1919–1931*, London, 1972. Vol. III *1931–1963*, London, 1974. *Naval Policy between the Wars, The Period of Anglo-American Antagonism 1919–1929*, London, 1968.
The War at Sea, Vol. I: *History of the Second World War*, H.M S.O., 1954.
Ross, Sir F. Leith, *Money Talks*, London, 1968.
Royal Institute of International Affairs, *Survey of International Affairs, 1926*, London, 1927.
Survey of International Affairs, 1932, London, 1933.
Survey of International Affairs, 1933, London, 1934.
Salter, Sir Arthur, 'China and the Depression, Impressions of a Three Months Visit', *China National Economic Council Special Series*, 1934.
Sansom, Katherine, *Sir George Sansom and Japan*, Talahassee, Fla, 1972.
Scalapino, R.O., *Democracy and the Party Movement in Pre-war Japan*, Berkeley, Cal. 1953.
Shigemitsu, Mamoru, *Japan and her Destiny*, London, 1958.
Schurmann, F. and Schell, O., *China Readings: Republican China*, Volume 2 of three volumes, London, 1968.
Steiner, Z.S., *The Foreign Office and Foreign Policy, 1898–1914*, Cambridge, 1969.
Storry, R. *The Double Patriots: A Study in Japanese Nationalism*, Boston, Mass., 1957.
A History of Modern Japan, London, 1960.
Strang, (Lord) W., *Home and Abroad*, London, 1957.
The Diplomatic Career, London, 1962.
The Foreign Office, London, 1955.
Swire, G.W., *The Coast and River Trade of China*, Data Paper for Institute of Pacific Relations, London, 1931 (Typescript).
Tamura Kosaku, *Genesis of the Pacific War*, Tokyo, 1944.
Tanin, O., and Yonan, E., *Militarism and Fascism in Japan*, London, 1934.
Taylor, A.J.P., *English History 1914–1945*, Oxford, 1965.
The Origins of the Second World War, 2nd edition, London, 1963.
Teichmann, Sir E., *Affairs of China: A Survey of the Recent History and Present Circumstances of the Republic of China*, London, 1938.

Templewood, Viscount, *Nine Troubled Years*, London, 1954.
Thomas, John N., *The Institute of Pacific Relations, Asian scholars and American politics*, Seattle, 1974.
Thompson, N., *The Anti-Appeasers*, Oxford, 1971.
Thorne, C., *The Limits of Foreign Policy: The West, the League and the Far Eastern Crisis of 1931–1933*, London, 1972.
'The Quest for Arms Embargoes: Failure in 1933' *Journal of Contemporary History*, v No. 4, 1970.
'The Shanghai Crisis of 1932: The Basis of British Policy', *American Historical Review*, Vol. LXXV, No. 6, October 1970.
Trotter, Ann, 'Tentative steps for an Anglo-Japanese rapprochement in 1934', *Modern Asian Studies*, Vol. 8, No. 1, 1974.
'The Dominions and Imperial Defence: Hankey's tour in 1934', *Journal of Imperial and Commonwealth History*, Vol. 2, No. 3, 1974.
Utley, Freda, *Japan's Feet of Clay*, 2nd edition, London, 1937.
Japan's Gamble in China, London, 1938.
Lancashire and the Far East, London, 1931.
Utley, Freda and Wills, D., *Japan can be Stopped*, London, 1937.
Vansittart, R., *Mist Procession*, London, 1958.
Van Slyke, L.P., *Enemies and Friends: The United Front in Chinese Communist History*, Stanford, Cal., 1967.
Walters, F.P., *A History of the League of Nations*, Oxford, 1952.
Watt, D.C., *Personalities and Policies*, London, 1965.
'Roosevelt and Neville Chamberlain: two appeasers', *International Journal*, Vol. XXVIII, No. 2, 1973.
'The Anglo–German Naval Agreement of 1935', *Journal of Modern History*, Vol. 27, No. 2, June 1956.
Wellesley, Sir V., *Diplomacy in Fetters*, London, 1944.
Woodhead, H.G.W., *A Journalist in China*, London, 1934.
Wright, M., 'Chinese History and the Historical Vocation', *Journal of Asian Studies*, Vol. XXIII, No. 4, August 1964.
Young, A. Morgan, *Imperial Japan*, London, 1938.
Young, Arthur N., *China's Financial and Economic Reconstruction*, New York, 1947.
China's Nation Building Effort 1927–37, Stanford, Cal., 1971.
China's Wartime Finance and Inflation 1937–1945, Cambridge, Mass., 1965.
Young, G.M., *Stanley Baldwin*, London, 1952.

JAPANESE LANGUAGE WORKS

Sato, Naotake, *Kaiko 80-nen* (Recollections of 80 years), Tokyo, 1963.
The Japanese Association of International Relations, the committee to study the Origins of the Pacific War (ed.), *Taiheiyō sensō e no michi: kaisen gaikō-shi* (The Road to the Pacific War), Volume I of 8 volumes, Tokyo, 1962–3.
Usui, Katsumi, *Nitchū Sensō* (Sino-Japanese war), Tokyo, 1967.

INDEX

support for, 138, 144, 148, 149; and currency crisis, 140, 185; and loans, 205, 208, 209, 210; and British policy, 211, 217

Chiefs of Staff; review 1933, 36–7, 39, *see also* Committee of Imperial Defence, Defence Requirements Committee

China; attitude of powers towards, 13–14; economic potential, 13, 19; and tariffs, 14; political situation 1920s, 14, 15; commercial relations with Japan, 23; industrial development, 25–26, *see also* Currency, Leith Ross mission, Loans, Silver, and various events, policies etc. by name

China Association, 26, 148

China Consortium; members, 62; Chinese attitude to, 62, 206; reaction to wheat and cotton loan, 64, 133; British attitude to, 65, 206; effect on loans to China, 133, 205–6; and invitation to send financial missions to China, 140–1

China Finance Corporation, 70

China lobby, 17–18, 24–7, 142, 144–9 *passim*, 206–7, *see also* Merchants

China, relations with Britain, 62, 85, 119, 120, 140, 211, *see also* Britain, China policy, Currency, Loans, Leith Ross mission, Reconstruction

Chinese Communist Party, 190, 196

Chinese Maritime Customs Administration, 19, 117n.11, 151, 179, 191; British determination to maintain its integrity, 19–20; question of British inspector general, 152, 156–7, 165, 181, 205, 206

Ching, General Teh-chin, 162n.64

Ching-Doihara Agreement, 162, 191

Clive, Sir Robert, 35; in Japan, 97, 101, 102, 103, 121, 157, 170, 174, 177, 181, 193, 194, 199, 200

Cliveden set, 212

Committee on Anglo-Japanese Political and Economic Relations, 136, 136n.25 146–7, 186

Committee of Imperial Defence, 37, 40–1, 95, *see also* Chiefs of staff, Defence Requirements Committee

Committee on the Naval Conference 1935, 54–5, 59

Communists; in China, 138, 190, 216,

see also Chinese Communist Party

Competition, commercial, *see* Anglo-Japanese competition

Control Faction, 178, 199

Craigie, Sir Robert; as naval expert, 9n.24, 38n.18, 98, 137, 172, 173–4, 175; and Norman Davis, 111n.99; and Yoshida, 195, 201

Cripps, Sir Stafford, 83

Crowe, Sir Edward, 117, 118, 118n.14, 123

Cunliffe-Owen, Sir Hugo, 142n.56

Currency; situation in China, 25, 64, 128, 130, 131, 142; Britain and Chinese currency, 128, 130, 131, 133, 134–44; Japan and Chinese currency, 139, 151–3, 159, 160, 214n.35; United States and Chinese currency, 139–40, 154n.30, 158, 159, 186, *see also* Leith Ross mission, Loans, Silver, Silver Purchase Act

Davis, Norman, 52, 53, 111n.99, 171, 174, 176, 215

Dawson, Geoffrey, 212

December memorandum, 15

Defence Requirements Committee; establishment, 39n.24, 91; report 1934, 40–1, 42, 88, 89, 90–2, 95; chairman, 95; report 1934, 169, *see also* Committee of Imperial Defence

Department of Overseas Trade, 8n.23, 116, 117, 118, 121, 142, 144

Disarmament Conference, 5, 41, 83, 88

Doihara, General Kenji, 162n.64

Dual Diplomacy; of Britain, 9, 211, 212–13; of Japan, 212, *see also* Foreign Office, Foreign policy, British far eastern, Leith Ross mission, Treasury

Dominions, 94, 95, 96, 97, 107, 108, 109, 202, *see also* Australia, Canada, New Zealand, South Africa

Dutch East Indies, 101, 103

East Asian Co-prosperity Sphere, 190, 214

East Asian Monroe Doctrine, 83, 214

East Hopei Anti-Communist Autonomous Council, 164

Eden, Anthony, 8, 35, 90; as foreign secretary, 166, 175, 180, 189, 194; and Pacific pact, 200, 202, 203; hard line 1937, 204

Lancashire; textile industry, 28; M.P.'s, 28, 32, 33n.29, 73; and Board of Trade, 29; delegation to India, 31–2; and Leith Ross, 148

Latham, Sir John, 109

League of Nations, 1, 3, 61, 62, 67, 106, 116; Japan's departure from, 1, 3, 34, 50, 118

League of Nations Union, 43, 44, 149

Lee, L. B., 142n.56

Leeper, A. W. A., 9n.24

Leith Ross, Sir Frederick, 147, 147n.78; mission, 148–61 *passim*, 176–88 *passim*; and loan to China, 205, 207, 209, 210; strong position, 212

Leith Ross Mission, 147, 147n.78; preparations, 148–51; in Japan, 151–3; and Chinese currency reform, 153–61; activity in China, 165–7; as a diplomatic mission, 176–7; return to Japan, 177–85, the report, 185–6; estimates of the mission, 186–7, 200; risks of, 213

Leith Ross Report, 185, 192, 211

Leith Ross Statement for cabinet, 185–6

Lindley, Sir Francis, 35, 78, 79, 80

Lo Wen-kan, 69

Loans; to China, 63, 70, 132–3, 154, 158, 160, 205, 206, 207; British policy on, 133, 134–5, 152, 154–5, 209–10; for Chinese railways, 166n.86 206, 209n.19; Japanese reaction to, 208, *see also* Wheat and Cotton loan Kung H. H., Leith Ross, Soong T. V.

Locock, Guy, 117, 118, 119, 123, 124, 126

London Naval Conference 1930, 47, 49

Lothian, Lord, 107, 108

Lukouchiao, 203

Lyons, J. A., 200

Lytton Report, 62, 124

MacDonald, Ramsay, 52, 53, 92

Macdonough, Sir George, 144n.66

MacGowan, Sir Harry, 117, 118n.14, 144, 148n.5

MacGowan Memorandum, 145, 146

Maisky Ivan, 125

Makino, Count Nobukai, 84, 105, 194n.22

Manchester Chamber of Commerce, 28, 28n.14, 148

Manchukuo; question of recognition, 33,

150, 151, 152, 153; trade prospects in, 115, 116, 117, 118–19; and A. H. F. Edwardes, 117, 129; FBI mission to, 120, 122; proposals for loans to, 124, 150, 151–2, 162; as a lever with Japan, 136, *see also* Manchuria, Manchurian crisis, Federation of British Industries

Manchuria, 1, 2, 3, 15, 16, 19, 23, 43, 115, 118, 134, *see also* Manchukuo, Manchurian crisis

Manchuria Petroleum Company, 115–16, 115n.4

Manchurian crisis, 5, 7, 15, 23, 34, 35, 44, 62n.4, *see also* Manchukuo, Manchuria

Marco Polo bridge incident, 186, 203, 205

Matsudaira Tsuneō, 66; and naval talks, 93, 96, 110, 111, 112; and British approaches 1934, 104–5, 105n.73, 106, 107, 173; and Warren Fisher, 137, 141; in Japan, 170, 177, 178, 179, 194

Maze, Sir Frederick, 132, 133, 181, 205

Merchants in China, 24–7, 141–4, 145, 185, 207, *see also* China lobby

Ministerial Committee on Disarmament, 57, 81, 88, 89–90, 91–2

Mongolia for the Mongolians campaign, 191, 196

Monnet, M. Jean, 66, 67, 70

Monsell, Sir Bolton Eyres, 43, 48, 89, 90

Morgenthau, Henry, 149

Nagai Matsuo, 173n.23, 174

Nagano, Admiral, 173n.23

Nanking Government, 62, 67, 86, 151, 154, 163, 183, 185, 191, 211, *see also* Chiang Kai-shek, Kuomintang

National Economic Council, 61, 62

Nationalism, in China, 2, 3, 14, 15, 20, 25, 196, 197, 216

Naval Conference 1935, 92, 98, 99, 102, 170–7, 187

Naval talks 1934, *see* Anglo-American, naval talks, Anglo-Japanese naval talks

Navy, *see* Royal Navy, Japanese Navy, United States Navy

New Zealand; defence of, 41, 91, 95; and pact with Japan, 102, 108, 109, 202n.56

Nine Power Treaty; conditions of, 13, 14, 73; possible breaches of, 64, 70; maintenance of façade, 68; Japan and, 78, 80, 83; Britain and, 103, 104, 173, *see also* Washington treaties

Nohara Daisuke, 66

North China, Japanese policy, 16, 69, 86, 190–1, 196

Norman, Montagu, 134

Oil; Japanese monopoly in Manchukuo, 115n.4, 119, 121n.29, 145

Okada Keisuke, 66, 96

One power standard, 47–8

Open door, 13, 16, 20, 24, 116, 217

Orde, Charles; head of far east department, 9; attitude to Amau statement, 72–3, 75, 80; and FBI mission, 123; and Neville Chamberlain, 176n.32; and China loan 1937, 209–10, 210n.26; experience, 212, *see also* Far East Department, Foreign Office

Osumi, Admiral, 96

Ottawa agreements, 17, 29, 30, 32n.28

Ozaki, Hotsumi, 216n.46

Pacific Pact; proposals for, 200–1, 202–3, 205; Japanese reaction, 200; Chinese reaction, 202; United States reaction, 202, 215

Pailingmiao, 196

Pearce, Sir George, 109

Phillips, William, 175

Piggott, Julian, 118, 118n.14, 119

Pratt, Sir John, 9, 26, 186, 212n.34

Railway loans, *see* loans

Rajchman, Dr Ludwig, 61, 67, 70, 84

Rapprochement; discussions about Anglo-Japanese and Sino-Japanese, *see* Anglo-Japanese rapprochement, Sino-Japanese rapprochement

Reconstruction; of China, 61–8, 70–1, *see also* currency, loans, Rajchman

Reconstruction Finance Corporation, 63

Rogers, Cyril, 148, 205, 208

Roosevelt, Franklin D., 11, 174

Rose, Sir Archibald, 144n.66

Ross, Sir Frederick Leith, *see* Leith Ross

Royal Navy; position in western Pacific, 12–13, and naval building, 16; in CID report 1933, 36, 37; role in far east,

45–6; and Washington treaties, 47–8, 51; question of size, 89, 90–1, 94, 95; cruiser requirements, 92; Hankey's view of, 96, *see also* Admiralty, Anglo-American, Anglo-Japanese naval talks, Britain, naval policy, Naval Conference 1935

Runciman, Walter, 44, 124, 143

Russia, 43, 45, 100, 103, 136, *see also* Russo-Japanese relations, 32, 40, 100, 121, 171, 189, 190–1, 216

Saionji, Prince Kinmochi, 102

Salter, Sir Arthur, 61

Sankey, Lord, 43

Sansom, George; his credentials, 35n.9, 35n.10, 35–6, 127; and Anglo-Japanese rapprochement, 105, 120–1, 172, 193; and FBI mission, 124, 125, 126

Sassoon's Bank, 134

Satō Naotake, 199, 214

Scott, Colin C., 142n.56

Seeckt, General Hans von, 84

Seligman, Sir Charles, 118, 121, 123n.41

Seligman Brothers Bank, 118, 124

Shanghai; May 30 incident, 14; British investment, 18; industrial development, 25; currency, 132, 134; Leith Ross in, 180, 185

Shansi, 164

Shantung, 164

Shidehara, Baron Kijūrō, 84

Shigemitsu Mamoru, 152

Showa Kenkyukai, 214n.46

Sian Incident, 186, 196, 199

Silver; China and United States policy, 128, 130, 132n.1, 154n.30, 158, 159; interdepartmental committee on problem, 133–4, *see also* Currency, Loans, Silver Purchase Act

Silver Purchase Act, 132

Simon, Sir John; and Manchurian crisis, 7; his temperament, 7–8, 10; opinion of Sansom, 35n.10, 127; and Japan 43–4, 45, 97, 98, 99, 100–1, 105–6, 107; and Amau statement, 74–8 *passim*, 80, 81, 82; and naval matters, 90, 105, 111, 111n.99, and Chinese currency crisis, 136–7; and China lobby, 147, *see also* Foreign Office

Singapore, 12–13, 31, 40, 49, 91, 95, 96

For EU product safety concerns, contact us at Calle de José Abascal, 56–1°, 28003 Madrid, Spain or eugpsr@cambridge.org.